D1559762

God on the Grounds

God on the Grounds

*A History of Religion at
Thomas Jefferson's University*

HARRY Y. GAMBLE

University of Virginia Press
Charlottesville and London

University of Virginia Press
© 2020 by the Rector and Visitors of the University of Virginia
Printed in the United States of America on acid-free paper

First published 2020

ISBN 978-0-8139-4405-0 (hardcover)
ISBN 978-0-8139-4406-7 (ebook)

9 8 7 6 5 4 3 2 1

Library of Congress Cataloging-in-Publication Data is available for this title.

Illustrations courtesy of the Albert and Shirley Small Special Collections Library, University of Virginia

Cover art: University chapel elevation and plans, from 1859 receipt, William Pratt, draughtsman. (Courtesy of the Albert and Shirley Small Special Collections Library, University of Virginia)

Contents

Illustrations

Preface

This is a book I did not intend to write. What I had in mind was a brief pamphlet that would answer a question I was often asked during a relatively long term as chair of the Department of Religious Studies at the University of Virginia. The question was: how did it come to be that, since Thomas Jefferson had excluded a professor of divinity from the faculty and the teaching of religion from the curriculum, the University of Virginia nevertheless now has the largest department of religious studies in a public university in the United States? I did not know the answer, but it was a good question, if only because the University customarily pays high deference to its founder, and his wisdom mostly goes unquestioned. This seemed, on the face of it, to be a large exception.

Finding an answer was far more challenging than I had imagined. No single decision, no particular event, and no obvious reason presented itself. I found myself being led further and further back into the history of the University, and finally to its very beginnings and the mind of its founder. In the process, the question itself grew larger. It was no longer why is there a department of religious studies at Virginia, but now: what had been the role of religion—both as studied and as practiced—in the history of the University? The answer to the former question can be found only by answering the latter. So I have ended up by writing what can be described as a history of religion at Jefferson's University.

It is surprising to discover that religion even has a history at the University, let alone that religion has played an influential role in the life of the institution, and that this was true virtually from the beginning, notwithstanding Jefferson's deep misgivings about religion and his careful measures against its intrusion. What we see, and what the following narrative documents, is the progressive importation, throughout the nineteenth century, of the study and practice of religion into the secular, public institution Jefferson established. This process began very soon after Jefferson's death, and within a couple of decades had succeeded in converting the University into a Protestant Christian institution.

It is especially interesting to see why this occurred. Jefferson's personal reputation as a freethinking infidel carried over to the institution he founded, and not without reason, for he intended that religion should have no recognition and play no role in the University. But that intention was wholly at odds with the warm piety that permeated the Commonwealth, and therefore from the outset the University was at a disadvantage, laboring under the popular perception that it was an irreligious and antireligious institution, potentially ruinous to the faith and morals of its students. This was a serious public relations problem. It threatened to deprive the University of the political patronage, the public support, and the prospective students that were critical to its success. If in the modern period the University is accustomed to lay proud claim to its Jeffersonian pedigree, it was not always so. In the nineteenth century Jefferson's legacy was a troublesome liability. Unless its irreligious reputation could be countered, one of the founder's proudest accomplishments was at risk of failure.

Consequently, when opportunities arose to make the University seem more friendly to religion by attaching to it some fixture of piety, the custodians of the institution—whether the faculty or the Board of Visitors or both—had a strong motive to do so. And that motive is almost always plainly stated or clearly implied, namely, to deflect the criticism that the University is a godless place intent on the destruction of religion. But adding agents and accessories of piety was not altogether easy, at least if their sponsors were attentive to the principles Jefferson had laid down. Adjustments, compromises, and redefinitions were required, and the result of these, over only a few decades, was to subvert the secular character of the institution.

It was only toward the middle of the twentieth century that the University belatedly realized how far it had departed from its founding principles, and began gradually to recover its secular character as a public institution and an agency of the Commonwealth. The reasons for this reversal were various: societal, cultural, judicial, and academic. But by century's end the University had managed to abandon its historical investments in piety and to take an indifferent stance toward religion, permitting its free expression but withholding any endorsement or support. So the narrative to follow charts two movements, first from secularism to religion, and then from religion to resecularization.

The focus of this study is admittedly narrow. My principal aim is to call new attention to the part played by religion in the history of the University, and even to emphasize its importance, because this has been a neglected dimension of the institutional past. Existing histories of the University, such as those of Patton or Bruce or Dabney, touch on the subject of religion, but only lightly and in passing, and with little indication of the issues at play, or the difficulties they posed, or the influence they had. I have tried to ferret out the available evidence on this subject, to trace a development, and to provide a coherent explanation of it. A full accounting is useful because it reveals the problematic interface of religious interests and secular principle in the developing life of the University. It also furnishes insights not only into the inner workings of the institution but also into its responsive relationship to its public constituency and its changing sociocultural context. And, lest this seem a merely parochial exercise, I also aim to indicate those developments within the University that relate in interesting ways to what was happening more broadly in American religious history and in the history of American higher education. Of course, a sharp focus on the theme of religion risks overemphasis. Although its role has been far more pronounced than many have realized, religion has been only one aspect of a much broader institutional history and needs to be correlated with other influential factors.

For their help in this project I am indebted to many people. I am very grateful to the late Rob Vaughn and the Virginia Foundation for the Humanities (now Virginia Humanities) for their interest in and support of this effort. Kurtis Schaeffer, the current chair of the Department of Religious Studies, has given me encouragement and helpful accommodations. I have been generously assisted by the University of Virginia Library, and especially by the able staff of its Albert and Shirley Small Special Collections division, who patiently helped me locate obscure materials. Among many who provided encouragement, suggested resources, read drafts, and saved me from a variety of embarrassments, I am grateful to several of my erstwhile colleagues in the Department of Religious Studies. I especially thank Jim Childress, who has been a wonderful colleague and steady friend for more than half a century. Matt Hedstrom and Heather Warren, specialists in American religious history, provided useful guidance in the expansive literature of that field and read drafts of some chapters. Among friends and colleagues outside the department I am indebted to Jon Mikalson and Tom Estes. Alexander "Sandy" Gilliam, longtime secretary to the Board of Visitors and special assistant to the president, whose knowledge of the University is exceeded only by his affection for it, has been an interested and engaging conversation partner. Not least, I thank my wife, Tamara, for both her well-tutored editorial eye and her tight-lipped tolerance for piles of books and papers.

Spring 2019
Charlottesville, Virginia

God on the Grounds

1

Jefferson and Religion

Thomas Jefferson, although far from being the most religious of the founding fathers, was the most interested in religion. He read about it, thought about it, and wrote about it more than any other. He was well aware of the plurality of world religions. "Let us reflect," he wrote, "that [the world] is inhabited by a thousand millions of people. That these profess probably a thousand different systems of religion. That ours is but one of those thousand."[1] Jefferson knew of all the major religions of the world, but he had only limited knowledge of the great religions of the East—Buddhism and Hinduism—and took no real interest in them. He was, of course, far more familiar with the religious traditions of the West—Judaism, Christianity, and Islam—but unevenly so. Jefferson owned a copy of the Qur'an and had diplomatic dealings with Muslim nations, but there were virtually no recognizable Muslims in America, and Jefferson apparently had a low regard for Islam.[2] Judaism was sparsely represented in the colonies, and although Jefferson knew some American Jews, he had an oddly anachronistic conception of Judaism, construing it as nothing different from the ancient Israelite religion found in the Hebrew scriptures. As a result, he had a decidedly negative view of Judaism, although he appreciated its monotheism.[3] Christianity was the religion that Jefferson knew best and spoke about most frequently, since it was almost exclusively predominant in his social and cultural environment.

Jefferson and Religious Freedom

Jefferson thought of religion in generic terms and regarded particular religious traditions as specific manifestations of the more general phenomenon. This is apparent not only from the quotation given above but also from his comments on his bill for establishing religious freedom, about which he says

> I had drawn in all the latitude of reason and right. It still met with opposition;
> but, with some mutilations in the preamble, it was finally passed; and a singular
> proposition proved that it's protection of opinion was meant to be universal.
> Where the preamble declares that coercion is a departure from the plan of the
> holy author of our religion, an amendment was proposed, by inserting the word
> "Jesus Christ," so that it should read "a departure from the plan of Jesus Christ,
> the holy author of our religion." The insertion was rejected by a great majority,
> in proof that they meant to comprehend, within the mantle of it's protection, the
> Jew and the Gentile, the Christian and Mahometan, the Hindoo, and infidel of
> every denomination.[4]

Jefferson would not permit "religion" to be limited to Christianity, which he referred to as the "particular superstition" of the American people (Thomas Jefferson to William Short, April 13, 1820),[5] nor would he permit religious freedom to have narrow application: it applied to any and all forms of religion.[6] In Jefferson's own environment, however, "religion" presented itself as the Christian religion, and this almost exclusively in its specifically Protestant configurations—Anglican, Congregationalist, Presbyterian, Baptist, Methodist, Lutheran, Quaker, or some other. Accordingly, for practical intents and immediate purposes, religious pluralism was for him less a matter of diverse *religions* than of diverse *sectarian forms of Protestant Christianity.*

The form of Protestant Christianity that was legally established in Virginia was the Church of England (the Anglican Church), but dissenting religious groups, especially Presbyterians and Baptists, were well represented. It was Jefferson's sensibility to this diversity of religious groups in his native Virginia, and to the disadvantages suffered by many under the establishment of the Church of England, that set him to work on what would become one of his proudest accomplishments, his authorship of the Virginia Statute for Religious Freedom. He drafted the bill proposing religious liberty in 1777 and introduced it in the General Assembly in 1779, but it was not enacted until 1786. At the time of its adoption, Jefferson was serving as minister to France, but the bill was powerfully advocated by James Madison in his "Memorial and Remonstrance" and was strongly supported by religious dissenters, above all Baptists and Presbyterians. Urging that "Almighty God hath created the mind free," and that all attempts to limit that freedom are futile and counter to the divine will, the bill maintained,

> No man shall be compelled to frequent or support any religious worship, place or ministry whatsoever, nor shall be enforced, restrained, molested or burthened in his body or goods, nor shall otherwise suffer, on account of his religious opinions or belief; but that all men shall be free to profess, and by argument to maintain, their opinion in matters of religion, and that the same shall in no wise diminish, enlarge or affect their civil capacities.

Since he was a tireless champion of religious freedom and the proud author of this statute, it is commonly supposed that Jefferson had a profound appreciation of and respect for religion, and even that he himself was a deeply pious man. But Jefferson's advocacy of religious freedom did not depend on his respect for religion per se, nor on his appreciation of any particular religion.[7] It was, rather, freedom of thought and liberty of conscience that he sought to protect. These included, certainly, the right of every individual to hold whatever religious views he or she might choose. The emphasis upon specifically *religious* freedom was a pointed recognition and rejection of the coercive power that religion in particular had historically exercised over people's minds. When "established," that is, when in league with the civil power (as it had almost always been), religion had often enforced its claims by disenfranchisement, repression, persecution, and violence. Jefferson viewed established religion as a violation of conscience, compelling consent and support irrespective of actual conviction, and thus, as he complained, making "one half the world fools, and the other half hypocrites."[8] Hence civil rights must in no way be dependent upon religious opinions.

But Jefferson was not only opposed to the alliance of religion and the state; he was also fundamentally critical of all ostensibly *revealed* religions—including Judaism, Islam, and Christianity in all its forms—because he believed that claims of revelation were themselves coercive in their own way. The assertion by any religion of authoritative revelation usurped the prerogative of reason and disenfranchised its judgment, whereas reason was, in his view, the only authoritative arbiter of all ideas, including religious ideas. Moreover, as we shall see, Jefferson considered the substance of allegedly revealed truths to be not simply beyond reason but contrary to reason and hence false. He believed that the untrammeled judgments of reason must be allowed to prevail in the sphere of religious convictions as in all other spheres. Thus religious freedom was needful not only in political life but also in intellectual life.

Given Jefferson's judgments that state-supported religion transgresses the rights of conscience and that revealed religions violate the prerogatives of reason, it is not surprising that most of Jefferson's extensive comments about religion are negative, for nearly all the religious postures with which he was acquainted fell into one or the other category, and most into both. In its traditional, most prominent and influential forms, religion itself was deeply problematic to him.

Much has been written about Jefferson and religion—both about Jefferson's concept of religious freedom, secured through the strict separation of church and state, and about Jefferson's personal religious convictions. It is perhaps too little recognized that these two aspects of the subject are closely connected. Jefferson insisted on religious freedom not only on the grounds of principle but in some measure also from self-interest: he desired it for himself on account of the unconventionality of his own religious ideas. For better or worse, he was a freethinker in matters religious, and this was generally for the worse since the Protestant Christian orthodoxy prevailing in his social and political environment did not smile on dissent.

Jefferson's Religious Ideas: Early Influences and Development

Despite extensive scrutiny, Jefferson's religious ideas have been very diversely characterized.[9] It has been argued that he was an atheist, a deist, a Christian, an infidel, and a heretic; that he was a deeply devout man, and that he was a thoroughgoing skeptic; that he was a complete secularist, and that he was a lifelong churchman. There are reasons for such differences of opinion, apart from the desire of some to sanctify Jefferson as a faithful Christian.[10] Jefferson was a private person, somewhat introverted, and unwilling to submit his religious views to public inspection. Only late in life did he reveal his personal convictions, and then only to sympathetic friends. As he remarked to Richard Rush (May 31, 1813), "Religion is a subject on which I have ever been most scrupulously reserved. I have considered it as a matter between every man and his maker, in which no other, & far less the public, has a right to intermeddle."[11] But in addition, Jefferson's religious ideas were not altogether static. As a freethinker who sought convincing truth, his ideas about religion were subject to revision or reformulation: some elements were constant more or less throughout his adult life, while others underwent reappraisal and, of course, some never found any resolution at all. For our purposes Jefferson's mature views, which are also in the clearest focus, are most relevant, since they were effective for his vision of the University of Virginia. Nevertheless, it is useful to sketch the background and development of those later ideas.

Jefferson was born, baptized, and brought up in the Anglican Church (or Church of England), which throughout the colonial period was the established church in his native Virginia and the normal ecclesiastical affiliation for members of the Commonwealth's upper or planter class, to which Jefferson belonged. But in Jefferson's native Piedmont region Anglicanism was not strongly ensconced: parish churches were small and widely separated, priests were few, and services were irregular. Dissenting groups, especially Presbyterians and Baptists, were active and influential.[12] He remained at least nominally Anglican all his life, never formally associating himself with, let alone converting to, any other organized religious body.[13] Nevertheless, Jefferson did not show any particular favoritism toward the Anglican tradition, and precisely because it was the established church and an arm of the British government, he had ample reason *not* to emphasize his association with it. Although baptized into a Christian church, from an early age Jefferson began to entertain serious reservations about fundamental Christian doctrines, and his reading and thinking led him ever further from traditional Christian convictions.

Jefferson gained his early education through private tutoring by two Anglican clergymen, first William Douglas and subsequently James Maury. Jefferson had small regard for Douglas, with whom he studied from 1752 to 1757, and found his instruction tedious and uninspiring. But Maury excited his mind, gave him a strong grounding in Greek, Latin, and ancient history, and opened his fine personal library to Jefferson's enthusiastic exploration. During his two years of instruction under Maury (1758–59), the classical world came into Jefferson's permanent and reverent possession. Of Maury he wrote to Joseph Priestley (January 27, 1800), "I thank on my knees him who directed my early education, for having put into my possession this rich source of delight; and I would not exchange it for anything which I could then have acquired, & have not since acquired."[14]

Thus prepared, Jefferson enrolled at the College of William and Mary in 1760 at the age of seventeen. The college was an establishment of the Church of England, and its charter required that the president and faculty "assent to the articles of the Christian faith, in the same manner, and in the same words, as the ministers of England are obliged to sign the [Thirty-Nine] Articles of the Church of England." Indeed, one of the founding purposes of the college was that the colony of Virginia "should be supplied with good ministers after the doctrine and government of the Church of England." Jefferson's intellectual horizons and religious ideas, far from being constrained by this ecclesiastical environment, found in it a particular stimulus. William and Mary had become a haven of Enlightenment thought in the colony, and Jefferson was fully exposed to it, particularly in its Scottish permutation, under the influence of Dr. William Small, a Scotsman and the only member of the college faculty who was not an Anglican clergyman.[15]

Jefferson considered that it was "my great good fortune and what probably fixed the destinies of my life" to study with Small.[16] It was Small, appointed as professor of mathematics, and subsequently also professor of natural philosophy, who introduced Jefferson to the salient ideas of the European Enlightenment. Jefferson quickly became Small's bright young protégé, and Small brought him into an intimate circle of sophisticated intellectuals in Williamsburg that included George Wythe, the professor of law, and Francis Fauquier, the lieutenant governor of the Commonwealth. Jefferson claimed to have gained "much instruction" from the dinner table conversations of this distinguished company.[17] It was during these college years that he became steeped in the progressive ideas of the Enlightenment.

Stimulated positively by the Scientific Revolution of the seventeenth and eighteenth centuries, and negatively by the drawn-out religious conflicts between Catholics and Protestants, the Enlightenment was a major intellectual and cultural watershed in European history. Although its manifestations differed somewhat from nation to nation, the Enlightenment had widely shared features.[18] Prescinding from the authority of both tradition and revelation, Enlightenment thinkers considered empirical experience and human reason to be the most dependable arbiters of knowledge. It has been widely thought that the Enlightenment was an antireligious movement that marked a transition from an essentially religious to an essentially secular conception of the world and human society.[19] But even if it was characterized by skepticism toward received ideas and an insistence on the authority of reason, the Enlightenment was not hostile to religion as such. Still, debate about the nature and reasonableness of religious belief and about the role of religion in society was a prominent aspect of the Enlightenment.[20]

With regard to religion the Enlightenment was multivalent. If some intellectuals made league with the radical Enlightenment and disavowed all religious ideas and principles, landing in atheism or agnosticism, others embraced the moderate Enlightenment and privileged reason along with revelation, either seeing them as complementary or rejecting what was contrary to reason but affirming certain revealed truths as "above" reason. Still others adopted a philosophical sort of piety that we have come to call Deism. Grounded in reason and empirical observation, Deism was characterized by its adherents as a "natural religion" (as distinct from a "revealed religion").[21] It retained the idea of a creator God and took the beauty, order, and lawful regularity of the universe as evidence of its intelligent and providential design. What can be known about God, therefore, is rationally deducible from the Creation. Ideas of supernatural interventions, miracles, and special revelations were, however, abandoned by most deists. Further, fundamental moral principles traditionally associated with religion and endowed with divine sanction were thought by deists to be rationally grounded and closely correlated with natural law, and thus required no intrinsically theological justification of their validity.[22]

Along with other dimensions of Enlightenment thought, the young Jefferson seems to have warmly embraced the deistic point of view. Although he never referred to himself as a deist, perhaps for fear of religious backlash (the label was a popular reprobation), he undoubtedly subscribed to the fundamental tenets of Deism, few as they were.[23] His youthful exposure to Deism precipitated a personal crisis of faith. Writing to J. P. Derieux (July 25, 1788), who had asked Jefferson to serve as a godparent to his child, Jefferson declined:

> The person who becomes sponsor for a child, according to the ritual of the church in which I was educated, makes a solemn profession, before god and the world, of faith in articles, which I had never sense enough to comprehend, and it has always appeared to me that comprehension must precede assent. The difficulty of reconciling the ideas of Unity and Trinity, have, *from a very early part of my life*, excluded me from *the office of sponsorship, often proposed* to me by my friends, who would have trusted, for the faithful discharge of it, to morality alone instead of which the church requires faith.

The "very early part of my life" mentioned here must refer to his days at William and Mary as the time when Jefferson, imbued with Enlightenment sensibilities, found himself strongly at odds with traditional Christianity. This is also shown by Jefferson's literary Commonplace Book, in which during his student days he made copious extracts from the works of Henry St. John, Viscount Bolingbroke, an English deist whose thoroughgoing rationalistic critique of Christianity the young Jefferson seems to have found irresistibly persuasive.[24] It is a fair assumption that from the 1760s until his acquaintance with the views of Joseph Priestley in the 1790s, Jefferson's thinking about religion made little or no advance beyond what he had absorbed from Bolingbroke. During those several decades Jefferson was an entirely typical deist who affirmed the existence of a creator God but rejected orthodox Christianity as incomprehensible to reason.

Deism enjoyed a measure of popularity in the colonies during the pre-Revolutionary and Revolutionary periods, but it was limited in its duration and in its constituency. It flourished in the interlude between two powerful revivalist movements that shaped American religious life: the Great Awakening and the Great Revival (sometimes called the Second Great Awakening).[25] The (first) Great Awakening originated with local manifestations in northeastern colonies in the 1720s, but by 1740 had become a robust religious fervor that spread throughout colonial America from New England to Georgia. Fueled by the open-air preaching of itinerant ministers, emphasizing personal religious experience and characterized by emotional extravagance, revival meetings attracted and energized thousands and effectively made evangelical Protestantism the religion of the American people. The energy, though not the effect, of the Great Awakening had largely dissipated by the late 1760s. But a fresh wave of revivalist enthusiasm, the "Great Revival," ensued about 1800, and while it affected all areas of the country, it aimed especially to evangelize the growing populations along the westward-moving frontier. It was in the decades of 1760–1800, the interim *between* these powerful revivalist movements, that Deism was fashionable among the educated elite and landed gentry.[26] Thus Jefferson was by no means peculiar in his embrace of Deism. Deism was not an organized movement, although it produced some energetic local societies and had its journalistic promoters. Nor was there ever a great multitude of deists in America, although many of them were prominent figures, including Ethan Allen, Benjamin Franklin, George Washington, Alexander Hamilton, and Thomas Paine.[27] Of these, Jefferson was the most sophisticated, well read, and articulate on the subject of religion. The deistic views that Jefferson had acquired from his teachers and his reading at William and Mary were doubtless reinforced during his service as minister to France (1784–89) through his acquaintance with various French *philosophes* who were deists, and strengthened still more with the publication of the most popular and influential of all deistic treatises, Thomas Paine's *Age of Reason, Being an Investigation of True and Fabulous Theology* in 1794.[28] Jefferson's deism nevertheless placed him in a religious minority, for in Virginia and in the new nation generally an evangelical Protestantism of a relatively orthodox and traditional sort held strong sway.

During this period of several decades most of what Jefferson had to say on the subject of religion—although it is not much—indicates a strong and consistent skepticism toward Christianity. In his famous letter to his nephew Peter Carr (August 10, 1787), Jefferson advised him to "Fix reason firmly in her seat, and call to her tribunal every fact, every opinion. Question with boldness even the existence of a god; because, if there be one, he must more approve the homage of reason, than that of blindfolded fear." Revealing a critical approach to the Bible, Jefferson suggested reading it

> as you would read Livy or Tacitus. The facts which are within the ordinary course of nature you will believe on the authority of the writer, as you do those of the same kind in Livy and Tacitus. . . . But those facts in the bible which contradict the laws of nature, must be examined with more care, and under a variety of faces. For example in the book of Joshua we are told the sun stood still several hours. Were we to read that fact in Livy or Tacitus we should class it with their showers of blood, speaking of statues, beasts &c., but it is said that the writer of that book was inspired. Examine therefore candidly what evidence there is of his having been inspired. . . . You will next read the new testament. It is the history of a personage called Jesus. Keep in your eye the opposite pretensions. 1. Of those who say he was begotten by god, born of a virgin, suspended and reversed the laws of nature at will, and ascended bodily into heaven: and 2. of those who say he was a man, of illegitimate birth, of a benevolent heart, enthusiastic mind, who set out without pretensions to divinity, ended in believing them, and was punished capitally for sedition by being gibbeted. . . . These questions are examined in the books I have mentioned under the head of religion, and several others. They will assist you in your enquiries, but keep your reason firmly on the watch in reading them all. Do not be frightened from this enquiry by any fear of it's consequences. . . . In fine, I repeat that you must lay aside all prejudice on both sides, and neither believe nor reject any thing because any other person, or description of persons have rejected or believed it. Your own reason is the only oracle given you by heaven, and you are answerable not for the rightness but uprightness of the decision.—I forgot to observe when speaking of the New testament that you should read all the histories of Christ, as well of those whom a council of ecclesiastics have decided for us to be Pseudo-evangelists, as those they named Evangelists, because these Pseudo-evangelists pretended to inspiration as much as the others, and you are to judge their pretensions by your own reason, and not by the reason of those ecclesiastics.

Jefferson's suggested perspective on the Bible was very much in accord with the approach of early deists and eighteenth-century pioneers of modern biblical criticism, who gave reason free rein in assessing the credibility and authority of the Bible.[29]

Jefferson's *Notes on the State of Virginia,* composed in 1782 and published in America in 1787, also offers some insight into his religious outlook. Particularly notable was the defense he gave there of the principle of religious freedom: "The legitimate powers of government extend to such acts only as are injurious to others. But it does me no injury for my neighbor to say there are twenty gods, or no god. It neither picks my pocket nor breaks my leg." Many readers took this less as an argument for religious liberty than as an expression of Jefferson's religious indifference: polytheism and atheism seemed equally unobjectionable to him. It was this statement more than any other that would soon become the basis of public suspicions about Jefferson's piety. But other passages in the *Notes* also expressed views that would provoke the pious. He doubted the reality of the Bible's universal flood; he called into question wide-spread theological opinion about the age of the Earth; he suggested that blacks may have been a distinct race from the Creation. To evangelicals, for whom the Bible was the irrefragable repository of divine truth, such insinuations were proof positive of Jefferson's irreligion. His proposal that the Bible should be kept out of the hands of children clinched the case.

Jefferson expressed his skepticism toward Christianity more clearly and specifically later on as he wrote more freely to trusted friends, and his skepticism often had a sharply polemical edge. Like other deists, he took explicit and strong exception to virtually all of the defining convictions of traditional, orthodox Christianity. Jefferson dismissed the doctrine of the Trinity as a mathematical absurdity born of philosophical mystification. Writing to John Adams (August 22, 1813) he commented that "it is too late in the day for men of sincerity to pretend they believe in the Platonic mysticisms that three are one, and one is three, and yet that the one is not three, and the three are not one" (an opinion in which Adams readily concurred). His ridicule of the doctrine of the Trinity was unrelenting.[30] For the sources of such an irrational concept he pointed to the dogmatic fourth-century Alexandrian bishop Athanasius, to the pernicious influence of Platonic philosophy on early Christianity, and to the self-serving obfuscations of the priesthood. In rejecting the doctrine of the Trinity Jefferson also rejected a correlative conviction of traditional Christianity, namely, the divine status of Jesus. If Jefferson was willing to ascribe to Jesus, as he wrote to Benjamin Rush (April 21, 1803), "every *human* excellence, and believing he never claimed any other," he would not go further. Years later, writing to William Short (August 4, 1820), Jefferson elaborated:

> That Jesus did not mean to impose himself on mankind as the son of god physically speaking I have been convinced by the writings of men more learned than myself in that lore. But that he might conscientiously believe himself inspired from above is very possible. Elevated by the enthusiasm of a warm and pure heart, conscious of the high strains of an eloquence which had not been taught him, he might easily mistake the coruscations of his own fine genius

for inspirations of an higher order. This belief carried therefore no more personal imputation, than the belief of Socrates, that himself was under the care and admonitions of a guardian daemon. And how many of our wisest men still believe in the reality of these inspirations while perfectly sane on all other subjects.

The notion of the divinity of Jesus was, for him, only another superstitious absurdity concocted by priests and theologians to bamboozle the gullible. Beyond these salient doctrines, Jefferson also rejected all ostensibly miraculous actions or occurrences, whether by Jesus or others, as merely fanciful imaginings. This point of view, held in common with virtually all deists of the period, was early expressed in the letter to his nephew Peter Carr (August 10, 1787), quoted above, but remained consistent throughout his life. In his letter to William Short (August 4, 1820), Jefferson regarded the miracles of the Gospels as falsifications, just as such events are to be judged when recounted by extrabiblical authors:

> When Livy and Siculus, for example, tell us things which coincide with our experience of the order of nature, we credit them on their word and place their narrations among the records of credible history. But when they tell us of calves speaking, of statues sweating blood, and other things against the course of nature, we reject these as fables not belonging to history.

Accordingly, the Bible as such is not to be granted any a priori authority, nor is its veracity to be taken for granted; rather, it is to be judged by reason, and not differently from any other body of ancient literature. In this same letter to Short, Jefferson appended as a footnote a list of additional elements of Christianity that he labeled "artificial systems":

> The immaculate conception of Jesus, his deification, the creation of the world by him, his miraculous powers, his resurrection and visible ascension, his corporeal presence in the Eucharist, the Trinity; original sin, atonement, regeneration, election, orders of hierarchy, &c.

Taking all this together, it is obvious that Jefferson vested no credence in Christianity in its traditional, historical form and as the vast majority of his contemporaries understood it. Although his disbelief is preponderantly expressed in his later correspondence, it undoubtedly began in his youth when he was a student at William and Mary. The Enlightenment ideas that he acquired there became foundational for him and remained constant for the rest of his life. Despite his reticence about his personal religious views, by the 1790s Jefferson had come to be regarded by many as a dangerous enemy to Christianity. This was mainly on account of his comments in *Notes on the State of Virginia* and his opposition to state support of religion.

The Influence of Joseph Priestley

Jefferson's steady antipathy for Christianity came under reconsideration, however, in the 1790s. The principal stimulus to this development was Jefferson's acquaintance with Joseph Priestley and his work.[31] Priestley (1733–1804) was an English polymath—clergyman, scientist, philosopher, historian—but he considered himself to be mainly a theological thinker. Originally a Presbyterian, Priestley's religious ideas became progressively unorthodox. At the same time, he advocated the toleration of religious diversity and the autonomy of congregations and opposed the idea of a state church. He was a prolific writer on religion, but his most influential and controversial work was his *History of the Corruptions of Christianity*, published in 1782.[32] His religious and political ideas led to his harassment and persecution in England, and in 1794 he emigrated to America, settling in Pennsylvania.[33]

Jefferson gained his initial personal acquaintance with Priestley when he attended the latter's lectures in Philadelphia in 1797. But several years earlier, perhaps in 1793, he had read Priestley's *History of the Corruptions of Christianity*, a work that had an enormous impact on him.[34] In it Priestley argued that Christianity, in its original and pure form, was a simple, straightforward, and rational religion proclaimed by Jesus, but that early on, his followers corrupted it by introducing various irrational doctrines that perverted the initial impulse and turned Christianity into a muddle of mysteries and a sponsor of superstition. On the basis of historical research, Priestley argued that Jesus and the earliest Christians were Unitarians, and that the doctrine of the Trinity was a subsequent imposition made in dependence on pagan philosophy and polytheism. Priestley also denied the divinity of Jesus, asserting that he was no more than a human being, yet one gifted with profound moral insight, a capacity to work miracles, and indeed even the power of resurrection and ascension. But the death of Jesus was not atoning, nor was any atonement necessary, for Priestley denied any original, innate, or inevitable sinfulness of human nature. Jesus' principal significance, therefore, was as a supreme moral teacher and exemplar. Other traditional or widely held Christian convictions, such as the preexistence of Christ, election/predestination, the plenary inspiration of scripture, transubstantiation, and the immateriality and immortality of the soul, Priestley likewise dismissed as corruptions of aboriginal Christianity. The real substance of Christianity, he urged, is responsiveness to the one God through obedience to the moral norms mediated by reason, conscience, and nature, and especially as expounded in the teaching of Jesus.[35] Moreover, a thoroughly accurate understanding of true Christianity was available to anyone through the freedom of conscience and the exercise of rational judgment. Clergymen and professional theologians were superfluous.

In Joseph Priestley, Jefferson came upon a like-minded rationalist dissenter, but one who was far more knowledgeable about scripture and about early Christian history and thought than Jefferson himself—a real "expert" upon whom he could confidently rely. Priestley provided not merely logical but also historical arguments for conclusions that comported closely, though not completely, with basic tenets of Jefferson's long-standing deism. And, by representing aboriginal Christianity as a rational, Unitarian, and essentially moral system, without much metaphysical baggage, Priestley had at last presented Jefferson with the previously unthinkable possibility of regarding himself as a Christian. As Jefferson put it, Priestley had succeeded in "simplifying the Christian philosophy—the most sublime & benevolent, but most perverted system that ever shone on man" (Jefferson to Joseph Priestley, March 21, 1801). In doing so, he enabled Jefferson to say, "To the corruptions of Christianity I am indeed opposed; but not to the genuine precepts of Jesus himself. I am a Christian, in the only sense he wished anyone to be; sincerely attached to his doctrines, in preference to all others" (Jefferson to Benjamin Rush, April 21, 1803). Still more emphatically, Jefferson wrote to Charles Thomson (January 9, 1816): ". . . I am a *real Christian,* that is to say, a disciple of the doctrines of Jesus, very different from the Platonists, who call *me* infidel and *themselves* Christians and preachers of the gospel, while they draw all their characteristic dogmas from what its author never said nor saw."

In short, Priestley critically redefined Christianity in a way that largely conformed to views that Jefferson *already* held, and thus gave Jefferson license to lay claim to the label "Christian," yet with virtually no alteration in his religious ideas. Accordingly, it was from this point on that Jefferson permitted himself to regard orthodox or traditional Christians as "mere usurpers of the Christian name, teaching a counter-religion made up of the *deliria* of crazy imaginations, as foreign from Christianity as that of Mahomet." Further, "their blasphemies have driven thinking men into infidelity, who have too hastily rejected the author himself, with the horrors so falsely imputed to him."[36] Jefferson had been one of those "thinking men," but Priestley gave him opportunity to reconsider Christianity and his attitude toward it.

Of course, Jefferson was not in agreement with the whole cloth of Priestley's representation of Christianity. Priestley believed that Jesus, though a human being, was the promised messiah with a divinely appointed mission to save humankind, but Jefferson affirmed only his humanity. Priestley allowed the possibility of miracles, including the resurrection and ascension of Jesus, which Jefferson did not, and he accepted the idea of judgment and life after death, about which Jefferson remained, at best, uncertain.[37] Moreover, Priestley affirmed the authority of scripture and gave strong credence to biblical prophecy (and would later become a fervent millenarian), which Jefferson's stricter rationalism precluded. Such large differences aside, Priestley had provided grounds enough for Jefferson to consider his own religious views no longer merely idiosyncratic and anti-Christian, but now, instead, as both precocious and authentically Christian.[38]

Priestley provided additional stimulus to Jefferson's religious thought with a little pamphlet entitled *Socrates and Jesus Compared,* published in 1803. In writing to thank him for sending a copy of it (April 9, 1803), Jefferson exhorted Priestley to enlarge that project so as to take account of a larger number of ancient moralists, including the Jews, and thus to demonstrate more fully the superiority of the moral teachings of Jesus, "the most innocent, the most benevolent, the most eloquent and sublime character that has ever been exhibited to man." It was only two weeks later that Jefferson wrote to Benjamin Rush (April 21, 1803), enclosing a "Syllabus of an Estimate of the Merit of the Doctrines of Jesus, Compared with Those of Others," which provided an outline of the more extensive treatment of the subject that he had recently proposed to Priestley. Some months later, Jefferson again wrote to Priestley (January 29, 1804) expressing his satisfaction that Priestley had now undertaken the more elaborate project Jefferson had suggested (which, however, was never accomplished). In that letter Jefferson went on to intimate that he himself had earlier "sent to Philadelphia to get two testaments Greek of the same edition, & two English, with a design to cut out the morsels of morality, and paste them on the leaves of a book," thus to furnish a kind of epitome of the moral teachings of Jesus.[39] In a much later letter to John Adams (October 12, 1813) Jefferson recalled the task of discriminating in the Gospels between authentic and spurious teachings of Jesus:

> I have performed this operation for my own use, by cutting verse by verse out of the printed book and arranging the matter which is evidently his, and which is as easily distinguished as diamonds in a dunghill. The result is an 8 vo. of 46. pages of pure and unsophisticated doctrines, such as were professed and acted on by the simple Christians of the first century, that is, before Platonizing priests and theologians began to corrupt the tradition.

Yet again, in writing to his longtime friend Charles Thomson (January 9, 1816), who had sent him a copy of a synopsis of the Gospels, Jefferson referred to having made

> a wee-little book from the same materials [the Gospels], which I call the Philosophy of Jesus; it is a paradigma of his doctrines, made by cutting the texts out of the book, and arranging them on the pages of a blank book, in a certain order of time or subject. A more beautiful or precious morsel of ethics I have never seen.

This little book of excerpts from the Gospels, fashioned in 1803–4 while Jefferson was president, was obviously stimulated by Priestley's work, and was the precursor of a later and fuller effort. In 1820, deep in his retirement, Jefferson returned to the project of making a digest of the teachings of Jesus. Using the same scissors-and-paste method, he arranged the texts of the passages he selected in four parallel columns of different languages—Greek, Latin, English, and French—with two columns per page. In this collection he included some narrative elements from the Gospels in addition to the chosen teachings, but excluded all miraculous elements and any texts suggesting that Jesus was more than human. Thus revised and enlarged—this version ran to 86 pages—it was also retitled "The Life and Morals of Jesus of Nazareth." This compilation later came to be popularly called the "Jefferson Bible."[40]

It is clear that Priestley provided the stimulus, the arguments, and the conceptual framework that enabled Jefferson to understand and represent his own long-standing and fundamentally deistic religious ideas as "Christian," and to dismiss his erstwhile Christian critics as themselves misguided. At the same time, Priestley gave Jefferson an opportunity to reassess the figure of Jesus and to come to a more positive appreciation of his moral teachings relative to the ancient philosophical moralists whom Jefferson had been accustomed to admire. Despite Jefferson's ready appropriation of many of his ideas, Priestley was not himself a deist, and he considered Jefferson's views to be extreme.[41]

Jefferson was all the more glad to embrace and exploit Priestley's ideas soon after the election of 1800, the first national election in which religion played a prominent part. In it Jefferson's political opponents relentlessly vilified him for his alleged impiety. The Federalist clergy of New England decried him as a heretic, atheist, or infidel, and as such a grave danger to the nation.[42] But with the aid of Priestley's construal of Christianity, Jefferson thought he could claim complete acquittal of such charges, and apparently found great satisfaction in doing so. It was he, after all, and not his critics, who adhered to "real" Christianity. In this confidence Jefferson began to express himself rather more freely on religious topics and to elaborate his conceptions, at least to his good friends, thus working to assure them, and no doubt himself as well, that he understood Christianity better than most and adhered to its true import.

Priestley's contention, that the simple teachings of Jesus had been corrupted by theologians and philosophers who introduced irrational doctrines, dovetailed nicely with a theory that Jefferson had acquired much earlier, namely, what he called "priestcraft." There is no more recurrent trope than this in Jefferson's discussions of religion. The theory of priestcraft had originated as an anti-Catholic theme in the Protestant Reformation of the sixteenth century, but it proved particularly useful in the seventeenth-century deistic critique of Christianity. The early deists alleged that an original, universal, natural, and rational religion had been co-opted and adulterated by priests, who turned it into an esoteric system of dogmatic mysteries and arcane rituals, which they manipulated to enhance their own power and wealth while deceiving the pious and depriving them of free judgment.[43] "Revealed religion" was thus merely a scheme contrived by the priestly caste to subjugate and exploit the ignorant. Jefferson was early exposed to this idea through Bolingbroke, but it is likely that his experience of vigorous French anticlericalism during his years in Paris and his irritation at clerical presumptions in America served to confirm and strengthen it.[44] Although the theory of priestly conspiracy had long been available to Jefferson, it seems to have come to the forefront of his thinking as a result of the attacks on him by the Federalist clergy in the elections of 1796 and 1800, and he would deploy it again later on as a result of clergy attacks on his plans for the University of Virginia.[45] His frequent broadsides against priests are not at all nuanced historically, theologically, or denominationally: any who would presume to speak officially and pronounce authoritatively about religion were included—Protestant preachers and pastors as well as Roman and Anglican priests. But the theory of priestcraft was valuable to Jefferson for two reasons. First, it explained the history of Christianity in a way that enabled him to dismiss those features of it that he disliked; second, it explained how "religion" came to be a state-supported establishment, colluding with monarchic governments to repress political liberty and freedom of thought. It was the league of priests and kings—the alliance of altar and throne—that had enslaved humanity to dogma and to tyranny, each reinforcing the other. At once a trenchant critique of Christianity and a baleful warning against melding church and state, "priestcraft" was a useful concept. But if Jefferson constantly recurred to this theme in his theological polemics, its function was almost entirely theoretical and rhetorical: it appears to have had no general or practical effect in his regard for or his relationships with individual clergymen, many of whom he admired and considered friends.

Jefferson's conception of Christianity, like Priestley's, was "restorationist"— that is, it aimed to reach back not only behind the formal doctrines of the Christian church but also behind the Bible in order to recover and restore what was presumed to be the pure, simple, and uncorrupted religion of Jesus himself, which was taken to be the true essence of Christianity. Although in Jefferson's case this "restoration" was hardly more than an unhistorical projection of his own views onto Jesus, it was also an ironic anticipation of another restorationist movement that would later acquire a large influence at Jefferson's University, namely the Disciples of Christ.[46]

Jefferson's Mature Religious Ideas

Priestley, though originally Presbyterian, had become a prominent and controversial Unitarian while in England; having crossed the Atlantic, he became an equally prominent and controversial Unitarian in America. Although there was a Unitarian church (King's Chapel) in Boston by 1785, and although Unitarianism was already gaining a foothold among the Congregational churches of eastern Massachusetts, Priestley became an important exponent of Unitarian thought during the decade of his American residence. As one of Priestley's earliest and most appreciative American followers, Jefferson wrote (November 4, 1820) to Jared Sparks, the noted Unitarian pastor and later president of Harvard, saying, "The religion of Jesus is founded in the Unity of God, and this principle chiefly, gave it triumph over the rabble of heathen gods then acknowledged. Thinking men of all nations rallied readily to the doctrine of one only God, and embraced it with the pure morals which Jesus inculcated." He expressed himself similarly in a letter to Timothy Pickering (February 27, 1821): "I have little doubt that the whole of our country will soon be rallied to the Unity of the Creator, and, I hope, to the pure doctrines of Jesus also." And with great enthusiasm he wrote to Benjamin Waterhouse (June 26, 1822): "the genuine doctrine of one only God is reviving, and I trust that there is not a *young man* now living in the United States who will not die an Unitarian." Later that same year, writing to Thomas Cooper (November 22, 1822), Jefferson remained fully confident of the progress of Unitarianism in America: "That this will, ere long, be the religion of the majority from north to south, I have no doubt." Jefferson actually refers to himself as a Unitarian in a letter written to Benjamin Waterhouse (January 8, 1825): "I am anxious to see the doctrine of one god commenced in our state. But the population of my neighborhood is too slender, and is too much divided into other sects to maintain any one preacher well. I must therefore be contented to be an Unitarian by myself, although I know there are many around me who would become so, if once they could hear the questions fairly stated." To the extent that, at least in its principal emphasis, Unitarianism approximated to deism, Jefferson seems to have thought that religion in America was tending strongly in his direction.[47] But he was mistaken.

If the deism of Jefferson's early decades was relatively popular in the colonies in the Revolutionary period, especially among the educated and affluent, by the time that Priestley had provided Jefferson with a means to label himself as "Christian" the tide of popular religious sentiment had already begun to sweep strongly ahead of him. Breaking out about 1800 was "the Great Revival" or "Second Great Awakening," a fresh wave of religious enthusiasm that would powerfully rejuvenate and promote evangelical Protestantism during the first half of the nineteenth century. Its intense emotionalism, strict biblicism, and doctrinal traditionalism were strong countercurrents to deism, which it washed away, and also to emergent Unitarianism, which it sought successfully to marginalize. Hence even with his newfound Unitarian "Christianity" Jefferson's religious ideas were destined to remain a small eddy outside the mainstream of popular religion. If his deistic views had been avant-garde in the pre-Revolutionary and Revolutionary periods, by the early nineteenth century they had passed out of fashion. And while many of Jefferson's contemporaries who in their younger years held deist views were now being reclaimed for evangelical Christianity by the Great Revival, Jefferson was repelled by its emotional fervor and regarded it as "a threatening cloud of fanaticism."[48] To a thoroughgoing rationalist, such religious enthusiasm could have no appeal.

There was, then, little actual development in Jefferson's religious ideas over the course of his life, from his collegiate days to his old age. In several letters written late in life to close and sympathetic friends Jefferson set out his personal religious convictions, which were few and straightforward: that there is one God, who is known in nature and through reason; and that morality, chiefly doing good to one's neighbors, is the essence of Christianity and indeed of all real religion.[49] This "ethical monotheism" was entirely in keeping with deism, but scarcely equivalent to Christianity. As we have seen, Jefferson was never able to make sense of, let alone affirm, those convictions that have historically been central to Christianity—the doctrine of the Trinity, the deity of Christ, the virginal conception, the resurrection and ascension of Jesus, and so on. For him these were merely Platonizing fabrications deserving of "euthanasia."

Moreover, in spite of having gained and professed admiration for the moral teachings of Jesus—or at least for those he regarded as genuine—Jefferson did not concur fully with Jesus, nor did he think the teachings of Jesus morally sufficient.[50] They required to be supplemented, and so Jefferson freely ranged alongside them the moral teachings of classical philosophers, especially of Epictetus and Epicurus. Writing to William Short (October 31, 1819), he noted that "Epictetus and Epicurus give laws for governing ourselves, Jesus [gives] a supplement of the duties and charities we owe to others." In the same letter he declared, "I too am an Epicurean," and attached a digest he had made of the principal doctrines of Epicurus, most of which stand in sharp tension with traditional Christianity, but Jefferson saw no incongruity with his own conception of Christianity.

Throughout his life Jefferson was an ardent opponent of doctrine and dogma, and this for several reasons. For one, dogma was authoritatively laid down, sought no endorsement of reason, and indeed usually appeared contrary to reason. Thus it violated freedom of thought. For another, doctrine produced sectarianism, encouraging divisions and disputes between Christians over fine points of theology or polity while minimizing the common affirmations of the existence of God and moral responsibility. But also, and not least important, doctrine and dogma made metaphysical claims and hence were merely speculative, whereas Jefferson, relying on empirical observation, maintained a profound distaste for metaphysics and speculative thought. In his view, metaphysics was the handmaid of spiritualists and mystifiers and produced nothing but foggy fantasies. When Sheldon Clark sent copies of some pamphlets he had written, Jefferson rather ungraciously replied (December 5, 1825):

> I revolt against all metaphysical reading, in which class your 'New pamphlet' must at least be placed. Some acquaintance with the operations of the mind is worth acquiring, but any *one* of the writers suffices for that. Locke, Kaims [*sic*], Hartley, Reid, Brown Tracy E'c. Those dreams of the day, like those of the night, vanish in vapour, leaving not a wreck behind. The business of life is with matter. That gives us tangible results. Handling that, we arrive at the knologe of the axe, the plough, the steam-boat, and every thing useful in life. But, from metaphysical speculations, I have never seen one useful result.

The basis of Jefferson's aversion to metaphysics was his materialism. As he wrote to John Adams (August 15, 1820), "to talk of *immaterial* existences is to talk of *nothings*. To say that the human soul, angels, god, are immaterial, is to say they are *nothings*, or that there is no god, no angels, no soul. I cannot reason otherwise: but I believe I am supported in my creed of materialism by Locke, Tracy, and Stewart. At what age of the Christian church this heresy of *immaterialism,* this masked atheism, crept in, I do not know. But a heresy it certainly is." Further, our acquaintance with matter is through sensation: only what we can feel or perceive with our senses is real, and sensation is the measure of religious truth as of other truth. In the same letter to Adams, he continued:

> Rejecting all organs of information, therefore, but my senses, I rid myself of all the pyrrhonisms with which an indulgence in speculations hyperphysical and antiphysical, so uselessly occupy and disquiet the mind. A single sense may indeed sometimes be deceived, but rarely; and never all our senses together, with their faculty of reasoning. They evidence realities, and there are enough of these for all the purposes of life, without plunging into the fathomless abyss of dreams and phantasms. I am satisfied, and sufficiently occupied with the things which are, without tormenting or troubling myself about those which may indeed be, but of which I have no evidence.

Together, materialism and sensation ensure the certainty, the intelligibility, and the usefulness of ideas.[51]

The conjunction in Jefferson's thought of rationalism, empiricism, materialism, and sensationism inevitably resulted in a radical devaluation not merely of metaphysics but of religious thought and theology generally. Hence it is unsurprising that in writing to Francis Van der Kemp (July 30, 1816) he remarked, "I rarely waste time in reading on theological subjects." If Jefferson thought there were perhaps a good many things that could be learned *about* religion, he did not think there was much to be learned *from* it. Theological claims, being essentially and inescapably speculative, are readily questionable and of small value. Thus in Jefferson's view religious ideas did not, as a rule, constitute genuine knowledge. Rather, religious doctrines were matters only of "opinion," not of knowledge, and could only be private and subjective, not public and objective.[52] Religion could not, therefore, be considered among what Jefferson regarded as "the useful sciences."

By contrast, the two fixed and fundamental elements of Jefferson's own religious outlook—the existence of a creator God and the existence of a moral order—were, to his mind, neither metaphysical nor speculative but based upon reason and experience. His theism was ostensibly empirical: he considered belief in a creator God to be a direct and necessary inference from the natural order itself. Because the universe could be comprehended by reason through scientific study, the creation must be the product of a rational Being. He wrote to John Adams (April 11, 1823) that

I hold (without appeal to revelation) that when we take a view of the Universe, in it's parts general or particular, it is impossible for the human mind not to perceive and feel a conviction of design, consummate skill, and indefinite power in every atom of it's composition, the movements of the heavenly bodies, so exactly held in their course by the balance of centrifugal and centripetal forces, the structure of our earth itself, with it's distribution of lands, waters and atmosphere, animal and vegetable bodies, examined in all their minutest particles, insects mere atoms of life, yet as perfectly organised as man or mammoth, the mineral substances, their generation and uses, [it] is impossible, I say, for the human mind not to believe that there is, in all this, design, cause and effect, up to an ultimate cause, a fabricator of all things from matter and motion, their preserver and regulator while permitted to exist in their present forms, and their regenerator into new and other forms.

The argument from design was decisive.[53] But notably, in this same letter to Adams, after asserting with great confidence the *existence* of God, Jefferson goes on to say: "Of the nature of this Being we know nothing." Notwithstanding this virtually complete agnosticism about the nature of God, he frequently characterized God not only as Creator but also as "intelligent" and "benevolent" and, sometimes, as "providential." Presumably, he considered such attributes to be implicit in the argument from design, and thus as correlatives of God's existence. All such statements, then, were predicated on the empirical observation of the universe. Jefferson's usual epithets for God are consistently general and abstract and do not connote any fuller or additional apprehensions of the divine nature. Absent appeals to revelation or metaphysical speculation, neither of which he condoned, knowledge of God was sharply limited for Jefferson. Even such knowledge as he asserted was, of course, open to question, for the argument from design was not persuasive to all.

Not less "empirical" than his theism was Jefferson's belief in a fundamental moral order, for the sense of right and wrong—the "moral instinct" or "moral sense" as he called it—seemed to be universal, innate to human beings, and readily accessible to everyone, though it required to be cultivated, exercised, and refined. But even if, as Jefferson thought, the moral sense was an endowment of the Creator, that did not make religion the basis or source of morality.[54] Rather, religion was, for him, essentially reducible to morality. As he wrote to James Fishback (September 27, 1809), "Reading, reflection and time have convinced me that the interests of society require the observation of those moral precepts only in which all religions agree (for all forbid us to steal, murder, plunder, or bear false witness), and that we should not intermeddle with the

particular dogmas in which all religions differ, and which are totally uncon-
nected with morality."[55] But whether or not behavior would be rewarded or
punished in a life beyond this world appears to be something of which Jefferson
remained uncertain. Such a prospect, however, he seems to have regarded at
least as a useful incentive to morality, and one provided by religion.

To Jefferson the appeal of an "ethical monotheism" such as was represented
by deism and subsequently by Unitarianism was not only rational; it was also
politically beneficial. Jefferson inhabited a religiously pluralistic society, even if
it was the pluralism mainly of diverse Christian sects, and he thought that this
sectarianism, fostered by competition and internecine debates over doctrines,
polities, and morals, threatened social cohesion and political consensus. Unitarianism seemed to offer a solution to the tensions and conflicts of pluralism. Because it embodied the least common denominator of all the sects, he supposed
it was a religious viewpoint in which all might agree. In this Jefferson under-
estimated the strength of sectarian loyalty, the importance vested in doctrine
and polity, and indeed the nature of religious experience and commitment in
traditional religious communities. Unitarianism might find a small place among
the sects, but it could not displace them. Nevertheless, a vague and minimal
deism such as Jefferson espoused did come to constitute the so-called civil
religion of the new nation, which saw itself standing under the overarching
providence of a benign creator God.[56]

For Jefferson, religion, like anything else, had to be thoroughly rational
to be tenable, respectable, and practical. His own religious ideas, he believed,
met this criterion. At the same time, religion for Jefferson seems to have been
an entirely intellectual matter. Like many other Enlightenment thinkers, he
viewed religion as a set of propositions seeking intellectual consent, and understood religious assertions to be on the order of factual claims comparable to scientific statements. Consequently, religion as he construed it seems not to have
been anything deeply *felt:* it appears to have lacked an affective dimension, a
deep inner conviction, or a forceful existential relevance. Regarding religion,
he seems to have been a man without passion, save in his polemics against
what he disapproved about it and in his insistence that it must be free. There
was little in his private life or his public life to indicate that he was a person of
strong piety.[57]

Although of the founding fathers Jefferson was among the most interested
in and knowledgeable about religion, his own religious views were minimalist
and, one might say, hardly "religious" in a conventional sense: his belief in
God was a philosophical postulate born of empirical inference rather than of
any personal apprehension of transcendent mystery, and his moral principles,

while broadly humanistic, neither claimed nor needed a religious foundation.[58] But it could not be otherwise, given his thoroughgoing rationalism: religion within the limits of mere reason is necessarily reductionist. In Jefferson's case it yielded primarily a divine sanction for political rights and a socially useful moral incentive, but little more.

Small wonder, then, that as Jefferson conceived the University of Virginia and labored to establish it, he envisioned an institution that was independent of any particular religious tradition, whether Christian or any other, and offered instruction in none. In matters religious what might be contemplated was only what all religions had in common, namely, the existence of God and fundamental moral principles. The focus of the University would be on useful knowledge gained by rational and scientific means. Religion, as a matter of private judgment and personal opinion, would lie as much beyond the purview of the University as it did beyond the dictates of the state.

2
Jefferson's Vision
A Secular University

Thomas Jefferson reckoned the founding of the University of Virginia among his three greatest accomplishments, the other two being the drafting of the Declaration of Independence and the authorship of the Virginia Statute for Religious Freedom. So it is not surprising that when Jefferson conceived the University of Virginia, he envisioned a public institution committed to the Enlightenment ideal of untrammeled reason, based on "the illimitable freedom of the human mind to explore and to expose every subject susceptible of its contemplation." No religion would have any formal status in the institution, and no religion would have any normative influence on its operations. The University would be a-religious, that is, without religion. Religion would be institutionally absent. This is what is meant when Jefferson's conception of the University is described as "secular."[1] It was precisely this intention to make the University independent of and indifferent to religion that generated the deepest reservations and the most strident criticisms before, during, and, as we shall see, long after the founding of the University.

By insisting that the University be subject neither to the authority nor to the influence of any organized religious body or particular religious tradition, and that no religious posture be endorsed or promoted, Jefferson was departing sharply from long tradition and common practice. Since the cathedral schools of medieval times, religion and education had been hand in glove. Virtually all the institutions of higher learning that had arisen in America during the colonial period were deeply enmeshed in religion, and indeed the majority of them were established by particular denominations with the principal aim of providing an educated clergy.[2] Thus Harvard (1636), Yale (1701), and Dartmouth (1769) were organs of the New England Puritan/Congregational churches; William and Mary (1693), Columbia (originally Kings College, 1754), and the University of Pennsylvania (originally the College of Philadelphia, 1755) were instruments of the Church of England; Princeton (originally the College of New Jersey, 1746) was a bastion of Presbyterianism, Rutgers (originally Queens College, 1766) of the Dutch Reformed churches, and Brown (originally, the College of Rhode Island, 1764) of the Baptists.

Even the state universities that were chartered and opened before the University of Virginia were under strong clerical and denominational influence. The public institutions of higher education established by Georgia (1785), North Carolina (1789), and South Carolina (1801) placed clergymen in positions of leadership, freely appointed ministers to faculty positions, were governed by boards heavily populated by devout men, and were responsive to denominational interests. These institutions, though publicly sponsored and supported, nevertheless took an explicit interest in the religious education and spiritual nurture of their students, and pressed religious belief and practice upon them through regulations requiring regular attendance at religious services.[3] Jefferson intended something different.

The Development of Jefferson's Ideas about the University

In his plan for the University of Virginia, Jefferson not only eschewed ecclesiastical sponsorship and denominational control but also sought to marginalize religion. He aimed to minimize the influence of religion upon its policies, faculty, or curriculum, and he imposed no religious expectations or duties upon its faculty or its students. In this Jefferson was variously guided by his own experience in relation to the College of William and Mary, by his long-standing convictions about religious freedom and the separation of church and state, and by his own religious ideas. All shaped his determination that religion would have no role at the University of Virginia.

In many ways Jefferson conceived of the University of Virginia in deliberate contrast to his own alma mater, the College of William and Mary. Jefferson had a poor regard for that institution, which during his own time there "was repeatedly disrupted by bitter internal and external quarrels, discredited by disorderly, drunken and licentious clergymen-professors, and embarrassed by a bibulous president who died a disgraced drunkard not long after Jefferson arrived."[4] Indeed, Jefferson subsequently found opportunities to press for changes at William and Mary.

As a member of the Virginia House of Delegates (1776–78) Jefferson drafted two bills: one was his well-known Bill for the More General Diffusion of Knowledge; the other was a Bill for Amending the Constitution of the College of William and Mary.[5] This latter bill proposed, among other things, to enlarge the number of professorships from six to eight, with the following purviews: moral philosophy, law, history, mathematics, medicine, natural philosophy, ancient languages, and modern languages. Notably, it made no provision for a professor of divinity, whereas at the time two of the six professors were professors of divinity.[6] The bill also provided for significant changes in the governance of the college, including reducing the number of Visitors from eighteen to five, adding three chancellors, all appointed by the legislature and in the exercise of their duties free not only from royal prerogative and English law but also "from the canons or constitution of the English Church." It is clear that with this bill Jefferson intended not merely that the curriculum should be enlarged but that the college should be reorganized on a secular basis.[7] The bill, however, failed of enactment on account of what Jefferson called the "religious jealousies" of dissenters.

In 1779 Jefferson was elected governor of Virginia, and became ex officio a Visitor at William and Mary. In these capacities he gained an opportunity to accomplish some reforms in the college, without the cooperation of the legislature, by promoting changes internally with the support of the college president, Rev. James Madison, his friend from childhood (not to be confused with the James Madison of constitutional and presidential fame), the board, and most of the faculty. These reforms aimed at a far-reaching makeover. They eliminated the professorial chairs of divinity and of oriental languages (which included the study of scripture), and added professorships in law, medicine, and modern languages to those of moral philosophy, natural philosophy, and mathematics. The grammar school, in which (among other things) the Christian catechism was taught, was abolished. Clearly, one of the most important objectives of these reforms was to deprive religion of both curricular representation and compulsory observance.[8] In Jefferson's view these were all progressive steps, but the changes did not last.

A decade after making these changes, when he returned to America from France, Jefferson found that the circumstances at William and Mary were as bad as before, and indeed worse: the grammar school had been reinstituted, the professorship of medicine was defunct, the professorship of law had been vacated by Jefferson's distinguished mentor, George Wythe, who found the conduct of some of his faculty colleagues intolerable, a degree in divinity had been established, and students were required to attend morning and evening prayers. If in the late 1770s Jefferson had hoped that William and Mary might be reformed and modernized so as to assume a respected place in a state educational system, by 1790 he seems to have abandoned that prospect. In his view the college was bound to the colonial past, enmeshed with ecclesiastical interests, saddled with cumbersome governance, and possessed of an undistinguished faculty. As such, it was beyond redemption.

We hear nothing more of Jefferson's educational ideas until 1800, when, during his term as vice president, he wrote a letter (January 18) to Joseph Priestley. Yet this letter makes it clear that Jefferson had not only continued to think about education but had been discussing it with his friends in Virginia: it had been "the subject of consultation among the ablest and highest characters of our State." He writes of William and Mary as "a college just well enough endowed to draw out the miserable existence to which a miserable constitution has doomed it." As a counterpoint, he expresses a wish to establish in Virginia "an University so broad and liberal and modern as to be worth patronizing with the public support, and be a temptation to the youth of other states to come and drink of the cup of knowledge and fraternize with us." Having washed his hands of William and Mary a decade earlier, Jefferson and his friends had begun to think in fresh terms. Now Jefferson solicited Priestley's ideas about a suitable academic plan—what subjects would be appropriate and how they might be arranged among a relatively small and affordable number of professors. Jefferson tentatively sketched out his own ideas of subjects that might be treated (he did not mention religion or divinity among these), but awaited the well-informed thoughts of Priestley. This letter was quickly followed up with another (January 27, 1800) in which Jefferson hastened to remedy his inadvertent omission of languages from subjects of study and to mention that although his earlier Bill for the General Diffusion of Knowledge, establishing a system of public schools statewide, had not been passed, nevertheless there were in Virginia a number of viable secondary schools upon whose instruction the curricular "superstructure" of a university might rest.

After retiring from the presidency and public life in 1809, Jefferson continued to pursue his educational ideas, now with hope of their practical implementation. But it was not until 1814 that things began to take shape. In March of that year Jefferson joined the board of trustees of Albemarle Academy. Albemarle Academy had originated in 1803 when the Virginia General Assembly authorized the establishment of a grammar school in Albemarle County and named a group of trustees, but provided no funding. For more than a decade it existed only on paper; nothing was done to bring it into being and put it into operation. But once Jefferson joined the board, he began to co-opt the moribund initiative to his own ends.[9] In May of 1814 he helped draft a petition to the General Assembly seeking funds for the school, but also asking the Legislature to recharter Albemarle Academy as Central College. In the autumn of that year Jefferson wrote to Peter Carr (September 7, 1814) with a full proposal of what might be taught "in the academy or college to be established in our neighborhood," but he also included a broad overview of the educational needs of the Commonwealth as a whole. The college, he proposed, should consist of general schools and professional schools. For the curriculum of the general schools Jefferson specifies three broadly construed areas of "useful science," namely, (1) Language (to include history, belles lettres, rhetoric, etc.), (2) Mathematics (to include also the natural sciences and medicine), and (3) Philosophy (to include ethics, law, government, and economics). The professional schools where advanced studies would be pursued include theology and ecclesiastical history, law, medicine, architecture, technical philosophy (i.e., applied skills), rural economy (i.e., agriculture), and the fine arts. Jefferson, in conclusion, grouped all these under only four professorships: a first, of languages and history, literature and rhetoric; a second of mathematics, including physics, anatomy, and medicine; a third of chemistry, biology, and mineralogy; and a fourth of philosophy. For our immediate interest, it is noteworthy that he mentions, among the professional schools, instruction in theology and ecclesiastical history. It need not be assumed that Jefferson intended this for Central College, for he prefaces the whole scheme with the comment that "we must ascertain with precision the object of our institution, by taking a survey of the general field of science, and marking out the portion we mean to occupy at first," and later says that "the sciences of the second grade [that is, of the general schools] are our first object," and makes no further mention of the professional schools. But even if it were intended for Central College, that institution was conceived as private, not public, and as funded by private subscriptions, not public funds, and on those terms the teaching of religion would be allowable.

Jefferson sent a copy of this letter to some friends, including Thomas Cooper (September 10, 1814), soliciting their suggestions about the curriculum. Cooper's letter in reply (September 22, 1814) strongly admonished Jefferson *not* to include religion among the subjects of study:

> I reject the Department of Theology: for reasons numerous and I think very
> weighty, but which need not be repeated. Where there exists a national system

of religion, there ought to be a church establishment to support it, and regular seminaries in which should be taught the dogmata and their defences which the nation has thought fit politically to adopt. If religion be politically necessary, then teach it without regard to the truth of the adopted system: but if you are to teach theology in your university on the ground of its truth, who is to judge which System is true? Suppose you teach Ecclesiastical History: any body can read it at home. Who can read it at all, with prejudices in favour of any System? Will you teach the Evidences of Christianity, internal and external? Is it not *fraud* unless you teach the objections also? What seminary will venture upon this? Avoid this: it is a Noli me tangere.

Jefferson responded to this stern warning by agreeing "a professorship of Theology has no place in our institution." He went on to say, however, "we cannot always do what is absolutely best. Those with whom we act, entertaining different views, have the power and right of carrying them into practice. Truth advances and error recedes step by step only."[10] Jefferson's political realism, his knowledge of traditional curricular design, and his sense of the strength of popular religious sentiment apparently made him uncertain whether religion could be excluded.

The 1814 petition to the General Assembly for a change in the charter of Albemarle Academy was approved and passed into law on February 14, 1816, and thus Central College was brought into existence in place of Albemarle Academy. But because the legislature failed to provide the requested funding, progress depended on voluntary public contributions. Those contributions were generous enough to enable the purchase of a tract of land and to undertake some initial construction.

At the same time, Jefferson continued to pursue the idea of a state university. Working with ideas formulated in connection with his earlier Bill for the General Diffusion of Knowledge, originally drafted in 1779 but never passed into law, he drew up a proposal for a system of public education that culminated in a state university. The proposal was submitted to the General Assembly, which passed a modified form of it on February 21, 1818, and made a small allocation of monies for the creation of an institution to be called "The University of Virginia." This action, though modest, raised a series of important questions: Where would the proposed university be located? On what design should it be constructed? What subjects would be taught? How would the institution be funded and governed? How would it be related to existing educational institutions in the state?

These were questions of interest to many people in the Commonwealth, and certainly not least to clergymen and their churches, who were strong in their opinions: first, that as a public institution the university would belong to the people of Virginia and should reflect their values and commitments, and second, that the university should therefore have a distinctly Christian character and orientation. That the university should promote religion, that is, promote Christianity, was not seen by them as a "reestablishment" of religion or as contrary to the constitutional guarantee of freedom of religion, for the idea was not to privilege any particular sect, but Christianity generally. Moreover, it was widely believed that moral formation was an essential aspect of education, and that moral discipline and the cultivation of virtue were predicated upon religious conviction. Learning, piety, and virtue go hand in hand. The popular persuasion that religion needed to be effectively incorporated into the university was sharpened by the knowledge that Jefferson was closely involved in the enterprise of creating the university, and hence by suspicions that his own unconventional religious ideas would have undue influence on it. As early as 1817, when Central College was merely one candidate among others to become the University of Virginia, Joseph C. Cabell, Jefferson's able point man in the legislature, wrote to him (December 29, 1817) that the Presbyterians "look with a scowling eye on the rising prospects of the Central College, and will use their whole influence against all our efforts to advance its interests. The pretext for opposition is that the Central College is under your government; that you are an infidel yourself and will cause your opinions to be introduced into the institution."

Cabell was undoubtedly referring to, among other Presbyterians, John Holt Rice, the most prominent and best-educated Presbyterian clergyman in Virginia.[11] Rice was a strong advocate of education and favored the development of a system of public education, including a capstone university for the state. As the founder, editor, and chief contributor of the *Virginia Evangelical and Literary Magazine*, Rice was also widely influential in and beyond Virginia. In the first volume of that magazine (1818) Rice wrote:

> Indeed there is not a literary institution of any note in the world that has not a
> decided character in reference to religion. The people of Virginia ought to know
> this; and in the whole plan of their university, have reference to the nature of
> man as a religious being. Should it finally be determined to exclude Christianity,
> the opinion will at once be fixed that the institution is infidel—Men according
> to their prejudices will affix to it different epithets—Some will call it the
> Socianian; others the Deistical or Atheistical University. Christians of various
> denominations will loudly complain, that, altho' they are citizens, possessing
> equal rights with others, and equally interested in this National school, their

opinions are disregarded, their feelings trampled on, and their money appropriated utterly contrary to their wishes.[12]

Jefferson had, of course, long since been variously labeled an infidel, Socinian, deist, or atheist, and Rice was clearly worried about the imposition of Jefferson's personal religious views on the university. In a subsequent issue of the magazine, Rice returned to the topic:

> All who love religion . . . should enquire with great anxiety, what is likely to be the religious character of the University. We do not mean at all, what sect will predominate there; because, as far as our wishes or exertions can go, this shall be the case with none. Let them be perfectly equal. But we wish to know whether infidelity or Christianity shall have sway; and whether the doctrines of the Reformation shall be acknowledged, or some new-fangled form of deism, under a Christian name, shall be the favoured system.[13]

Rice's concerns and suggestions, though forceful, seem relatively moderate when compared to those of a fellow clergyman, Rev. Conrad Speece. Speece was a Presbyterian preacher who became pastor of Augusta Church near Staunton in 1813, remaining there until his death in 1836. In 1818 he collected and published as a book a series of essays and sermons he had written between 1813 and 1816. His proposals about the role of religion in the university must be quoted at length:

> The more extensive the influence of any seminary may be in the formation of character, and in giving the tone to public sentiment and manners, so much the more necessary is it that in such seminary religion should be honoured and inculcated. In applying this idea to the University of Virginia, I trust my readers will not understand me to mean by religion, the little peculiarities of sects and parties; but the grand doctrines and precepts of our common Christianity, in opposition to infidelity and atheism. Under these impressions I think the following rules should be adopted as sacred and unalterable.
>
> Every professor, or other teacher, in the university, from the highest to the lowest, should be required, before his induction into office, solemnly to avow his belief in the existence of one eternal, all-perfect God, the Creator and moral Governor of the world; in the divine authority of the scriptures of the Old and New Testaments, as a revelation from God, the infallible rule of faith and practice; in the trinity of persons in the Godhead, Father, Son and Holy Ghost; and in Jesus Christ as the mediator between God and man, the great propitiatory sacrifice for sin, our only Redeemer from eternal punishment.
>
> Every professor, or other teacher, should be liable to dismission from office, on proof of his having written or spoken any thing in opposition to the above

profession, or to any part of it. And the same penalty should be annexed to his being found guilty of any immoral conduct and especially of his persisting in such immorality.

It should be the duty of some professor, say the professor of moral science, to deliver, within the limits of every session, a course of lectures on the evidences of religion, natural and revealed; and these lectures all students should be bound to attend. Such discourses, without being numerous or tedious, might be exceedingly useful in fortifying the minds of the young against the assaults of infidelity.

Public prayer to almighty God should be performed every morning and evening by the professors in the hall of the university, accompanied with the reading of a portion of the scriptures. And every student should be required to attend these exercises.

The students should be obliged to attend the worship of God at church, if practicable, every Sabbath, with a decent and respectful behavior; and to keep the whole of that day sacred from worldly studies, and every other profanation.

Every student should be bound to have in his possession a copy of the holy scriptures, ready at all times to be exhibited on demand.

The students should be made liable to speedy expulsion for malignant or contemptuous language concerning God, his word, or any of the essential doctrines of religion; whether such language be uttered by speech or writing. And in the laws established for regulating the moral deportment of the students, profane swearing, cursing, and every other mode of taking the name of God in vain, should be marked as crimes of a high grade, and punished accordingly.[14]

Many Virginians would have applauded the piety-promoting prescriptions set forth by Rev. Speece, wishing like him that the university then being planned would energetically advance the cause of religion—which is to say, traditional, orthodox, evangelical Protestant Christianity. One does not have to imagine how Jefferson would have reacted to such urgings: he made his views plain both in actions and in words.

The Rockfish Gap Report

The role that religion would play, if any, in the prospective university was only one of many questions to be answered. Its location, constitution, organization, and curriculum were also at stake. To deliberate and resolve those issues Governor James Preston named a commission of twenty-four men, one from each of the senatorial districts of the Commonwealth. The membership included Jefferson.[15] Convening on August 1, 1818, at a tavern in Rockfish Gap, this group (hence known as the Rockfish Gap Commission) issued a detailed report to the legislature. Although both Hampden Sydney College and Washington College (later Washington and Lee) bid strongly to be designated and developed as the University of Virginia, the commission, persuaded by Jefferson's argument that Charlottesville was the most central location, proposed that Central College be named as the site of the university. The commission went on to recommend to the legislature that the university take the architectural form of pavilions "arranged on each side of a lawn" and "united by a range of dormitories"; that it have ten schools, each comprehending a set of coherent subjects to be taught by a single professor; and that it be administered by a board of visitors. The commission's report, in full and final form, was dated August 4, which means that it was produced in only four days. It is not to be assumed, of course, that a commission of twenty-four people could have debated and resolved all the issues in its charge in only four days, nor did it. In fact, the only question debated at length by the whole commission was the matter of location. And since the report's recommendations comport in all particulars with Jefferson's own ideas and wishes as they had taken shape over many years, it is clear that Jefferson came to the meeting with a proposal that was already fully worked out, and thus spared the commission much labor.[16] The commission, however, had its uses, mainly in giving official collective endorsement to Jefferson's personal vision.

The Rockfish Gap report refers to religion only two times. One of these appears in the discussion of architecture for the university.

> It is supposed probable that a building of somewhat more size in the middle
> of the grounds may be called for in time, in which may be rooms for religious
> worship under such impartial regulations as the Visitors may prescribe, for
> public examinations, for a library, for the schools of music, drawing, and other
> associated purposes.

The reference, of course, is to the intended Rotunda. There is here an assumption about religious worship on the Grounds, but it is not clear what was in the minds of Jefferson or the commissioners save that worship would not take place in a traditional chapel, and that the nature of any such worship must be "impartial," which means not favoring any one religious viewpoint.

The report's second reference to religion, and the most interesting for our purposes, has to do with the teaching of religion:

In conformity with the principles of our Constitution, which places all sects of religion on an equal footing, with the jealousies of the different sects in guarding that equality from encroachment and surprise, and with the sentiments of the Legislature in favor of freedom of religion, manifested on former occasions, we have proposed no professor of divinity; and the rather as the proofs of the being of a God, the creator, preserver, and supreme ruler of the universe, the author of all the relations of morality, and of the laws and obligations these infer, will be within the province of the professor of ethics; to which adding the developments of these moral obligations, of those in which all sects agree, with a knowledge of the languages, Hebrew, Greek, and Latin, a basis will be formed common to all sects. Proceeding thus far without offence to the Constitution, we have thought it proper at this point to leave every sect to provide, as they think fittest, the means of further instruction in their own peculiar tenets.

In the university as Jefferson conceived of it there was to be "no professor of divinity." This was one among other curricular innovations proposed by Jefferson, including the lecture method, the elective system, an emphasis on the sciences, and so on. But the exclusion of a professor of divinity was consistent with Jefferson's Bill for Amending the Constitution of the College of William and Mary, drafted in 1779 but never passed, which made no provision for a professor of divinity, and also with the reforms he enacted as governor when he eliminated the professors of divinity and of Oriental languages at William and Mary (even though they were later reestablished). Jefferson was aware of the popular and traditional convictions that education entailed character formation, that character and virtue were predicated on religion, and that therefore it was important to teach religion. The absence of a professor of divinity, he knew, would be a cause for complaint. But in the end he took the risk.

The rejection of a professor of divinity is said to be "in conformity with the principles of our Constitution." The reference here is probably to the Constitution of the Commonwealth (Article I, Section 16) rather than to the federal Constitution, but in substance it does not matter, since they agree in the points made here: no establishment ("equal footing") and free exercise (freedom of religion). The report speaks of "all sects of religion." In accordance with Jefferson's conception of religion, this must mean "all forms of religion" or "all religions," not merely "all denominations of Christianity," for Jefferson excluded no religious viewpoint, non-Christian or Christian, from the right of religious freedom. In addition, Jefferson believed that all religions had some things in common, namely, the acknowledgment of a Supreme Being whose existence sanctions morality, and some basic principles of social morality, whereas in matters of doctrine religions were widely divergent. The report proposes that, absent a professor of divinity, what is taught touching the topic of religion shall be within the province of a professor of moral philosophy, and shall consist only of those points "on which all sects agree." Of course, in Jefferson's immediate context religious diversity was manifested less by multiple religions than by a variety of Protestant Christian denominations, but they were regarded as having the same lowest common denominator as religions in general, namely, theism and morality. Thus ancillary to these topics are the languages (Hebrew, Greek, and Latin) that enable access to the primary sources upon which the various sects rely as authoritative.[17] To the extent that the "sects" in view here include those Protestant Christian groups that predominated in the population of the Commonwealth (namely, in descending order of numbers, Episcopalians, Presbyterians, Baptists, and Methodists), it must be pointed out that, however much these groups may have differed from each other in doctrine and polity, they had a great deal more in common than the Rockfish Gap Report acknowledges. Its highly distilled representation of what they shared corresponds much more closely to the basic convictions of Jefferson himself than to the common credo of the several Christian sects in question.

The Rockfish Gap Report was accepted by the Virginia legislature, and Central College was chartered as the University of Virginia, on January 25, 1819. Jefferson, of course, had anticipated, planned, and worked toward this result for many years, and despite the uncertain prospects, he had much earlier set about trying to acquire a faculty for the institution of his dreams. Those efforts would give additional alarm to persons who were anxious about the role religion would play in the University.

The Early Search for a Faculty and the Cooper Affair

As a cultivated intellectual and a strong proponent of education, Jefferson's attention had always been drawn to persons of intellectual merit, and over the years he had become acquainted with a number of men he thought would make fine members of the faculty of the University of Virginia. He had strong admiration for Dr. Samuel Knox (1756–1832), who was born in Ireland, educated in Scotland, and settled permanently in America in 1795. Knox was a Presbyterian minister and served churches in Maryland, but he became notable as an educator. In 1796 he took second prize in a competition sponsored by the American Philosophical Society to design the best system of education for the United States, and his treatise got Jefferson's attention.[18] His view, as expressed in that treatise, agreed with Jefferson's that religious education should be excluded from public education. Jefferson appreciated him yet more when, during the bitter presidential election of 1800, Knox published a vigorous defense of Jefferson against those who attacked him on religious grounds.[19] Knox served as principal of the Frederick (Maryland) Academy from 1797 to 1803, and as principal of Baltimore College from 1808 to 1820. In July of 1817 the board of Central College, aspiring to become the University of Virginia, voted to offer Knox appointment as professor of languages, belles lettres, rhetoric, history, and geography, but hearing that Knox had retired, the board rescinded the invitation a few months later. It appears that Knox never knew of the offer, and he remained at Baltimore College.[20]

Only a few months later, on October 7, 1817, the board, with the strong urging of Jefferson, invited Dr. Thomas Cooper to become professor of chemistry and law at Central College. Cooper was an Englishman, educated at Oxford, who had migrated to the United States in 1794 along with his father-in-law, Joseph Priestley. Jefferson admired Cooper for his legal, scientific, and philosophical knowledge, but also appreciated his political and religious views. The two had begun corresponding as early as 1801, during Jefferson's presidency. In a letter to Cooper written on January 16, 1814, Jefferson mentioned, "I have long had under contemplation, and been collecting materials for the plan of a university in Virginia which should comprehend all the sciences useful to us, and none others." He went on to say that should such a plan materialize and a university be established, "it would offer places worthy of you, and of which you are worthy." Later that year (August 25, 1814), Jefferson wrote to Cooper again, asking for his ideas on what subjects should be taught in such an institution, and Cooper replied (September 22, 1814) with a curricular conspectus. Thus Jefferson had had Cooper in mind for some time as a potential member of the faculty. With the 1819 incorporation of Central College as the University of Virginia, Jefferson wanted to make sure that Cooper would still be available. He mentioned this in a letter to Cabell (February 19, 1819), but Cabell responded (February 22, 1819) that Cooper was "unpopular in the enlightened part of society," which found him wanting "either in point of manners, habits, or character," and urged that no decision be made until it had been discussed by the new Board of Visitors.[21]

The offer to Cooper was sustained, but it turned out to be a serious mistake that had many repercussions. Although the appointment of Cooper was made in late 1817, not much was known or made of it until early in 1820. In February of that year John Holt Rice published in the *Virginia Evangelical and Literary Magazine* a lengthy review of Cooper's *Memoirs of Dr. Joseph Priestley to the Year 1795, written by himself; with a continuation to the time of his decease, by his son, Joseph Priestley. And observations on his writings, by Thomas Cooper, President Judge of the 4ᵗʰ District of Pennsylvania; and the Rev. William Christie.*[22] Priestley's *Memoirs* had been published long before, in 1806. The only reason Rice provided a review of it in 1820 was to publicize and criticize opinions that Cooper had expressed in his long appendix to the *Memoirs* commenting on Priestley's ideas. Rice gave copious quotations from Cooper's excurses to show, among other things, that he was a materialist who denied the immateriality and immortality of the human soul, and also denied postmortem rewards and punishments; that he thought a person can be a good member of society irrespective of his religious opinions, and hence that atheism is not necessarily a danger to society; that he believed that the freedom of the will and the doctrine of the Trinity were untenable doctrines not deserving of public discussion. Characterizing these views as "rash, dogmatical and preemptory," Rice concluded that "we cannot wish that a man who obtrudes such sentiments on the public should have the direction of our young citizens, yea and be placed foremost among those who are to afford instruction in our University."[23]

Rice's essay provoked a strong backlash against the appointment of Cooper, especially among evangelical, principally Presbyterian, clergy in Virginia, who proceeded to denounce it among their congregations. Jefferson, who had been stringing Cooper along through various postponements until the University could be built and become operational, now had to contend with the mounting opposition of public opinion. In April of 1820 he wrote to Jose Francesco Correa da Serra that

> there exists indeed an opposition to it [the University] by the friends of William and Mary, which is not strong, the most restive is that of the priests of the different religious sects, who dread the advance of science as witches do the approach of day-light; and scowl on it as the fatal harbinger announcing the subversion of the duperies on which they live. In this the Presbyterian clergy take the lead. The tocsin is sounded in all their pulpits, and the first alarm denounced is against the particular creed of Doctr. Cooper; and as impudently denounced as if they really knew what it is.

Notwithstanding Jefferson's own enthusiasm for Cooper, there were reservations about him even among some close associates of Jefferson. As noted above, already early in 1819 Joseph Cabell had warned Jefferson about Cooper. It was after reading Rice's indictment of Cooper that William H. Cabell wrote to his brother Joseph, "I fear that Cooper's appointment will do the University infinite injury. His religious views are damnable, as exhibited in a book published by him shortly after the death of Priestley. You will have every religious man in Virginia against you."[24] Some members of the Board of Visitors also took strong exception to Cooper. John Hartwell Cocke, owner of Bremo plantation on the James River in Fluvanna County, was himself a devout, evangelical Christian layman and a friend of John Holt Rice. Even before Rice penned his poison piece on Cooper in the *Virginia Evangelical and Literary Magazine,* he had written to Cocke expressing his aversion to Cooper, and saying that if Cooper were to come to the University, he would "call forth a strong decided opposition from all branches of the Christian church in Virginia."[25] Cocke in turn wrote to Cabell saying that, in spite of Jefferson's very warm regard for Cooper, he himself felt bound to oppose Cooper's appointment. He was joined in his opposition to Cooper by yet another member of the board, Chapman Johnson.

Cooper himself, after reading Rice's attack on his views, wrote to Jefferson, expressing his reluctance to become involved in a situation where he would have to contend with the hostility of the clergy and offering to resign the appointment. "I know the inveteracy of the *odium theologicum,*" he wrote, "and I dread to meet it at the close of life."[26] In response, Jefferson tried to assure Cooper that the opposition was not so strong or general as he supposed.

> The Presbyterian *clergy* alone (not their followers) remain bitterly federal and malcontent with their government. They are violent, ambitious of power, and intolerant in politics as in religion and want nothing by licence from the laws to kindle again the fires of their leader John Knox and to give us a 2d blast from his trumpet. Having a little more monkish learning than the clergy of the other sects, they are jealous of the general diffusion of science, and therefore hostile to our Seminary, lest it should qualify their antagonists of the other sects to meet them in equal combat. Not daring to attack the institution with the avowal of their real motives, they peck at you, at me, and every feather they can spy out. The snarle of Mr. Rice issues from the spirit of his *priesthood;* having himself as much candor as his gown will tolerate. A dozen or two fanatics or bigots of his sect in this state may read his Evangelical magazine: but he would not more effectually have hidden his diatribe than by consigning it to that deposit.[27]

But Jefferson was too optimistic. Opposition to the Cooper appointment persisted and increased, and soon even Jefferson realized that sustaining the appointment would bring far more harm than good to the University and its reputation.[28] Cooper's resignation was accepted. The religious interests had won. This was a bitter pill for Jefferson to swallow: the dark suspicions he had long harbored about the motives and interests of the clergy found ample confirmation in the Cooper affair. Cooper himself went on from the faculty posts in chemistry he had held at Dickinson College (1811–14) and at the University of Pennsylvania (1818–19) to the University (then College) of South Carolina, of which he became president in 1821. But there Cooper's views on religion continued to arouse objections, and for that reason he finally resigned from the presidency at South Carolina in 1833, and from his professorship in 1834.[29] Meantime, Jefferson returned to the business of acquiring a faculty.

Cooper had scarcely tendered his resignation when in 1820 the Board of Visitors of the University, still searching for prospective faculty members, initiated negotiations with two other scholars, Nathaniel Bowditch and George Ticknor. Bowditch (1733–1838), of Salem, Massachusetts, although largely self-taught, was an eminent mathematician who made important contributions to the sciences of navigation and astronomy. He had already been offered professorships at Harvard and West Point but had declined them both. The much younger Ticknor (1791–1871), from Boston, was a specialist in language and literature, who had become professor of belles lettres at Harvard in 1817, but Jefferson had previously known and admired him and hoped to bring him to Virginia. The Cooper affair had, however, put sectarian bodies on high alert to the possible encroachment of Unitarianism within the University and upon the Commonwealth. Fears of this were provoked again, at first by the mere fact that Bowditch and Ticknor were both from Massachusetts, regarded by southern Protestants as a hotbed of Unitarianism. Word reached the Presbyterian Synod held in Staunton in the autumn of 1821 that Jefferson had said he expected Unitarianism to make some progress in the South. The remark gave consternation to the Presbyterians and also to other denominational interests. Joseph Cabell reported the situation to Jefferson in a letter of January 14, 1822:

> I have had a very long interview with Mr. Rice. He and myself differed on some points; but agreed in the propriety of a firm union between the friends of the University and the Colleges, as to measures of common interest, and of postponing for future discussion and settlement points on which we differ. I think this safe ground. We shall be first endowed; and have the vantage ground in this respect. . . . They have heard that you have said they may well be afraid of the progress of the Unitarians to the South. This remark was carried from Bedford to the Synod, beyond the Ridge, last fall. The Bible Societies are in constant correspondence all over the continent, and a fact is wafted across it in a few weeks. Through these societies the discovery of the religious opinions of Ticknor and Bowditch was made. Mr. Rice assured me that he was a warm friend of the University; and that, as a matter of policy, he hoped the Visitors would, in the early stages of its existence, remove the fears of the religious orders. He avowed that

the Presbyterians sought no peculiar advantage, and that they and the other sects would be well satisfied by the appointment of an Episcopalian. I stated to him that I knew not what would be the determination of the board; but I was sure no desire existed any where to give any preference to the Unitarians; and, for my own part, I should not vote against anyone on account of his being a professor of religion or free-thinker.

As it happened, negotiations with both Ticknor and Bowditch were unsuccessful, a result that probably spared the University from yet another fusillade of religious objections. But here was another indication that religious interests stood in Jefferson's way.

A Clever Ploy? Religious Schools on the Margins

The religiously inspired protests that had been raised against the University beginning in 1817, well before it even opened, did not abate. In January of 1822, Joseph Cabell had written to Jefferson,

> In reflecting on the causes of the opposition to the University, I cannot but ascribe a great deal of it to the clergy. William and Mary has conciliated them. It is represented that they are to be *excluded* from the University. There has been no decision to this effect; and, on full reflection, I should suppose that religious opinions should form no test whatsoever. I should think it improper to exclude religious men, and open the door to such as Dr. Cooper. Mr. Johnson [Chapman Johnson] concurs with me in this view. And I have publicly expressed the opinion. The clergy have succeeded in spreading the belief of their intended exclusion, and, in my opinion, it is the source of much of our trouble. I am cautious not to commit yourself, or Mr. Madison, or the board. I have also made overtures of free communication with Mr. Rice, and shall take occasion to call on Bishop Moore. I do not know that I shall touch on this delicate point with either of them. But I wish to consult these heads of the church, and ask their opinions.[30]

And in May of 1822 John Holt Rice, having succeeded in the campaign against Cooper, pressed a more general point:

> The University has been regarded not merely as an institution for the rich; but as an institution for a party. And certain circumstances in the history of its management, have arrayed religious prejudices against it. Whether with reason or not, we shall not now undertake to decide. We only state what we know to be a fact. And it is our full conviction that, until efficient measures have been adopted

to remove these prejudices, the University will labour under public disfavour. The whole religious part of the community will unite against any institution, which it is supposed will have influence in propagating error. And the opposition made by a warmly religious people is always formidable. That which smiles at the wheel and the stake, and triumphs in the flames, is not to be trifled with or despised.[31]

Thus warned by friend and foe, Jefferson and the board had to take seriously the "religious prejudices" that had now developed against the University, and felt constrained to return to the subject of religion and its relation to the University. The Rector (the chair of the Board of Visitors) and Visitors of the University were required by law to submit to the Directors of the Literary Fund annual reports detailing the financial transactions and general condition of the University. In the fourth of these reports, approved on October 7, 1822, they brought up once more the subject of the teaching of religion in the University. After quoting the relevant paragraph from the Rockfish Gap Report, the board first defended the rationale of the policy there proposed.

It was not, however, to be understood [from the Rockfish Gap Report] that instruction in religious opinions and duties was meant to be precluded by the public authorities as indifferent to the interests of society; on the contrary, the relations which exist between man and his Maker, and the duties resulting from those relations, are the most interesting and important to every human being, and the most incumbent on his study and investigation. The want of instruction in the various creeds of religious faith existing among our citizens presents, therefore, a chasm in a general institution of the useful sciences; but it was thought that this want, and the entrustment to each society of instruction in its own doctrines, were evils of less danger than a permission to the public authorities to dictate modes or principles of religious instruction, or than opportunities furnished them of giving countenance or ascendancy to any one sect over another.

The board thus rejected the inference that religion is a matter of indifference to society and strongly asserted the importance of religion; nevertheless, it reiterated that religion was not to be taught in the University, for that would infringe religious freedom, violate the separation of church and state, and tend to the preferential treatment of one or another denomination.

Beyond such clarifications, the board realized that something more needed to be done by way of meeting the criticism by a pious public, and so they went on to tender a possible solution to the conundrum of how to handle religion:

A remedy, however, has been suggested, of promising aspect, which, while it excludes the public authorities from the domain of religious freedom, would give to the sectarian schools of divinity the full benefit of the public provisions made for instruction in the other branches of science. . . . It has, therefore, been in contemplation, and suggested by some pious individuals, who perceive the advantages of associating other studies with those of religion, to establish their religious schools on the confines of the University, so as to give to their students ready and convenient access and attendance on the scientific lectures of the University; and to maintain, by that means, those destined for the religious professions on as high a standing of science, and of personal weight and respectability, as may be obtained by others from the benefits of the University. Such establishments would offer the further and great advantage of enabling the students of the University to attend religious exercises with the professor of their particular sect, either in the rooms of the building still to be erected [the Rotunda], and destined to that purpose under impartial regulations, as proposed in the same report of the Commissioners, or in the lecturing room of such professor. To such propositions the Visitors are prepared to lend a willing ear, and would think it their duty to give every encouragement, by assuring to those who might choose such a location for their schools that the regulations of the University should be so modified and accommodated as to give every facility of access and attendance to their students, with such regulated use also as may be permitted to the other students of the library which may hereafter be acquired, either by public or private munificence, but always understanding that these schools shall be independent of the University and of each other. Such an arrangement would complete the circle of useful sciences embraced by this institution, and would fill the chasm now existing on principles which would leave inviolate the constitutional freedom of religion, the most unalienable and sacred of all human rights, over which the people and authorities of this State, individually and publicly, have ever manifested the most watchful jealousy; and could this jealousy now be alarmed, in the opinion of the Legislature, by what is here suggested, the idea will be relinquished on any surmise of disapprobation which they might think proper to express.[32]

It is not known what "pious individuals" may have suggested this "remedy." The idea may have come to members of the board from outside acquaintances, or it may have originated within the board.[33] In any event, it was certainly not Jefferson's own idea. He could accept it only with deep reluctance, as a concession of sorts to critics of the nonreligious curriculum of the University, as a means, he wrote to Cooper, to silence the "calumny" that the University "is an institution, not merely of no religion, but against all religion."[34] But he could tolerate the prospect only on the condition that such religious schools would be and remain strictly independent of the University and of each other. It is obvious that Jefferson was by no means strongly committed to the proposal, for he was ready to abandon it upon "any surmise of disapprobation." The suggestion, then, is very tentative, and the discussion of it is entirely abstract and theoretical.

Even if the notion of religious schools near the University had been conceived in good faith by whoever proposed it, the use made of it in the 1822 Report to the President and Directors of the Literary Fund appears to be a matter of pure political expediency, calculated to mollify religious opposition so as not to endanger important funding requests that had been made but not yet granted. At the time, a major allocation of money was urgently needed for the construction of the Rotunda/Library, which Jefferson regarded as indispensable, but above and beyond religious opposition, there was much discontent around the Commonwealth about the large sums of money that had already been allocated to the University.[35] It cannot be accidental that reference is made here to "the further and great advantage" of affording students opportunity to attend religious services "in the rooms of *the building still to be erected* [the Rotunda], *and destined to that purpose under impartial regulation*" (emphasis added). This statement introduces religion as an additional and important incentive to fund the construction of the Rotunda. Of course, the Rotunda itself was not, in fact, "destined to" the purpose of religious exercises; rather, only one of its lecture rooms was allowed to be used on Sundays for such a purpose. (The sentence fosters some ambiguity about this, probably deliberately.) Given the reluctance of the legislature and the citizenry to provide yet more money toward construction, Jefferson and the board recognized that nothing was gained by giving unnecessary offense to uneasy clergy or pious citizens. Thus, holding out the possibility that sectarian schools might adjoin the University was a sop to evangelical sentiments more than it was ever a plan to be implemented.[36] That the suggestion indicates a welcoming attitude toward religion by Jefferson, as is sometimes claimed, overlooks the tardiness, tentativeness, and reluctance with which it was put forth.

Despite the rhetoric employed, the proposal would not "complete the circle of useful sciences embraced by this institution," for the University's curriculum would still not include religion, and, of course, Jefferson never considered religion to be among "the useful sciences." And even if adjacent seminaries were to be built, it is emphasized that they must be entirely independent of the University and the University entirely independent of them. Further still, it was clearly Jefferson's thought *not* that they would influence the University, but rather that the University would influence *them*. As he wrote to Cooper (November 2, 1822),

> I think the invitation will be accepted, by some sects from candid intentions, and
> by others from jealousy and rivalship. And by bringing the sects together,
> and mixing them with the mass of other students, we shall soften their asperities,
> liberalize and neutralize their prejudices, and make the general religion a religion
> of peace, reason and morality.

That is, to the extent that positive educational benefit was thought to lie in the proposal of religious schools close to the University, it would be to bring sectaries around to a more Jeffersonian type of piety.

Having made this proposal, the Board of Visitors had to keep it in mind. And so, two years later, at its meeting in October of 1824, the board enacted a variety of regulations, among which were the following two, having to do with the possibility of adjacent seminaries:

> Should the religious sects of this state, or any of them, according to the
> invitation held out to them, establish within or adjacent to the precincts of
> the University, schools of instruction in the religion of their sects, the students
> of the University will be free, and expected, to attend religious worship at the
> establishment of their respective sects, in the morning and in time to meet their
> school in the University at its stated hour.

And,

> The students of such religious schools, if they attend any school of the Uni-
> versity, shall be considered as students of the University, subject to the same
> regulations, and entitled to the same rights and privileges.[37]

Thus the prospect of religious schools in proximity to the University was sustained, and the related enactments remained on the books. But they never had any effect or application, although in later years they were sometimes usefully invoked "to refute the charge from time to time launched against the University of wielding an influence hostile to religion."[38] No denomination ever took up the offer, and only one ever gave it any serious consideration.[39] The University remained intent on offering a curriculum that did not include the study of religion, and on fashioning a faculty that did not include a professor of divinity.

Gilmer's Faculty Search and Jefferson's Anticlericalism

The early efforts to attract distinguished American scholars to the faculty having failed, at least partly because of religious opposition, and the construction of the University approaching its completion, in May of 1824 Jefferson dispatched his estimable young friend Francis Walker Gilmer to England to recruit the necessary men. The recourse to the Old World for faculty members was widely disapproved, either as insulting to American scholarship or as importing an outworn worldview.[40] No letter of Jefferson to Gilmer requesting that he undertake this task has been preserved.[41] What has been preserved is a sheet of Jefferson's notes, an "agenda" listing characteristics to be sought in prospective faculty members. These were apparently talking points for Jefferson's instructions to Gilmer. Among the stipulations is "no clergyman."[42] This was a very constricting provision because in that period clergymen were heavily represented among the best educated, more or less regardless of subject matter. Whether or not their exclusion reflects Jefferson's long-standing and often expressed anticlerical bias, it must at least result from the recognition that any clergyman would inevitably be associated with some particular religious viewpoint, and the university that hired him would be seen as favoring that position. In any case, it seemed safest to Jefferson to avoid any and all clergymen, and so he instructed Gilmer, who was scrupulous on this point.[43] Gilmer succeeded in hiring five faculty members in Europe: George Long, professor of ancient languages; Robley Dunglison, professor of anatomy and medicine; Charles Bonnycastle, professor of natural philosophy; Thomas Key, professor of mathematics; and George Blaetterman, professor of modern languages. All were British save Blaetterman, who was German. The remaining three of the eight original members of the faculty were American recruits: George Tucker, professor of moral philosophy; John Emmet, professor of chemistry; and John Lomax, professor of law. Although a number of these men were religiously inclined and affiliated with one sect or another, none was a clergyman.[44]

As noted earlier, in declining to have a professor of divinity, Jefferson assigned any teaching concerning religion and morality to the professor of moral philosophy. In nineteenth-century higher education, "moral philosophy" was a portmanteau of subjects—social, psychological, political, economic, religious, and moral. It was taught, usually as an integrative "capstone" course and usually by the president of a college or university (who was customarily a clergyman), by way of illustrating the unity of knowledge, that is, the compatibility and mutual reinforcement between religion/morality and natural science ("natural philosophy") and other disciplines, and contributing to the moral formation of students.[45] Contemplating an appointment to this professorship, Jefferson wrote to James Madison (November 30, 1824):

> I am quite at a loss for a Professor of Ethics. This subject has been so exclusively confined to the clergy, that when forced to seek one, not of that body, it becomes difficult. But it is a branch of science of little difficulty to any ingenious man. Locke, Stewart, Brown, Tracy for the general science of the mind furnish material abundant, and that of Ethics is still more trite. I should think that any person, with a general education rendering them otherwise worthy of a place among his scientific brethren might soon qualify himself.

In his reply (December 3, 1824), Madison proposed George Tucker for the post. Tucker was a lawyer, then serving in the House of Representatives (1819–25). He had a special interest in political economy, but he was also a writer of essays and novels. In Tucker's background or in his areas of interest there was nothing whatever that touched on religion. That he was appointed to the chair in moral philosophy shows just how much—or rather how little—importance Jefferson attached to religion within the large scope of moral philosophy. But after all, in Jefferson's view there was little needing to be taught on the subject: only the existence of God, which Jefferson thought was irresistibly self-evident from the Creation, and morality, knowledge of which Jefferson considered innate.[46] Jefferson's rather casual attitude about the field of moral philosophy tends to belie the statement in the 1822 report to the Directors of the Literary Fund that the subjects of religion and morality are "the most interesting and important to every human being, and the most incumbent on his study and investigation."

The principle of excluding clergymen from the faculty of the University was firmly maintained by Jefferson, but soon after his death it came into question. In 1827 Chapman Johnson wrote to his fellow board member John Hartwell Cocke (both of them devout Christians), saying it was high time for the University to hire someone who had been educated for the ministry: "Tell Cabell it is time to give up his old prejudice upon this subject, the offspring of the French Revolution, long since a bastard by a divorce of the unnatural alliance between liberty and atheism."[47] James Madison, having succeeded Jefferson as Rector, corresponded in 1828 with other board members about a successor to Charles Bonnycastle as professor of natural philosophy. An offer of appointment to a Mr. Richie, a British scientist, was being contemplated with some enthusiasm, but there was uncertainty whether Richie was a clergyman. If he were, Madison wrote to Chapman Johnson (March 24, 1828), it would be an "insuperable" objection. Nevertheless, Madison wondered whether, if Richie were a clergyman, the problem might be sidestepped "by a distinct understanding that in the event of his appointment he is to be considered as de facto, without any ecclesiastical character, or functions in the University?"

Johnson's response of April 21, 1828, written after consultation with Cocke, is striking. He says that "we" (himself and Cocke)

> should not think that Mr. Richie's being a minister of the church would constitute a valid objection to his appointment. On the contrary, it would, in our estimation, be rather a recommendation; for whilst we would guard the University, with jealousy, against all manner of agency in propagating sectarian doctrines, and would not consent that it should have any connection with ecclesiastical affairs, *we would anxiously protect it, from the injurious imputation of being a school for infidelity, and a nursery of irreligion, and would gladly see among our professors, those who, by their daily example, would recommend the observance of a Christian community to the respect of the rising generation.* (emphasis added)

It bears emphasis that Jefferson's exclusion of clergymen from the faculty is here dismissed out of hand in favor of preserving the University from allegations of impiety.

Uncertainty about Richie's status persisted and gave Madison opportunity for further reflections, which he communicated to Chapman Johnson (May 1, 1828). On the question whether or not Richie is a clergyman, he says,

> It seems pretty certain that he is not; and if otherwise, and he should not adopt a course obviating objections, my view of the subject may be more singular than I had supposed. I cannot but think, nevertheless, that desireable as it may be that the Professors should be exemplary in a proper respect for Religion as in everything else, it will be better to have that benefit separated from than united with the Ecclesiastical profession, in an institution, essentially unsectarian. If Clergymen be received at all into the Professorships, they must be rec[eive]d indiscriminately, and considering the probabilities of qualification, not infrequently; should they happen to be all of the same denomination, a jealousy and discontent could not fail to be excited among the Sects not having the same advantage in an Institution equally theirs: should they be of different denominations; to say nothing of like feelings among the Sects less fortunate, it would be against all experience, if controversial scenes and religious parties did not arise, detrimental to the Establishment, and disturbing that harmony in the Faculty, so much to be desired, yet allways but too much exposed to danger, without the addition of so pregnant a cause.

Thus, unlike Johnson and Cocke, Madison remained committed to the Jeffersonian principle. Although he considered the appointment of a clergyman to be not impossible if done on very strict terms, it remained highly undesirable because it would precipitate sectarian conflicts and disrupt collegial relations within the faculty.[48]

In this exchange we see, for the first time after Jefferson's decease, a particular manifestation of a dilemma that would be long-term, namely, between honoring the founder's secular intention and responding to the Commonwealth's religious climate. In the event, Jefferson's firm stance against hiring clergymen was sustained for nearly two decades but was gradually softened. It was not until 1845 that a clergyman became a member of the faculty. He was William Holmes McGuffey, an ordained Presbyterian minister, hired as professor of moral philosophy. No other clergyman became a member of the faculty until early in the twentieth century. By that time the anticlerical disposition inherited from Jefferson had almost entirely disappeared.

The Problem of Public Opinion

The absence of a professor of divinity and the lack of instruction in religion in the University, together with the widespread popular view that Jefferson himself was, if not an outright atheist, then an infidel or a heretic, was readily exploited to represent the University as a bastion of impiety and immorality. Well before it even opened its doors in 1825, the University of Virginia was widely regarded, not as a public institution with a nonsectarian policy, but as an avowedly and aggressively secular institution that was, and was intended to be, actively hostile toward Christianity and toward religion generally. A summary of the Rockfish Gap Report published in the liberal *North American Review* in 1820 referred to the absence of a professor of divinity and of instruction in religion—"probably the first instance in the world without any such provision"—as a "hazardous experiment."[49] There were many pious souls in Virginia who thought that the University was a far more insidious project than that. In 1825 George Pierson, a schoolteacher in Fredericksburg, wrote to his brother Albert that the University was "a school of infidelity—a nursery of bad principles, designed in its origin to crush the Institution of Religion in V[irgini]a."[50] The University was widely represented and reputed as Jefferson's chosen instrument for the propagation of his own antireligious views. Rev. Francis L. Hawks (1798–1866), an Episcopal clergyman and editor of the *New York Review and Quarterly Church Journal,* gave sharp expression to this opinion. In a review of George Tucker's biography of Jefferson, Hawks said that Jefferson intended the University to "lend its powerful aid to the maintenance of a refined and civilized heathenism." Jefferson's aim for the University was "poisoning the stream at the fountain. Ardent, generous, gifted and unsuspecting youth was here made the victim of a deliberate, cold-blooded, calculating design for its corruption." In Jefferson's own "hatred of Christianity," he was "ready enough to make proselytes to his opinions."[51]

Only a few years later, in 1840, Rev. Stephen H. Tyng (1800–1885), a leader of the evangelical wing of the Episcopal Church, offered an equally harsh judgment in the *Episcopal Recorder:*

> This institution was established through the influence of Mr. Jefferson and was an object of deep interest with him. While his principles and plans are so well known in the community, and the exclusion of the influence and the preaching of the Christian religion from this place under these plans was so entire, I presume it is not unjust to say, that this university was set up in a direct and designed hostility to Christianity. It was considered, and it was undoubtedly intended to be, an infidel institution, and a school in which the principles of infidelity, negatively at least, should be taught. I believe this character was maintained during the life of its founder. But it did not secure or promote the prosperity of the institution, and God has overruled in part, and I doubt not will overrule more completely, the important instrument of literary power which has been here created, to the promotion of the faith which it was intended to destroy.[52]

George Tucker, the University's professor of moral philosophy whose 1837 biography of Jefferson was so strongly attacked in the *New York Review* by Reverend Hawks, responded in that same journal with an equally strong defense of his biography and its subject. There he comments that Hawks

> denounces him [Jefferson] for having designed to make this institution [the University] a place "where the minds of young and unsuspecting youth were to be poisoned with the venom of atheism"—where they "were to be taught that the Sabbath was to be abolished"—"that God Almighty was not the Lord of the universe"—"and where a deliberate attempt was to be made to overthrow the whole fabric of the Christian religion," etc. Now, can it be believed possible, that there is not the slightest foundation for all this overwhelming mass of accusation—this charge of conspiracy so gigantic against the religion of half the world—this purpose so Satanic in its conception and means of execution? Never did one word, that we have ever heard, reach the ears of the public, respecting the religious opinions which were to be taught at the University! Mr. Jefferson never contemplated the establishment of a professorship in any way connected with the subject of christianity; and in the original plan embracing the different departments of the college, not one syllable is to be found upon the matter.

Never in the appointment of professors, was any inquiry made, that we have known, in allusion to their peculiar principles of religion. Never in any of his [Jefferson's] various official and private conversations with them, from the origin of the institution up to the day of his death, did we ever hear (and we were ourselves a student there for many years) that he had expressed any wish or desire, in any way connected with his peculiar views upon the subject. So utterly and entirely destitute of foundation is this whole fabric of the pious writer's imagination, that even Mr. Jefferson's ideas of christianity were ever a matter of doubt among the young men of the University.[53]

But such protestations were ineffective, and the clergy nevertheless had their revenge upon Jefferson and the University. The root of their objections was not merely Jefferson's own religious opinions, objectionable as they were to Christian preachers; it was also the simple fact, forthrightly acknowledged by Tucker, that in regard to religion the position of the University was one of deliberate and official indifference. This indifference was predicated upon Jefferson's conception of religious freedom, long since enacted into law in the Virginia Statute for Religious Freedom, and upon a correlative impartiality toward the various forms of religion. But to clerical critics and their congregants, a studied indifference was tantamount to a practical hostility toward religion—an assertion that religion did not matter. Thus it was, in John Holt Rice's phrase, an "atrocious impartiality."

In the minds of its critics the University's religious lacuna created yet a further anxiety, namely, that the University would give no moral formation to its students. Impiety would be accompanied by immorality. It was axiomatic in most eighteenth- and nineteenth-century educational theory that morality rested upon and was effectively promoted only by religious conviction, and that a large part of the educational objective was the molding of character.[54] Moral education was essential to the civic virtue needed in a free society. This was not a matter of pedagogy only, but also of institutional discipline. Unsurprisingly, John Holt Rice, whose criticisms had subverted the appointment of Thomas Cooper, was also a vocal critic of the absence, in planning for the University, of a system of student discipline. He wrote,

We have been particularly desirous to see, and are greatly disappointed in not having seen a *Code of Laws* for the internal government of the University. We have heard it insinuated, indeed, that there is to be no such thing; that the institution is to be governed by an application of the laws of the land to the cases of disorder that may occur. . . . Youth at college need to be under a different sort of government. One that, while it is conducted on fixed principles, and according to laws not to be changed by the caprice or passion of the professors, ought to mingle with all its details as much of the paternal government as possible. It is at best, a hazardous and fearful experiment, to separate boys from the influences of domestic life, from the restraints composed by the presence of mothers and sisters, and all the softening effects of that sort of female society, and to place them in constant contact with boys similarly situated.[55]

Jefferson himself, in a letter to Thomas Cooper, allowed that

the article of discipline is the most difficult in American education. Premature ideas of independence, too little repressed by parents, beget a spirit of insubordination, which is the great obstacle to science with us, and a principal cause of its decay since the revolution. I look to it with dismay in our institution, as a breaker ahead, which I am far from being confident we shall be able to weather.[56]

Although this worry would prove to be prophetic, Jefferson was a man of principle, and he applied his philosophy of civil government to the governance of the student body. As Professor George Tucker put it, "believing that the authority of government is often needlessly exerted, and the restraints of law are too much multiplied, [Jefferson] allowed more latitude and indulgence to students than was usual" and attempted "to conduct a body of youths by appeals to their reason, their hopes, and to every generous feeling, rather than to the fear of punishment, or dread of disgrace."[57] Some, perhaps most, thought that Jefferson's approach to student governance was naive and destined to fail.[58] And fail it did: despite the idealistic aspirations, the student body very quickly ran amok. During its first two decades the University was frequently disrupted by student violence, acts of vandalism, riots, and revolts against faculty authority, including even the murder of a faculty member.[59] To the detractors of the University, the freewheeling misbehavior of the students proved conclusively that the absence of religion meant also the absence of morality. The pseudonymous "Philodemus" who penned a series of letters to the Directors of the Literary Fund in the *Virginia Evangelical and Literary Magazine* maintained,

Many a promising youth, the light of his parents' eyes, the joy of their hearts, and the subject of their fondest hopes, has brought on them the bitterest disappointments, and hastened their sorrowful progress to the grave, merely because the due culture of his moral feelings had been totally neglected. A cold and callous-hearted philosopher heeds not this suffering. He has formed his theory. He steadfastly maintains that learning and science will ensure virtue and wisdom; and pursues his plans while the morality of the state is continually lowering its standard, and she is daily losing her influence. . . . It is time to attempt a change. When infidelity spread its poison through the land, then many of the practical maxims which made our fore-fathers equal to the foremost men of all the world, were abandoned; . . . The work of education is only half performed, when man's moral powers are uncultivated. . . . Permit me to ask, in tones of deepest earnestness, is the banishment of religion from seats of learning, likely to subserve the true interests of virtue, science, and literature among us?[60]

Even though patterns of rank misbehavior were commonplace in nearly all American colleges and universities of the early nineteenth century, including those where religion had a strong institutional presence, this did not prevent a particular obloquy from being assigned to Mr. Jefferson's university.[61]

The University's reputation as a haven of impiety and immorality had important consequences. Enrollments in the early years were disappointing. Jefferson had anticipated in 1822 that within six months of its opening the University would have more than 200 students and would soon afterward outgrow its facilities. In 1824 he was yet more optimistic, expecting as many as 500 students in the first year of operation. The actual numbers turned out to be far smaller. In the first session of 1825 there were only 123 students, and ten years later only twice that number. Jefferson's assumption of 500 students was not realized until the 1850s. A principal reason for such modest enrollments between 1825 and 1850 was the University's irreligious reputation. Many young men of Virginia or other southern states who aspired to a higher education were deterred from the University in Charlottesville precisely because of their—or their families'—reservations about its religious and moral environment. Henry Tutwiler, who entered the University in 1825, reported that "a most excellent clergyman said to a gentleman who was about to send his son here [to the University], 'Much as I love your son' (he had been a favorite pupil) 'I would this day rather follow him to his grave than to see him enter the University.'"[62] An essay in the *Virginia Evangelical and Literary Magazine* in 1828, entitled "Is it safe for a pious parent to send his son to college?" answered the question with a decided "no." It goes unnamed, but the writer clearly had Jefferson's university in view.[63] Robert Lewis Dabney, a student from 1839 to 1842, commented that the University opened "under infidel auspices, without prayers, chaplain, Bible classes, Sabbath school—yea we may say, without Sabbath; so that almost all godly parents kept their sons away from it with a pious dread."[64] It was a widespread fear of parents that their sons' attendance at state universities, as opposed to denominational colleges, would be injurious to their religion and morality, and this fear attached especially strongly to the University of Virginia.[65]

When Jefferson wrote to Cooper that the University was criticized as "an institution not merely of no religion, but against all religion" he crisply caught the heart of the matter: what Jefferson himself intended was "an institution of no religion," that is, an entirely secular establishment that was indifferent to religion. But critics saw this neglect as "against all religion," and their judgment was influential. The reputation of the University as an irreligious, indeed antireligious, institution was strong and long-lived: it arose well before the University opened; it haunted the University not just in its earliest decades but throughout the nineteenth century; and it persisted even into the twentieth century.

Jefferson's conception of the University as a secular institution was shaped through a long period of gestation. But he sought to bring it into being in the midst of the most powerful, widespread, and consequential revival of religion that America has ever seen, before or since—the Great Revival or Second Great Awakening, a movement that infused the whole country with a vibrant religious enthusiasm, most strongly during the first three decades of the nineteenth century, but with effects persisting through the Civil War. The Great Revival arose against a climate of religious depression. The period between the Revolutionary War and Jefferson's presidency (1783–1800) marked a low ebb in the history of religion in America. Indifference and apathy were widespread: it is estimated that less than 10 percent of the population had church affiliation, and in large areas of the western frontier there was no religious presence at all. Enlightenment ideas that had been fertile in the field of politics were inhospitable to traditional religious interests and inclined to skepticism, deism, and atheism. The Great Revival was a revolt against both irreligion and enlightened religion. It energetically mobilized an evangelical Protestant piety that had moved beyond strict Calvinism, with its tenets of divine election to salvation and the total depravity of human nature, to reassert the capacities of the human will and the improvability of personal character. This newfound voluntarism was key to revivalism. The Great Revival was characterized by large and emotionally intense gatherings, with charismatic preachers proclaiming the availability of personal salvation, calling for repentance from sin, encouraging dramatic experiences of spiritual rebirth, and emphasizing the self-discipline of a righteous life. Thousands were converted. Baptists and Methodists, previously small dissenting groups, gained heavily, and by the 1830s they had become the nation's largest denominations. Presbyterians also benefited, and even staid Episcopalians acquired an evangelistic aspect. Denominationalism became a prominent feature of American religious life, and among the denominations the competition was strong.

The Great Revival and its results represented almost everything that Jefferson disliked about religion. It played to emotionalism and was little given to rational reflection. It promoted the presence and power of the supernatural, claiming present-day miracles. It was emphatically biblicist, confidently reliant on the authority and truth of the scriptures. It focused on the individual and personal redemption through faith. It stood by traditional Christian doctrines, and at the same time fueled sectarian diversity. This sort of evangelical Protestantism constituted the religious environment of Virginia when, in the period from 1814 to 1825, Jefferson labored to establish his secular University. It is hardly surprising that he met strong religious objections.

The popular perception of the University as inimical both to piety and to morality was not lost upon either the Board of Visitors or the faculty. In this respect, Thomas Jefferson proved to be a heavy practical liability to the institution he fostered. Over the course of the nineteenth century the board and the faculty found themselves torn between fidelity to Jefferson's idea of the University as a secular institution indifferent to religion on the one hand, and responsiveness to a strong evangelical Christian culture and constituency on the other. In this uncomfortable circumstance the board and the faculty began early on to seek ways of mediating the conflict. Although their efforts were conscientious and looked to what they considered the best interests of the University, the pressure of the religious culture was not to be resisted. The Board of Visitors and the faculty would be inclined to be receptive to nearly any measure that might improve the University's standing in the eyes of the pious. Consequently, the progression of the nineteenth century saw the University draped ever more fully in the garb of evangelical Protestant Christian piety until, eventually but paradoxically, it became a sponsor of religious life and activity. How this transpired will be the subject of the following chapters.

3

The Early Years

Preachers, Professors, and Public Opinion

When it opened in 1825 the University stood more than a mile from the small village of Charlottesville. Since there were no churches in Charlottesville or within easy reach of the University, Jefferson provided for one of the lecture rooms in the Rotunda to be used for religious services as occasion arose.[1] But because religious services, if held, were to be entirely voluntary, Jefferson made no arrangements for scheduling or staffing them. Such minimal attention to the matter of religious worship was a token of the founder's intention that the University be a secular institution, independent of and indifferent to religion. Only thus would it be possible for the University not to infringe upon the religious freedom of its students.

James Madison, who succeeded Jefferson as Rector and served in that role from 1826 until 1834, was himself a staunch champion of religious freedom, but he was also probably more religiously inclined than Jefferson had been.[2] Writing to board member Chapman Johnson (May 1, 1828), Madison confirms that there were no arrangements of any sort for religion, but he hoped that some might be made:

> I have indulged . . . the hope that provision for religious instruction and
> observances among the Students would be made by themselves or their Parents
> and Guardians, each contributing to a fund to be applied in remunerating the
> services of Clergymen of denominations corresponding with the preference
> of the contributors. Small contributions would suffice, and the arrangement
> would become more & more efficient & adequate as the Students become more

numerous; whilst being altogether voluntary, it would interfere neither with the characteristic peculiarity of the University, the consecrated principle of the law, nor the spirit of the Country.

"The characteristic peculiarity of the University" to which Madison refers was, of course, its secularism, and "the consecrated principle of the law" was freedom of religion. Madison supposed that both could remain inviolate if students or their parents would contribute toward the support of a minister. But his wish that "religious instruction and observances" might be made available in this way went unfulfilled.

Without initiative from the students themselves or their parents, the chairman of the faculty, George Tucker, was suddenly burdened with the task of making arrangements for religious services. This was nothing that had been envisioned among the duties of any faculty member, and it seems likely that Madison urged this concern upon Professor Tucker. In any case, Tucker recorded in the *Journal of the Chairman* that on December 14, 1828, "Mr. Hatch was this day spoken to for the purpose of learning whether he could not preach to the University twice in the month, in the fore rather than in the afternoon of the day, as the attendance was so irregular," and Mr. Hatch agreed to do so. Frederick W. Hatch (1789–1862) was an Episcopal clergyman who served in the Charlottesville area from 1820 to 1830.[3] From the chairman's notice it can be inferred that religious services had previously been held only once monthly, in the afternoon or evening, with small and unreliable attendance. How long this may have been going on is unclear, but perhaps only for a few months. Tucker clearly wished to increase the frequency of services, for he indicated in his *Journal* that the next day (December 15, 1828), at a social gathering, he proposed to his faculty colleagues that he inquire "whether Mr. Hatch and Mr. Bowman might not be able to preach in the morning on alternate Sundays," and the faculty concurred. Francis W. Bowman (1795–1875) was the Presbyterian minister in the Charlottesville area.[4] On being contacted by Professor Tucker about preaching at the University, Bowman agreed, and thus an arrangement was made for services to be conducted each Sunday morning, with Hatch and Bowman alternating as preachers. Their preaching was presumably compensated by the voluntary contributions of those who attended the services.

This system worked for a while, but not reliably well. Hatch and Bowman were not always able to be present on the Sundays for which they were scheduled, and services were not always held at the same time. Tucker's *Journal* entry for May 3, 1829, expressed great frustration at this and emphasized the importance of strict regularity, complaining that poor attendance at the services was caused by the irregular hours of the clergymen. The clergymen themselves seem to have been dissatisfied with the arrangement, for Bowman wrote to Tucker on May 17 stating "his inability to preach any longer at the University." Tucker's plan for weekly Sunday morning services thus lasted less than six months.

It appears, then, that the first stirrings of religious interest at the University originated with James Madison, and that the first arrangements for worship services were made by the chairman of the faculty, and with the concurrence of the faculty.

A Bishop's Challenge

During the session of 1828–29 the University was ravaged by an outbreak of typhoid fever. Many students were sickened, some died, and others withdrew from the University for fear of infection, and so it was decided to close the University for two months. After the contagion had been brought under control and the University reopened, the faculty invited the Reverend William Meade, then assistant bishop for the Episcopal Diocese of Virginia, to preach at the University on May 24, 1829. To a substantial gathering of faculty and students the bishop preached a sermon purporting to offer a Christian interpretation of the epidemic that had brought about the deaths of nine students, the suffering of many others, and a long interruption of the academic schedule. Expounding the text of Amos 3:6, "Shall a trumpet be blown in the city, and the people not be afraid? Shall there be evil in the city and the Lord hath not done it?," Reverend Meade made clear at great length (the sermon's printed version was 20 pages long!) that the affliction suffered by the University community was to be understood as a divine judgment upon, and a rebuke to, the impiety of the institution and, by unmistakable implication, of its founder:

> The design of God, therefore, in these dispensations, and the use to be made of them by us, are as plain as they are important. When God visits us with the rod of affliction, it is that we may search our hearts, and try our ways, and turn to him. When his judgments are abroad in the earth, it is that the inhabitants may learn righteousness. Does it not, then, become all concerned in this institution to ask, may not these judgments have been intended to stir us up to more zeal in rendering it holy and acceptable to God? Should they not ask, with what views and hopes have we entered upon this work? Did we acknowledge the Almighty and feel that, without his blessing, we could not prosper; or was our hope from the talents and favor of man?[5]

The bishop went on to propose the appropriate remedy:

> O might I be permitted to speak to all the friends, and patrons, and directors of
> this college in the language of plain but affectionate entreaty. I would beseech
> them as they would have it to find favor with God and man, and be a mighty
> blessing to our state and country, that they solemnly dedicate it to Almighty
> God and place it under his guardian care. In his name and by his laws let them
> rule over it. Let them see that the high motives and awful sanctions of religion
> be continually and eloquently presented to the minds of the youth committed
> to their care. Let the divine philosophy of the Bible be here studied. Let the
> morality here taught, be the morality of the Bible. Let the Bible, the Bible which
> is the religion of Protestants, be the textbook of first esteem and most constant
> reference. . . . Let it not merely be said that nothing is taught contrary to Christi-
> anity; that the mind is left free to its own choice; rather let it be announced to the
> world that every thing which can be said is said in its [Christianity's] behalf, and
> every thing which can be done is done in order to lead those immortal souls who
> come hither for the high improvement of their faculties, to the saving knowledge
> of him who is "the true God and eternal life."[6]

In the bishop's view, the University should have been a professedly Christian
institution encouraging instruction in Christian teaching and observance of
Christian worship. This oration stood in a well-developed tradition of deep
misgivings among the pious, and especially among the clergy, about the secular
character of the University, but the bishop gave those suspicions more detailed
articulation than they had previously received as well as a far sharper application. But his remarks had two large yet rather different effects.

First and most immediately, the faculty, all of whom heard the bishop's
sermon, took umbrage at some of his insinuations. At a meeting on the very
next day the faculty adopted a resolution: "Whereas the discourse of the
Rev. Dr. Meade delivered yesterday in the Rotunda by the invitation of the professors of the University contained an important erroneous statement of the
motives which dictated that invitation, as well as other exceptionable passages,
RESOLVED therefore that a committee be appointed to consider what course
it might be proper for the faculty to pursue on the occasion." The committee
appointed comprised Professors Patterson, Bonnycastle, and Lomax.[7]

The "erroneous statement of the motives" for inviting him was Meade's
imputation to the faculty of his own view and his claim that they had publicly
declared that view. Meade had said in his sermon that, "despairing to find any
secondary cause [of the disease] which might be brought within the reach of

man and be removed by human skill, they [the faculty] have looked up to the great cause of all causes, and humbly bowing before it, have said, and publicly said it, 'This is a visitation of divine providence: the hand of God hath done it.' As such they have resolved at this religious meeting, to acknowledge and celebrate it; and I come before you this day, with a feeble effort to make the desired improvement."

We cannot be entirely sure what course the faculty committee pursued to counter the bishop's ideas, but it seems highly likely that the faculty sent him a letter of objection. Meade himself later acknowledged the criticism of his sermon:

> At this discourse much offence was taken by some, and many misrepresentations went forth through the State. It was charged against it that, besides undertaking to interpret and apply the judgments of God in a way which had been most carefully avoided, a personal attack had been made on the Professors and Visitors of the University, and especially on its chief founder, whose opinions, having been published to the world, were known to be contrary to those expressed in the sermon.[8]

The sermon, as it was published in July of 1829, carried an appendix consisting of seven extended "notes" which in various ways qualified, corrected, or elaborated statements in the sermon as delivered. In Note A, Meade admits both to having been mistaken "as to the public declaration said here [in the sermon] to have been made by the Faculty" and to having erroneously inferred that the faculty regarded the epidemic as a divine visitation. Despite these concessions, Meade did not revise his own opinions about the cause of the epidemic or about its remedy. Indeed, John Minor later indicated that the bishop's view was not at all idiosyncratic, but that the epidemic "was very generally regarded as a token of divine displeasure, provoked by the supposed anti-religious character of the institution."[9]

Nevertheless, the bishop's sermon made him persona non grata to many in the University, and he was not invited to return for quite some time.[10] The reason may have been the offence taken not only by those who valued Jefferson's secular conception of the University but, conversely, also by those in the University who had in the immediately preceding years had arranged to introduce religious worship.

In this light it is not surprising that Bishop Meade's sermon had a second, slightly later but more far-reaching consequence. In the aftermath of his broadside, the idea took hold among faculty and students that, as Meade had suggested, the University would indeed fare better if piety were given more scope and encouragement. Thus Professor Dunglison wrote in the *Journal of the Chairman of the Faculty* on October 31, 1829, that

> The chairman has encouraged the performance of divine service by Mr. Smith, a clergyman of Philadelphia regularly at the University, and has permitted him to board and lodge within the precincts. Today he [Mr. Smith] issued a notice that divine service could be performed tomorrow at 10. The chairman considers it important that the students should have an opportunity afforded to them for this purpose, whilst he is equally aware that it must be a private arrangement of the Faculty.

Here there emerge a few points of interest and importance. The effort to provide more frequent and regular religious services at the University was now renewed. Chairman Dunglison, who was the chief executive officer of the University, thought that he was obliged to provide students with the opportunity for religious worship, although he recognized that the use of that opportunity was voluntary. It is acknowledged that the faculty must make private provisions for this, since as a public institution the University could not officially sponsor religious services. If the faculty could act collectively and officially in representing the institution, it could also act individually and unofficially to promote activities that were considered desirable, even if not among institutional prerogatives or priorities. Some fine distinctions are at work here, but they are important and, as we will see, were more or less closely observed in the subsequent history of the University.

Unlike the Reverends Hatch and Bowman, who were local clergymen, Edward Dunlap Smith (1802–83) was a Presbyterian minister from Philadelphia and a graduate of Princeton College (1822) and Princeton Theological Seminary (1826). He had served as a Presbyterian missionary in Georgia in 1828 and 1829, and it was apparently in that same capacity that he was "regularly at the University." It was exceptional, however, that Reverend Smith was allowed to live within the University precincts, since it was the rule that only those who had official status within the institution might do so; the permission extended to him by Dunglison was tacit recognition that he had quasi-official standing. This is the first instance of a regular clerical presence on the Grounds. Because he was reliably available, as Bowman and Hatch had not been, the chairman saw in him a ready resource for the regular performance of religious services. Smith is nowhere officially designated as chaplain to the University, but he apparently functioned as such in 1830, although he was not the only clergyman to hold services at the University in this period.

About the same time there is a passing mention in the chairman's *Journal* of a proposal that—fortunately—came to nothing. The room in the Rotunda that had been made available for religious worship on Sundays was used as a classroom during the week, and many thought it unsuitable for religious gatherings. In the autumn of 1829 some thought was given to holding religious services in the "library room" (that is, the Dome Room) instead. This idea arose when some pious and well-meaning person suggested to Dunglison that an organ might be placed in the Dome Room, provided that the instrument could be subscribed by contributions and presented to the University.[11] The chairman seems to have been intrigued with this scheme, and was of the opinion that divine service could indeed be performed in the library room, "provided no damage would be done to the books." However, nothing at all is subsequently heard of this proposal. Other members of the faculty probably vetoed it out of respect for the library. It seems certain that Jefferson himself would have shuddered at the prospect of worship in the Dome Room, let alone the installation of an organ there.

Not until the autumn and winter of 1830 does the chairman's *Journal* make any further reference to preachers and religious services. During that period, several notations indicate that various preachers other than Reverend Smith—Reverends Armstrong, Cotton, and Speece among them—"preached at the Rotunda on my invitation." This shows that Dunglison took it upon himself to select preachers, although the candidates may not have been especially numerous. The dates in the session of 1830–31 on which these preachers performed their duties were widely spaced: one in September, two in December, another in March, and another in June, so services were apparently infrequent. In the following session, of 1831–32, we read in the *Journal* of other preachers—Reverends Rice, Swift, Boyd, Cobbs, Hamet [misspelling of Hammett]—but the schedule of services was again sparse: only one is mentioned in each of the months of September, October, January, April, May, and June, but two in February.[12]

Thus from some point in 1828 up to 1832 arrangements for religious services and officiating clergymen were made by the faculty, acting through its chairman, but they were ad hoc and irregular. As described by Robert Lewis Dabney, who knew the situation well, "There was no chaplain, nor religious observance of any kind. Occasional public worship had been held perhaps, by transient ministers of distinction; and the sound religious sentiment which distinguishes the bulk of our people, was beginning to make itself felt among the governors of the institution; so that they were not unwilling to pay the tribute of some outward religious observance to this public opinion."[13]

The Chaplaincy

At the beginning of the 1832–33 session the infrequency and irregularity of services, and perhaps also some reminiscence of Bishop Meade's sermon, prompted a group of students, led by one McClung Wickham, to submit to the chairman of the faculty the following petition:

> We the undersigned, desirous of having stated preaching in the University of Virginia by some suitable minister of one of the four denominations of Christians who hold in common the fundamental truths of Religion, and wishing, if practicable, to obtain a minister of a different denomination each succeeding session of the University within every period of four years, in order to guard the more effectually against even any appearance of sectarianism, are willing to make the appropriations annexed to our respective names, to be Paid out of our funds deposited in the Patron's hands—such appropriations in no case exceeding one dollar and fifty cents.[14]

The petition was signed by thirty-four students, thirty-three of whom subscribed $1.50, the other $1.00. The chairman at the time, George Tucker, noted in his *Journal* that the students "wished the approbation of the Faculty as well as their co-operation. I stated at the foot of their resolutions my cordial approbation of the plan, and that I would contribute 20 dollars a year certainly towards it, and thirty if required."

This proposal was brought before the faculty by Professor Tucker, and then, with faculty support, was submitted to the Board of Visitors. At its meeting in July of 1833 the board gave a florid endorsement to this student initiative, seeing in it "a flattering evidence of that sobriety of mind and that deep sense of the higher duties of man, which in youth, give the fairest promise of a virtuous and useful life and in all are the surest guarantee of elevated character and lasting happiness." The board proceeded to resolve upon "procuring the services of a minister of the Gospel," saying that although it recognized that public monies could not be used for the purpose, "the Visitors individually, will cheerfully contribute to that object."[15] With members of the faculty and the Board of Visitors adding $20 each to the student pledge, private funds enabled the creation of a regular chaplaincy at the University.

Thus originated in 1833 the position of University chaplain. Henceforth it was the practice of the University to appoint a chaplain each year for a one-year term, the candidate being selected by a vote of the faculty. Moreover, as the students had proposed, the appointment was to rotate regularly among the four principal religious denominations of the state: Episcopal, Presbyterian,

Baptist, and Methodist. The first chaplain to be appointed under this scheme was Rev. William Hammett (1799–1861), a Methodist pastor, who served in 1833–34. He was followed by Rev. Nicholas Cobbs (1796–1861), an Episcopal priest and evangelist, who served in 1834–35. Rev. Robert Ryland (1805–99), a Baptist, served in 1835–36,[16] and in 1836–37 a Presbyterian, Septimus Tustin (1796–1871), held the position. Then the rotation began again.

The purpose of this denominational rotation was obviously to maintain religious neutrality, avoid the identification of the University with any particular construal of Christianity, and sidestep the controversies and polemics that arose in sectarian competition. Nevertheless, in various ways the arrangement marked an extremely important shift in the conception of the University and the place of religion in it. The secular character of the institution, intended by Jefferson to preserve religious freedom, is here reconceived as "nonsectarianism," a notion that was destined to do long duty in legitimizing the University's engagement with religion. Jefferson does not seem to have used the term nonsectarian (although he spoke of impartiality toward religion), but had he done so, it would have meant *not supporting any particular religion, Christianity included*.[17] But now, in the hands of the faculty members and board members, nonsectarianism was taken to mean *not favoring any particular denomination of Christianity*. Put differently, it was supposed that the nonreligious character of the University meant no more than that it was nondenominational. Thus the originally secular character of the University was suspended. This same tendency in the interpretation and application of the separation of church and state was more broadly manifest in Virginia's legislative activity and political culture during the first half of the nineteenth century.[18] On this assumption, it was further supposed that the principle of nonsectarianism could be satisfied by recognizing the *four Christian* denominations that were most populous in the Commonwealth—Episcopalians, Presbyterians, Baptists, and Methodists. Of course, this construal of nonsectarianism was itself sectarian because it recognized only Christianity, and indeed only Protestant Christianity, and Protestant Christianity in only four of its iterations. "Nonsectarianism" replaced the secular nature of the University, and made it, de facto, a Christian institution.[19] To be sure, the chaplaincy was supported with private donations, not public money, and attendance at the services was voluntary. Nevertheless, with the establishment of the chaplaincy regular religious observances were introduced into the University by the mutual agreement and support of the faculty, the board, and some students.

Despite the rotational scheme of the chaplaincy, denominational jealousies made themselves felt almost right away. In accordance with the policy adopted by the faculty and endorsed by the Board of Visitors, Reverend Hammett, a Methodist, had been elected to a one-year term, but he quickly became very popular among the students, and there was some interest in reelecting him. As the next election was contemplated, partisans of Reverend Hammett began to lobby on his behalf, believing that the Presbyterians were maneuvering to replace him with one of their own. A meeting of Hammett supporters was planned, but the chairman of the faculty, Professor Tucker, who believed the meeting intended disrespect to the Presbyterian Synod that was then convened in Charlottesville, refused to provide a room and asked that the meeting be postponed until the Synod had adjourned.[20] It was the faculty, then, who insisted on maintaining the regular rotation by way of forestalling sectarian strife, despite the students' personal attachment to Reverend Hammett.

An entry in the chairman's *Journal* in June of 1834 refers to a meeting of the faculty on June 24 "chiefly called to obtain the final assent of the professors to the terms whereon the Rev. Cobbs had been invited to preach at the University." Professor Bonnycastle, who was chairman at the time, went on to say,

> The invitation of a minister has always been considered as a private matter that
> does not appear upon the records of the Faculty, and this chiefly on account
> of the option which must be left to each Professor in regard to the pecuniary
> compensation that he is willing to contribute. But as the invitation of a minister
> is now looked for at the Chairman's hands; is made in his name; and might be so
> abused as to become injurious to the University, I have deemed it right to place a
> copy of this correspondence where it will be open to the inspection of the Board.

Here we see an admirable scrupulousness both to maintain the privacy of professorial support for the chaplain and to ensure that the chairman's power of appointment is not abused. There follows a copy of the letter of the chairman to Mr. A. Garrett, a delegate to the Episcopal Convention scheduled to meet in Staunton, requesting that he bring to the attention of the bishop the University's need of an Episcopal minister, but also spelling out the nature of the position. The letter contains this paragraph:

> The act of establishing this University leaves, as you are aware, the religious
> instruction of our youth open to all the persuasions established in the Common-
> wealth: the University belongs to the whole state; and it appears to have been
> deemed improper to limit a subject of such momentous importance as religious
> instruction by any other restrictions than those which the judgment of the people
> at large has approved: acting under this impression, and anxious that all our
> students should participate in the benefits resulting from a solemn and regular

performance of divine service, we have endeavored at the close of each session, to procure the attendance of an eminent minister from one of the four churches whose tenets are most prevalent in this state.[21]

Here the line between private and institutional sponsorship—fine to begin with—threatens to disappear. In addition, the pressure of public opinion is acknowledged.

The principle of nonsectarianism was tested again in January of 1835. The current chairman of the faculty, John A. G. Davis, remarked in the chairman's *Journal*,

> The Rev. Mr. Goss of Charlottesville, having a few days ago written to me, in behalf of Dr. Thomas of Richmond, for leave for that gentleman, who is a Campbelite [*sic*] Baptist, to preach here; I today replied to his letter, and declined to grant the permission asked, on two grounds; first, because to such applications from persons of whom we know nothing, or to whom it would not be proper to extend the indulgence, I have adopted as a rule for my own government whilst Chairman, to grant authority to preach here to none but those who are invited by the Chaplain or myself, and in no case to give such authority upon application; and secondly, because it is not proper to allow the University to be made the arena of religious controversy, which might, and probably would, be the consequence of granting Dr. Thomas's request. These objections I stated in as civil a manner as I could, and being sufficient, I did not think it necessary to state others of a more personal nature.[22]

Davis rejected the request not simply on principle (although that would have sufficed), but also because Dr. Thomas was a Campbellite Baptist. Davis's worry about involving the University in "religious controversy" had reference to this fact, for the Campbellite movement (which today we call the Stone-Campbell movement), then in its very early days, had already acquired a reputation for theological disputation and aggressive proselytism, both of which had become manifest in Charlottesville itself. Davis was no doubt aware that the Baptist church in Charlottesville had been riven by religious controversy in the months immediately preceding, thirty to forty of its members having been expelled on the charge of "Campbellism." The University chaplain at this time was Rev. Robert Ryland, who was a Baptist and a member of the Charlottesville Baptist church. J. W. Goss, a minister of the Charlottesville Baptist church who had cast his lot with the Campbellites, wrote that Ryland had

> contended against that portion of the church which he denounced as heretics and followers of A—— C——. We called upon him to state the heresies which we

held, and challenged him to show that we entertained a sentiment or maintained a practice which the Scriptures did not teach or sanction. But all to no effect. He offered as an apology for declining, that our doctrines flourished by controversy! Let a man be branded with the charge of C——ism, and many suppose that justice is not due him.[23]

Professor Davis had no intention of importing such sectarian strife onto the University Grounds,

Only a few years later, in 1838, an application was made by Alexander Walker and Robert Johnson for Rev. Alexander P. Campbell himself to preach in the Rotunda. Alexander Campbell was the son of Thomas Campbell, and with his father was a founder of the Campbellite movement; by 1838 he had become its principal leader and spokesperson. In support of the application it was urged both that many students were anxious to hear Reverend Campbell, and also that he would preach on the evidences of Christianity without introducing any controversial sectarian topics. In spite of these inducements, the chairman, now Gessner Harrison, declined to invite Campbell, appealing to the policy earlier laid down by Professor Davis. Harrison anticipated that there would be student discontent with his decision, and so he called a meeting of the faculty to back him up. The faculty adopted the following resolution:

> The Chairman, having consulted the Faculty in reference to the application made on behalf of Mr. Alexander P. Campbell to be allowed to preach in the University; Resolved, That the application cannot be granted without departing from the principles, which have been adopted by the Faculty, sanctioned by the Board of Visitors, and approved by the public, respecting the performance of religious services in this institution; and that therefore, as well as because of the inconvenient precedent which the granting of it would establish, the Chairman be advised to decline a compliance with such application.[24]

The faculty's refusal to welcome Campbell did indeed offend the students who had been eager to hear him preach. They announced a protest meeting in the Rotunda, but when Chairman Harrison caught wind of it he instructed the bell ringer, who controlled access to the Rotunda, not to allow its use. The meeting went off anyway, with a majority of the students who attended voting to condemn the faculty's decision. A different group of students, who supported the action of the faculty, asked to use the Rotunda the next evening. They were given permission to do so and voted to endorse the faculty's decision, which would have stood in any case.[25] But the incident showed that sectarian controversy was almost impossible to avoid.

If the University was now presuming to satisfy its nonsectarian policy by acknowledging the four principal Christian denominations in the Commonwealth, that policy was itself sectarian, not only by virtue of recognizing Christianity alone, but also by virtue of favoring just those denominations of Christianity. There were, after all, other Christian denominations in the Commonwealth, and new ones, such as the Campbellites, could always appear. What the University chiefly feared about the Campbellites and their preachers was that they would provoke religious controversy, but in its actions regarding Dr. Thomas and Reverend Campbell it is obvious that the policy of nonsectarianism was discriminatory, readily denying equal privilege to minority religious groups. The safeguard against their intrusion was that the opportunity to preach at the University came by invitation only, whether from the chairman of the faculty or, as later, from the chaplain. Applications were not accepted.

A rich irony resides in these early repudiations of Campbellism by the University. The Campbellite movement, sometimes known as the Restoration Movement, had as one of its primary objectives to transcend the denominational divisions of Protestantism by returning to the practices of primitive Christianity as described by scripture. It sponsored a kind of "lowest common denominator" form of Protestantism, appealing only to what all Protestants agreed to be authoritative, namely, the explicit teaching of the Bible. In this sense, Campbellism was itself quintessentially nonsectarian. Disavowing sectarian divisions and denominational labels, Campbellites preferred to call themselves simply "Christians." In the course of the nineteenth century the Campbellites evolved into one of the earliest forms of Protestantism indigenous to the United States, namely the Disciples of Christ (also known as the Christian Church).[26] The irony of the University's refusal to let Alexander Campbell preach is that it was precisely the Disciples of Christ who, in the late nineteenth and in the early twentieth centuries, came to exercise the predominant religious influence within the University.

When the chaplaincy was inaugurated, the primary responsibility of the chaplain was to officiate at a single religious service on Sunday morning. Over the course of only a few years, however, the responsibilities grew and religious occasions multiplied. Already the first regular chaplain, Reverend Hammett, sought permission to use the general lecture room in the Rotunda for an additional hour each Sunday "for the purpose of instruction in Psalmody."[27] Soon a Sunday evening service was added. The devout McClung Wickham, one of the students who had initially petitioned for a chaplain, now asked also for a Sunday school to be held, and permission was given.[28] As early as 1835 prayer meetings were regularly held on Sunday afternoons in the Rotunda, and prayer meetings were also hosted during the week by faculty members in their Pavilions. Soon daily services of morning prayers were being conducted before breakfast during the week. Furthermore, a Bible Society had been established. An address was given before the Bible Society in 1835 by Henry L. Pinckney, a congressman from South Carolina. Referring to that occasion, and introducing an excerpt from Pinckney's speech, a report in the *American Annals of Education* said that the University was "an institution designed by some of its projectors, to furnish an example of the power of *unassisted human philosophy*, but whose officers, according to the account of Mr. Pinckney, have imbued it with the spirit of Christianity."[29]

Remarkably, within a mere decade of the opening of the University, occasions of religious observance and study had proliferated, had been supplied with a regular clergyman, and had been endorsed and subsidized by the faculty and the Board of Visitors. There was, therefore, ample reason for Professor Minor to write,

> From about the year 1835 a very apparent change in the aspect of things was manifest. The prevailing spirit became progressively more friendly to Christianity. Infidelity ceased to be aggressive. Apathy gave place to rational inquiry. The Scriptures, as they were more studied, asserted their wonted power to convince and persuade. Sectarian peculiarities were softened to an all-embracing catholicity, founded on pure Bible teaching, and an ardent activity in good works attested by its fruits the divine genuineness whence they sprang.[30]

Minor, himself a deeply devout man, had been a student in the University from 1831 to 1834, and afterward was its professor of law for fifty years (1845–95). He had witnessed the developments he spoke of, and obviously approved of them.

This sense of the rapid development of piety at the University is confirmed by observations of the Episcopal clergyman Stephen Tyng, who believed that the University had been "set up in direct and designed hostility to Christianity." In 1840 Reverend Tyng preached twice to students of the University and observed that "God has overruled in part, and I doubt not will overrule yet more completely, the important instrument of literary power which has been here created, to the promotion of the faith which it was intended to destroy."[31] Another commentator suggested that the University

> should have been planned and executed in reliance upon Divine aid and direction; for nothing can be truer than except the Lord build the house, they labor in vain who build it. Without being superstitious, the overruling hand of Providence must be acknowledged; and apprehensions sometimes arise lest Heaven

has decreed the fall of the University, in order to prove to man the folly and impiety of founding such institutions, without invoking its blessing. Religion cannot be safely separated from any human undertaking. . . . The system of Mr. Jefferson has been abandoned; and there are now regular religious services twice a week, and the students pay marked respect to the minister.[32]

Even Bishop Meade, who had found fault with the ungodliness of the University in 1829, said that it brought him happiness "to see, only a few years after, all the offensive features of [my] sermon adopted into the administration of the College, as far perhaps as is practicable under the circumstances of its existence as the common property of all denominations of Christians and all citizens of the State."[33]

Contemplating a Chapel

Given the rapid profusion of occasions for religious worship and increasing enthusiasm for them, the absence of any adequate or appropriate space for that purpose quickly became evident. Jefferson had departed from tradition in failing to provide for a house of worship in his architectural plan for the University. Colleges and universities of the colonial and early federal periods, including state institutions, routinely included a chapel, usually in a central location with other buildings oriented around it. In Jefferson's scheme, what stood in the place that would normally have been reserved for a chapel was the Library, that is, the Rotunda, modeled upon the Pantheon of Rome. It was not lost on those who regarded the University as an infidel institution that its focal structure evoked a pagan temple rather than a Christian church.

Only a month after the University opened its doors Arthur Brockenbrough, Proctor of the University, had proposed to Jefferson that permission be given for the lecture room of Pavilion I "to be used regularly for prayers and preaching on Sundays" by the Episcopal and Presbyterian congregations of the town of Charlottesville, who had no church buildings and were accustomed to meet in the Albemarle County Courthouse. Jefferson's response was that University buildings must not be used "to other than University purposes."[34] Jefferson's objection seems to have been against the use of University facilities by outside groups, since he allowed some provision of space for religious gatherings for students. Even so, from an early point in the history of the University the absence of a proper chapel was a matter of dissatisfaction, and not only among the institution's external constituency. Jefferson had thought it sufficient to make available a lecture room in the Rotunda for the use, on Sundays, of those members of the University community who might choose to hold a religious service, but those who did so found the room—with its benches, blackboards, graffiti, and quotidian associations—ill suited to the purpose and wished for something better.[35]

So it was that a mere ten years after the University opened, the faculty expressed its desire for a chapel. In March of 1835 George Tucker, the professor of moral philosophy, sent a letter to each member of the Board of Visitors. It read:

> Sir,
>
> The members of the Faculty, having long felt the want of a building in the university devoted exclusively to religious worship, and believing that the funds required for the erection of a chapel could be obtained by voluntary contribution throughout the state, have formed themselves into a Board. . . . They have accordingly, in this character, selected as the most eligible site, the ground to the south of the Lawn and immediately in front of the Rotunda. They have procured from an architect of high reputation the plan of a church or chapel of the Gothic style, which being large enough to contain 800 persons, and so finished as to be not unworthy of the place and occasion, is estimated to cost $20,000.

This missive is astonishing for several reasons. It is surprising to find the faculty, apparently as a unanimous body, thinking that a chapel was needed and taking such strong initiative, having gone so far as to select a site and obtain architectural drawings. Moreover, the site selected was very prominent, and the building style proposed (Gothic revival) very much out of character with its surroundings.[36]

Several months after receiving Professor Tucker's letter, the Board of Visitors, at its meeting in July 1835, received from the faculty the following formal preamble and proposed resolution:

> The proceedings of the professors having in view the adoption of measures for the erection by private contributions, of a chapel on the grounds of the University for the more convenient and appropriate performance of the religious services already provided for by an arrangement which has received the sanction of the Board of Visitors, being presented:
>
> Resolved, that the board, duly estimating, as their predecessors have done, the importance of religious worship to the well-being of the Institution over which they preside, & finding that the apartment heretofore allotted and occupied for that purpose is totally inadequate to the accommodation of the students and professors and their families, who have shown an earnest desire to attend on the

religious services which have for some years been regularly performed there, do cheerfully assent to the proposed building of a chapel on the grounds of the University; reserving to their future decision, upon a more deliberate consultation with the professors, the precise designation of the site for the chapel, and it being well understood that the same jealous care to maintain a strict impartiality and equality between the several religious denominations in their relations to this institution, shall continue to be scrupulously and sacredly preserved.

In this resolution's statement of "the importance of religious worship to the well-being of the Institution" we hear echoes of Bishop Meade's admonishments. It is clear as well that the faculty, evidently more than the students, was very desirous of a chapel. But it can also be noticed that the faculty has modified some of the presumption present in Tucker's earlier letter. In particular, greater deference is accorded to the board, no reference is made to a specific plan, and the question of location is left open. The faculty hoped, and probably expected, that its proposed resolution, thus revised, would meet with the board's approval. The minutes of the board note, however, that "some difficulty" arose concerning it, and that the resolution was "laid over" or tabled for consideration at a later meeting.[37]

If the faculty was eager to have a chapel, the board seems to have been reluctant to contemplate such an innovation. This was not merely because not all members of the board were present. We cannot be sure what constituted "some difficulty arising" within the board about the faculty's proposal, but we can conjecture several issues that it may have raised. One was probably a persistent recollection by at least some members of the board that Jefferson intended the University to be a nonreligious institution, and hence without a chapel. Other members may have thought that the faculty was exercising an authority that belonged not to it but to the board, or at any rate was to be shared.[38] Another question was where on the Grounds such a structure might be located. Still another issue must have been whether it was appropriate to modify Jefferson's architectural design of the University *at all*.[39] In 1835 a chapel would have been the first non-Jeffersonian building on the Grounds. Yet a further reservation might lie behind the heavy emphasis on denominational neutrality: perhaps it was feared that a building would be more susceptible to claims of denominational ownership, or hegemony, than a lecture room in the Rotunda, depending in part on who contributed the building funds.

Whatever its hesitations, the Board of Visitors did not soon return to this subject. The next reference in the board's minutes to the faculty's proposal of a chapel appears only after three more years (!). At the meeting of July 1, 1838, it was resolved that the secretary of the board send to each member a copy of the 1835 "application of the Professors of the University for permission to build a Chapel on the grounds of the University," and this with a view to acting on the matter at the board's next meeting.[40] The subject did not come up, however, at the next meeting (1839), or even at the next after that (1840). The faculty's proposal to build a chapel would languish for six years after it was first submitted.

Despite the board's foot-dragging, faculty and student interest in a chapel building remained strong. Benjamin Blake Minor, a graduate of the University of Virginia and the College of William and Mary, published an essay on the University in the *Southern Literary Messenger* in 1842, in which he said, among other things,

> In the University the services are performed in the lecture-room, which is very inconveniently arranged, and where the mind is diverted by a thousand perceptions and associations. Everything in connection with the *spirituel* of that institution would show, if we did not know the fact, that the introduction of religion was an afterthought. In all her extensive arrangements, there is not a single accommodation for religion. . . . The first thing to be done is to erect a suitable chapel. The faculty are anxious for this to be effected, and presented a memorial to the Visiters on the subject. At the request of the writer, Professor Bonnycastle drew up an eloquent memorial to be presented on the part of the students; but, as circumstances prevented the signatures from being obtained, it was not handed in. A chapel is not only necessary for the religious services, but for public occasions, anniversary orations, the use of societies, and for important meetings of the students, when they wish to do honor to the memory of a departed fellow-student or professor. It will also be useful as an ornament,—and this dreadful hiatus, so painfully obvious to every Christian friend of the institution, should be speedily supplied.[41]

By the time this opinion was published, at least part of its concern had been anticipated and addressed by the Board of Visitors. At its July meeting in 1841, when it finally came back around to the question, the board implicitly rejected the idea of building a chapel when it resolved that "the apartment which is now in a course of execution [i.e., renovation] in place of the Eastern gymnasium be fitted up and appropriated to the general meetings of the University and as a place of religious worship for the professors, officers and their families and of the Students of the University, and that it be placed under the direction of the Faculty." The reference is to the eastern basement area of the Rotunda, previously used as a gymnasium, which was more commodious than the lecture room on the main floor that had originally been designated for occasional use for religious services. By repurposing the gymnasium space, the board deflected the faculty's persistent enthusiasm for a separate chapel building. In effect, the idea was tabled indefinitely, while the original arrangement of allowing religious services to be held in the Rotunda was continued, only now in a different space, renovated to make it more suitable for religious gatherings as well as general meetings. This room was subsequently sometimes referred to as "the chapel."[42] As we shall see, the new arrangement did not extinguish the desire for a separate chapel building.

A Parsonage

The chaplaincy of the University was appealing to younger clergymen. Methodist and Baptist preachers especially, who typically came from modest backgrounds and were not well educated, regarded it as an opportunity for study, for intellectual and social self-improvement, and thus as a path to professional and social advancement.[43] But the University's ability to attract and retain capable chaplains, including experienced clergymen with families, was hampered by the brevity of the appointment, by the absence of adequate housing, and by relatively modest compensation. The first problem was addressed when it was determined that a longer appointment would be to the benefit of both the chaplain and the University community. It was decided that, beginning with the 1846–47 session, chaplains would be appointed to two-year terms, but the rotation among the four denominations would be continued.

The second issue, the lack of accommodations, was a larger challenge. Since 1843 the chaplain had resided in some rooms of Pavilion V. Students and faculty members believed that a larger and permanent on-Grounds residence was needed for the chaplain, and in 1851 they sought permission from the Board of Visitors to raise money for the purpose of constructing a parsonage. According to its minutes for June 25, 1851, the board resolved,

> Permission is hereby granted to erect by voluntary contribution, on such site
> upon the grounds of the University, as the Executive Committee shall approve,
> a house for the residence of the Chaplain, biennially chosen by the Professors &
> supported by the Professors & Students.

At this point, however, concerns arose within the board about whether such action was ultimately compatible with the principles originally laid down about the role of religion in the University. References to and long extracts from the Rockfish Gap Report and the 1822 report of the Board of Visitors to the Directors of the Literary Fund were entered into the board's minutes.

Having reviewed the principles expressed there and apparently finding no obstacle, the board repealed the resolution adopted earlier and substituted another, as follows:

> Resolved that the Professors of the University be authorized to open a subscription for donations to be received by the Board of Visitors in trust for the University for the erection of such *houses as may be necessary for the religious worship* of the Professors & Students on such sites upon the grounds of the University as the Executive Committee shall approve. (italics added)

Here the responsibility is explicitly assigned to the faculty, not to the board, which is only to hold contributions "in trust." But it is striking that the object is no longer simply "a house for the residence of the Chaplain," but instead "such houses as may be necessary for the religious worship" of the University community. This seems to mean, at least potentially, not only a residence (or residences) for a chaplain (or chaplains) but also a house (or houses) of worship. By this time the indifference to religion intended by Jefferson had been conveniently swept under the rug by faculty and board alike.

The subscription for a parsonage was immediately undertaken. Members of the faculty, especially Professors James L. Cabell and William H. McGuffey, were leaders in this effort. The letter of solicitation read as follows:

> Dear Sir:
>
> The undersigned respectfully beg leave to invoke your aid in furtherance of a scheme, which has for its object to facilitate and insure the ministrations of our holy religion at the University of Virginia.
>
> It being contrary to the uniform policy of the Government to make any special provision for the performance of religious services in any of the institutions belonging to the State, the Faculty of the University for many years past have adopted the expedient of appointing a Chaplain for a term of two years, selected in turn from the four principal religious denominations in the State and supported by the voluntary contributions of the members of the Faculty and of such of the Students as may choose to co-operate. From the want of a suitable house for the residence of a family, the choice is practically restricted to a very small class in each denomination, namely the younger members of the ministry, who cannot be expected to bring to the discharge of the duties of the Chaplaincy those qualifications which previous ministerial experience alone can adequately give. On a recent occasion the Faculty failed to secure the services of an Episcopalian Chaplain, and were constrained to pass over to another denomination, although more than

one of the clergymen to whom the office was tendered, expressed a desire to accept it, if provision were made for the accommodation of their families. It is proposed, therefore, to raise by subscription, a sum adequate to the erection of a suitable parsonage on the University grounds.

The Professors and others connected with the University will aid with their pecuniary contributions according to their means and the justness of the claims upon them. Forming by themselves a very small community, and contributing statedly towards the support of the denominational churches to which they are respectively attached, they cannot be expected to bear the whole burden of an enterprise intended mainly for the good of those who are temporarily confided to their care, and whose spiritual welfare must be supposed to be an object of yet nearer concern to their parents and other relatives. In this view, it has been thought admissible to invoke the aid of clergymen and other influential friends of Christianity, in procuring contributions from the fathers and mothers of Virginia youths, or from other persons who feel an interest in, and are willing to lend a helping hand to this enterprise.

It is hoped that the speedy erection of the contemplated building will stand as an abiding monument, bearing testimony that its fortune-favored patrons are imbued with the belief, that the Christian religion and science must go hand in hand and co-operate, in order to effect the grandest results in the promised design of Divine Providence, for the future ameliorization of the condition of man.

The Board of Visitors have granted permission to place the proposed building within the precincts. It is estimated that a suitable structure can be erected at a cost not exceeding $3000. We again respectfully, but earnestly solicit your active co-operation in the way of collecting subscriptions. For this purpose a subscription list is subjoined on presenting which to any of your friends it is suggested that you explain the grounds of the application and the claims of the enterprise as set forth in the foregoing statement. Remittances may be made to either of the undersigned or to Wm. S. Kemper, Proctor of the University.

This carefully crafted letter was signed by several students, by John H. Cocke as a member of the Board of Visitors, and by faculty members Gessner Harrison, James. Cabell, and William McGuffey. Notable in it are the emphases on Christianity (as "our holy religion"), on the separation of church and state, on impartiality among the four denominations, and on the co-operative power of Christianity and science to improve the human condition. These themes, though not comfortably coherent with each other, accurately represent the position at which the University had arrived by midcentury.

The solicitation rapidly raised the needed funds, and in 1854–55 the parsonage was built. Its first occupant was Rev. John A. Broadus, a prominent Baptist clergyman and, at the time, pastor of the Charlottesville Baptist church. The parsonage remains intact today as 4 Dawson's Row, known as the Luther P. Jackson House, and is the home of the University's Office of African-American Affairs.

Contemplating a Chapel—Again

The provision of a parsonage and the increase in the number of students contributing to the chaplain's salary went a good way toward improving the attractiveness of the chaplaincy to men of maturity with families and greater experience. But a real chapel was still lacking. That lack must have been pressed upon William A. Pratt, an architect and engineer hired by the University in 1855 to help oversee the physical property of the University, a responsibility that previously had rested entirely with the Proctor. Three years later the Board of Visitors created the position of Superintendent of Buildings and Grounds and made Pratt its first incumbent. By then Pratt had drawn up a design of a chapel for the University. It was for a Gothic Revival structure of somewhat unattractive proportions, to be situated at the south end of the Lawn, facing the Rotunda. In these respects it was highly reminiscent of the faculty's 1835 proposal. In order to solicit funds, a large certificate was prepared, showing both the front elevation and the floor plan, beneath which were spaces for the name of the donor and the amount of the donation. It was signed by J. C. Cabell as treasurer and William A. Pratt as architect.[44]

At its meeting on July 4, 1860, the Board of Visitors resolved,

> That permission be granted to the Faculty and such others as may unite with them to build by private subscription upon the precincts of the University a house to be used as a place of religious worship. The location and plan of the building shall be subject to the approval of the Executive Committee and the house shall be the property of the University and at all times subject to the control of the Visitors.

It should be noted that although the faculty and other interested parties are here authorized to solicit contributions toward the construction of a chapel, no approval is given either to a particular plan or to a specific site for the building,

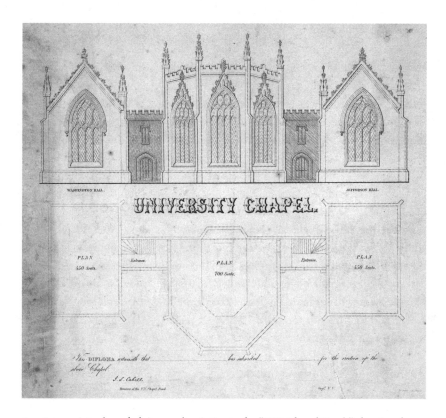

An 1859 receipt acknowledging a subscription to the "U.V. Chapel Fund," showing the elevation and plan for a proposed chapel at the University of Virginia, William Pratt, draughtsman

those decisions being reserved to the board and to the future. Further, the stipulation that, once built, the chapel will be the property of the University and under the control of the board is intended to guard against possible proprietary claims by any religious group that might contribute heavily toward the cost. Funds for a chapel began to be collected immediately and with some success, but the campaign was interrupted only nine months later by the outbreak of the Civil War. At that point it was decided that the money so far donated for the chapel should be devoted instead to the war effort. Accordingly, the funds were invested in Confederate bonds, and most of the money was subsequently lost. Thus although no chapel was built in the antebellum period of the University, the strong and irrepressible desire for one, emerging as early as 1835 and persisting until the war, is an index of how vigorous religious interest and activity had become by the end of the University's first decade.

The Piety of Professors

It would be a mistake, however, to think that the creation of the University chaplaincy was the only means, or even the primary means, of infusing religion into the early life of the University. Professors were at least equally influential. One might perhaps have expected this from the presence of a professor of moral philosophy, to whom Jefferson, in the Rockfish Gap Report, assigned the responsibility for teaching "the proofs of the being of a God, the creator, preserver, and supreme ruler of the universe, the author of all relations of morality, and of the laws and obligations these infer." And one might more especially expect it because the 1822 report to the Directors of the Literary Fund, asserts that "the relations which exist between man and his Maker, and the duties resulting from those relations, are the most interesting and important to every human being, and the most incumbent on his study and investigation." But in fact the subjects grouped together under the topic of "moral philosophy" were "ideology, general grammar, ethics, rhetoric, belles lettres, and the fine arts."[45] Religion goes unmentioned. And, as noted earlier, Jefferson was determined not to hire a clergyman as professor of moral philosophy, even though they were best suited to it, and so he appointed George Tucker, a lawyer who had no training in religion and little interest in it. But if religion received scant attention from Professor Tucker, it found other enthusiastic supporters and expositors.

Given that Jefferson excluded from the faculty not only a professor of divinity but also any clergymen at all, it is noteworthy that throughout the nineteenth century there were many deeply pious members of the faculty, and some members of the Board of Visitors, who were strong and influential advocates of religious conviction and religious practice, whether in the classroom, or by their own examples, or through their activities and associations, or in their favored causes.

First to be mentioned in this connection is John Hartwell Cocke (1780–1866), who served on the Board of Visitors from 1819 until 1852—the longest term on record—and is often regarded, along with Joseph Cabell, as an indispensable associate of Jefferson in the creation of the University.[46] Educated at William and Mary, Cocke had served with distinction as a general of American forces in the War of 1812 and owned the large Bremo plantation on the banks of the James River. Although Cocke left William and Mary as a deist, the death of his wife in 1816 and the force of the Great Revival propelled him into evangelical Christianity, and he became a devout believer. As such, he was a zealous and dependable supporter of many evangelical causes, including Bible societies, Tractarian missions, Sunday school societies, and foreign missions.

But his most sustained efforts to put his religious principles into practice had to do with what he regarded as two great social evils of his day: slavery and alcohol. He considered slavery to be "the great cause of all the evils of our land" and pressed for a constitutional amendment to end it. He was a dedicated member of the American Colonization Society and served for half a century as its vice president. In accordance with its policy of promoting the return of enslaved blacks to Africa, Cocke manumitted some of his own slaves who were capable of supporting themselves, paid their passage to Africa, and maintained contact with them after their return there. (He retained other slaves who he thought were dependent on him for their welfare.)[47] As to alcohol, Cocke took the temperance pledge in 1828, and thereafter worked tirelessly to stop the production and consumption of intoxicating drink.[48] He became vice president of the Virginia Society for the Promotion of Temperance in 1830, president of the first Virginia Temperance Society in 1834, and served as the first president of the American Temperance Society from 1836 to 1843. He was perhaps the most active and prominent advocate of temperance in the Commonwealth and in the nation during the second quarter of the nineteenth century. Cocke was also concerned, of course, to eliminate the consumption of alcohol by students

John Hartwell Cocke, collaborator with Jefferson in the construction of the University, and member of the Board of Visitors from 1819 to 1852, the longest term on record

at the University and was the primary impetus leading to the establishment in 1852 of a University Temperance Society—The Sons of Temperance—and he was the principal contributor of money for the construction of Temperance Hall in 1856. Although Cocke was finally unsuccessful in his crusades against both slavery and drinking, his long tenure on the Board of Visitors assured that his religious principles had strong representation in the University's policies and practices during the antebellum period.

Closely allied with Cocke on the Board of Visitors was Chapman Johnson (1777–1849), a Staunton attorney who served in the state senate from 1805 to 1831. Johnson was a member of the board from 1819 to 1845 and its Rector from 1836 to 1845. It was noted previously that as early as 1828 Johnson, with Cocke, had urged Madison to abandon Jefferson's opposition to naming any clergyman to the faculty. Johnson believed that a clergyman on the faculty would protect the University "from the injurious imputation of being a school for infidelity, and a nursery of irreligion." It is unsurprising, then, that when a clergyman was finally appointed to the faculty, Johnson was the Rector. Although Cocke and Johnson were not the only advocates of religion on the board, they were the most long serving, outspoken, and influential.

Almost all of the original members of the faculty were men of some religious inclination and affiliation. They willingly made provisions for voluntary religious worship to take place, but they did not become advocates of religion within the University. As they were replaced, however, new members of the faculty took a greater interest in religion and a more active role in promoting it among the student body. Especially prominent among these during the antebellum years were Gessner Harrison, James L. Cabell, William H. McGuffey, John B. Minor, Francis H. Smith, and John A. Broadus. Each of these men was in his way a powerful religious force within the institution.

Gessner Harrison (1807–62) was a member of the first class of the University and a graduate in both ancient languages and medicine. When the original professor of ancient languages, George Long, tendered his resignation in 1828 in order to become professor of Greek at the University of London, he recommended to members of the board that they hire Harrison, who at the time was only twenty-one years old and very provincial, never having traveled outside Virginia. The board hired Harrison on a one-year trial basis, but then made the appointment permanent. Gessner Harrison was a devout Methodist. His father was a deeply committed Christian and a decided Methodist, and his early teachers were Presbyterian clergymen, so a strong evangelical piety had been bred into him from a young age. The story is told that during his student days, when Jefferson invited him and his brother to come to Monticello for lunch on a Sunday, they declined the invitation out of deference to their father, who had instilled in them a strict observance of the Sabbath.[49] When a chaplain was appointed in 1833 (William Hammett, a Methodist) it was largely through the influence of Gessner Harrison, who at the time was the only member of the University faculty who openly professed his religious faith.[50] Harrison served on the faculty until 1859, when he resigned with the aim of opening his own academy, but the war preempted his progress, and he died soon thereafter. But he was a man of piety and virtue. His memorialist, who was also his son-in-law, John Broadus, recalled that Harrison "was a fervently devout Christian. . . . With no loud professions, he was always outspoken as a Christian, ready for every good word and work, and making the impression upon all, and most deeply on those who knew him best, that religion was the strength of his life."[51]

James L. Cabell (1813–89), a nephew of Joseph C. Cabell, who had been Jefferson's legislative point man in the establishment of the University, was a student at the University from 1829 to 1833. After attending medical school at the University of Maryland and further study abroad, he was appointed professor of anatomy, physiology, and surgery at Virginia in 1837, a post he held almost until his death. Cabell, an Episcopalian, was elected in 1840 to the vestry of Christ Church, the first church built in Charlottesville.[52] A man of formidable

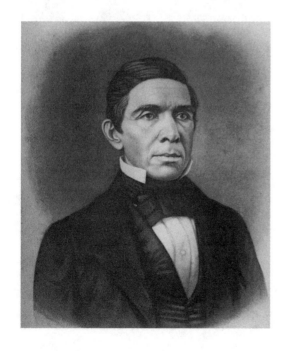

Gessner Harrison, Professor
of Ancient Languages,
1828–1859

piety and deep moral sensibility, Cabell was known for his attentiveness to the spiritual welfare of those around him. One of his memorialists recalled that "the ennobling feature of his character was his deep and abiding religious faith," which was "the inspiration of all his thoughts and acts" and "filled his private life with charity and benevolence."[53] Another remembered that "to his intimate young friends, in the retirement of his closet, he set lessons of personal religion. He taught a Bible class for years, with the door open to all."[54] Cabell was also an indefatigable supporter of the effort to build the University Chapel and served as treasurer for the Chapel Aid Society that worked to raise the necessary funds, although he did not live to see that effort completed.

William Holmes McGuffey (1800–1873) was professor of moral philosophy from 1845 until 1873, succeeding George Tucker in that post. McGuffey was the first clergyman to be appointed to the University faculty, and a Presbyterian at that—a member of the selfsame "irritable tribe of priests" against whom Jefferson had often fulminated. The appointment of a clergyman only twenty years after the University opened indicates that its founding principles were eroding,

James L. Cabell, Professor of Medicine, 1837–1889

for Jefferson, as we have seen, disqualified clergymen from serving on the faculty. It is an interesting question whether, as some have supposed, McGuffey was hired in order to deflect criticism of its irreligion by the Commonwealth's evangelical population. The University had been experiencing violent and disruptive student behavior, one result of which had been the murder of Professor John Davis in 1840, and this situation was widely taken as proof that there was no moral discipline at the University. Thus perhaps McGuffey's appointment "was more due to a desire to restore public confidence in the state university and recoup losses in enrollment, than to any deep conviction on the part of trustees that there ought to be a closer relation between religion and education in state universities."[55] But since religion and morality were generally thought to be closely correlative, McGuffey's presence would certainly have gone some way toward countering negative perceptions of the institution.

McGuffey was educated at Washington College (later Washington and Jefferson) and graduated with honors in 1826. He then became professor of ancient languages at Miami University in Oxford, Ohio, and subsequently professor of mental philosophy there. During his time at Miami he was ordained as a minister of the Presbyterian Church. He went on to become president of Cincinnati College from 1836 to 1839, and then president of Ohio University

William Holmes McGuffey,
Professor of Moral
Philosophy, 1845–1873,
the first clergyman to be
appointed to the University
faculty

from 1839 to 1843. After a brief tenure at Woodward College in Cincinnati he came to the University of Virginia. By the time of his appointment at Virginia, McGuffey was a mature scholar and had already had a distinguished career. His renown, however, had little to do with moral philosophy; instead, he was famous for his authorship of McGuffey's Readers, a graduated series of reading textbooks he had begun to produce in 1836. By the end of the nineteenth century these readers would become the most widely used resource in the history of American education, selling well over a hundred million copies, educating five generations of Americans and earning for McGuffey the epithet "Schoolmaster to the Nation."[56] The readers incorporated a strongly theological and moral aspect and aimed at the spiritual formation of students as much as their literacy.[57]

McGuffey's reputation at the University of Virginia came to rest, however, not on his famous readers but on his strong religious influence. He has been well described as "an inflexible and militant Christian, a man of the tough Covenanter fibre, who would have cheerfully gone to the block rather than have abjured his religious principles."[58] If George Tucker, his predecessor in the chair of moral philosophy, had taken scant interest in religion, McGuffey took immensely more. A student recollected that

> nothing could have been grander than the continued attacks he made upon atheism and infidelity. . . . Which one of his students can ever forget his touching and graphic description of the sublime and beautiful doctrine of Him who, clad in an humble fisherman's garb, taught by the wayside in Galilee and Judea! Though an earnest and loyal Presbyterian, nothing seemed to delight him more than to attack the world's prevalent idea of predestination. He pounded it with ridicule, stamped it with sarcasm, and made what predestination really meant so plain that no one could misunderstand his version of it.[59]

In addition to his courses in moral philosophy, it was reported that McGuffey had imported theological studies into the University. The *Virginia Historical Register, and Literary Advertiser* quotes a certain "Clericus," writing for the *Watchman and Observer,* to the effect that, "The Professor of Moral Philosophy performs an extra service in conducting a small class of five in a Theological course of instruction for the ministry."[60] This appears to have been extracurricular and done on Sundays, but McGuffey evidently wanted the University to be of direct service to prospective ministers.

McGuffey exercised his clerical standing fully and freely outside the classroom too. It was he who instituted daily morning prayers at the University. He also held forth in his regular lecture room on Sunday mornings at eight o'clock with lectures on the Bible, which drew up to a hundred students. He was instrumental in promoting Sunday afternoon prayer meetings as well, which also met in his lecture room and for which he maintained a "book of remembrance" recording the names of all those attending over a period of thirty years (1846–76). Although McGuffey had no regular pastorate during his professorial tenure at Virginia, he preached very often from pulpits—local, regional, and national, both Presbyterian and non-Presbyterian—and he himself estimated late in his life that he had preached about three thousand sermons.[61] He preached from time to time to students in the chapel room of the Rotunda, but often also to gatherings of African American residents of Charlottesville, and even went into the hills and hollows around Charlottesville and preached, sometimes in the open air, to gatherings of country folk. Together with other faculty members, McGuffey was a strong supporter of the Young Men's Christian Association from its origins until his death. As one who knew him remarked, "No one ever forgot that Dr. McGuffey was a clergyman. There was nothing of ecclesiastical bombast or pretension about him; but somehow all who saw and heard him felt that here, to use a good old phrase, was a Man of God."[62]

Jefferson's provisions against clergy on the faculty and against the teaching of religion may have suddenly seemed prescient when, in 1859, a student in McGuffey's course wrote a letter to the Baptist journal *The Religious Herald* charging that the University "is beyond question a sectarian institution, has been for the last several years, and will continue to be so, while Dr. McGuffey holds a connection with it." The student, a Baptist, claimed that McGuffey, a Presbyterian, had called "a bigot" anyone who maintained (as Baptists did) that "there is only one apostolic mode of baptism." Sectarian offence was apparently easily given and easily taken.[63]

Joining the University faculty soon after McGuffey was John B. Minor, professor of law for a half century, from 1845 to 1895. Minor (1813–95), an Episcopalian and a vestryman at Christ Episcopal Church in Charlottesville, was a deeply religious man and a stern moralist. It was said of him that "his religion dominated absolutely his life . . . and his every act, apparent and concealed, was but a manifestation or expression of that ennobling sentiment."[64] Minor, like McGuffey and other faculty members, sometimes led religious services in place of the University chaplain. For years before the Civil War he supervised and taught a Sunday school for the slave population in and around the University. With the end of the war Professor Minor began a Sunday morning Bible class for students at the University, which he taught from 9 to 10 a.m. in his lecture room right up to the end of his life.

John Barbee Minor,
Professor of Law, 1845–1895

To this all students had access, in fact were invited, but none was desired who would not study the subject and profit by the teaching. Consequently only those religiously inclined and legal students desiring to know something of the sacred writings constituted the class. It was well understood that Professor Minor recognized the Christian life as the only one, and that he considered an acquaintance with the Bible essential to every lawyer, looking with special favor and interest upon those in his department of like opinion—who earnestly attended and studied these Scriptural lectures. Realizing this, few law students inclined to incur his disfavor through what apparently seemed at the beginning of the course a slight extra tax upon time, that which, however, developed into no little responsibility as the session advanced, owing to the thoroughness of instruction and amount of material included.[65]

It is said that Professor Minor "probably never lost an opportunity to press on his pupils in private, with gentle and engaging manner but with his own impressive certainty of conviction, the claims of personal religion."[66] Between them, Cabell, McGuffey, and Minor brought about an enormous increase of religious zeal in the University, laboring to strengthen the presence of Christianity among the student body and within the University as an institution.

A strong interest in religion is perhaps less to be expected in a mathematician and scientist such as Francis H. Smith (1829–1928), but such an assumption proves false. After attending Wesleyan University, Smith studied at the University of Virginia from 1849 to 1851, earning an M.A. He then served as an assistant to the professor of mathematics from 1851 to 1853 before being appointed professor of natural philosophy, a post he held for more than half a century, from 1853 until 1907. Known for his broad knowledge, thorough scholarship, and engaging personal manner, Smith was also a deeply devout Christian of the Presbyterian variety. In a period of major scientific advances marked by such skepticism-inducing works as Lyell's *Principles of Geology* (1830–33) and Darwin's *On the Origin of Species* (1859), Smith took it as his task to be a staunch defender of Christianity. In the antebellum period Protestant clergymen and theologians were fond of appealing to the "evidences of Christianity," which were taken to include both the evidence of scripture and the evidence of nature, the two being understood as equally "factual," complementary, and mutually reinforcing.[67] That scientific findings were fully compatible with Christianity was the position of most scientists up until about 1860, when Darwinism complicated the picture. Darwin notwithstanding, Professor

Francis H. Smith, Professor
of Natural Philosophy,
1853–1907

Smith consistently emphasized throughout his career the harmony of science with the Bible, and wrote a lengthy volume on that topic with the title *Christ Regarded as the Centre of Science*.[68] Smith also did much to encourage religion within the University. It was said of him that "in all the religious activities of the University community . . . he bore a distinguished part." This was an arena in which "his energies were unwearied and effectual."[69] He was a constant and devout participant in University services of worship, and an energetic advocate for the construction of the University Chapel.[70]

The only man to serve both as a member of the faculty and as chaplain—though not simultaneously and neither for long—was John A. Broadus (1827–95). Of a strong Baptist background, Broadus was a student at the University from 1846 to 1850, studying ancient languages, moral philosophy, and mathematics, and earning an M.A. Immediately after his graduation he worked briefly as a tutor in the family of John Hartwell Cocke at Bremo, but then returned to the University in 1851 as an instructor, assisting the professor of ancient languages, Gessner Harrison, whose daughter Maria was married to Broadus. At the same time, Broadus also served as the pastor of the Baptist church in Charlottesville. In 1853 he resigned his position on the faculty to give

John Albert Broadus,
University Chaplain,
1855–1857, and pastor of
the Charlottesville Baptist
church, 1851–1855 and
1857–1859

all his energies to his pastorate, but in 1855 he accepted a two-year appointment as the University's chaplain and took up residence in the newly constructed parsonage. While many of the University's chaplains were men of large ability who commanded the respect of the faculty as well as of students, none was more highly regarded or more effective than Broadus, and during his time in Charlottesville he was a major religious force in both the town and the University. An eloquent and powerful presence in the pulpit, Broadus would later come to be nationally known as the most outstanding Baptist preacher of the nineteenth century. His fourteen lectures entitled "The Apostle Paul," given in the Baptist church in 1853, "created a sensation and thronged the church to overflowing with professors and students from the University and people of all denominations from Charlottesville."[71] In 1857–58 his revivalist preaching provoked a great surge of religious enthusiasm among students, faculty, and townsfolk, one lasting result of which was the establishment of the University chapter of the YMCA. In a decision that was very difficult for him, Broadus left Charlottesville and the University in 1859 to become one of the founding professors of the Southern Baptist Theological Seminary, of which he became the second president in 1888.[72]

It was through the agency of these institutional officers that in the several decades preceding the Civil War religion was steadily and strongly introduced into the University and naturalized in its life. There was no question in their minds that Jefferson's university should give the greatest possible encouragement to religious conviction, emphasize the authority of the Bible, and staunchly advocate the truth of Christianity.

The Public

All of these men were evangelical Protestants, and evangelical Protestant Christianity was the religious orientation that early came to be dominant, indeed almost exclusively so, at the University. This was in keeping with the religious demography of the Commonwealth at large. The intrusion of other religious traditions was much resented, as two faculty appointments showed.

When the University's second professor of mathematics, Charles Bonnycastle, died at the young age of forty-three in 1840, the Board of Visitors appointed James Joseph Sylvester to the post. Sylvester was a young Englishman who at the age of twenty-seven had already achieved academic distinction and had a brilliant mathematical future ahead of him. Sylvester was also Jewish. Also in 1840 George Blaetterman, the University's first professor of modern languages, retired from the faculty, and the Board of Visitors appointed in his stead Charles Kraitsir (or Kraitzer), a Hungarian who had also fought as a Polish patriot, and who was fluent in many European languages. Kraitsir was a Roman Catholic. Both men joined the University faculty in 1841. Before either Sylvester or Kraitsir had even arrived in Charlottesville there appeared in religious periodicals of the Commonwealth articles that were severely critical of their hiring. One of these articles began with the assertion that the University "belongs to the people of this Commonwealth," and that the University should therefore reflect its public constituency, a theme often struck when the University was founded. Few Catholics and even fewer Jews were to be found in the Commonwealth. Thus the appointments of Sylvester and Kraitsir were deemed "exceedingly unfortunate and undesirable." The article went on to say:

> [The Board of Visitors] met and gave one vacant professorship to a Jew of London and another to a Hungarian Papist. This is the heaviest blow the University has ever received. Some things clergymen have not a good opportunity of learning, but we are not deceived in saying that public sentiment in Virginia will not sustain such a procedure. It was wholly unnecessary. We are informed on what we regard as good authority, that there were more than thirty candidates for one of these vacancies, and more than forty for the other. Among them were some of the most gifted and best cultivated minds in our country, minds too adorned with Christian virtues and Christian principles. . . . We have often said that as infidelity became ashamed of its own colors, it would seek to form alliances with Papism, Unitarianism, Judaism, and other errors subversive of Christianity.[73]

In making these appointments, the Board of Visitors was clearly more liberal than the public—certainly than the Presbyterian public. So was the faculty. In regard to this and similar attacks, William Rogers, professor of natural philosophy and at the time also chairman of the faculty, wrote to his brother Robert in September of 1841:

> I have been mortified and provoked too, at finding so much illiberality among a portion of the community here on the subject of religion, as displayed in the bigoted publications which appeared during the summer respecting the appointments of Sylvester and Kraitzer. Would you believe it, that a series of essays has been published condemning the Visitors for the appointment of a Jew and a Catholic, and sweeping charges at the same time made against the character, literary as well as moral, of the University! These have been chiefly published by

two of the religious papers, but have not passed without eliciting the sympathy of some of the other prints, though in the main condemned by them.[74]

Sylvester remained at the University for less than five months, resigning in March of 1842. The ostensible reason for his resignation was a disagreement with the faculty over student discipline: students had been disrespectful and unruly in his classes, and Sylvester insisted that one of them be expelled, whereas the faculty would agree to no more than a reprimand. Subsequently, Sylvester suffered a physical attack from some students. It is unclear to what extent religious prejudice played a role in the offense given to Professor Sylvester: it appears that he was warmly welcomed by the students upon his arrival, but foreign-born professors were often resented, and his Jewishness contributed to his otherness. Given the anti-Semitism of evangelical Christians and the religious press, motives of religious bigotry cannot be excluded.[75] Professor Kraitsir, for his part, remained at the University two years longer than Sylvester, resigning in 1844. Far less is known of his experience at the University, and "Papist" though he was, he seems not to have been subjected to any explicitly religious prejudice within the University community. But in both these cases bigoted public sentiment sought to apply religious pressure on the University in the matter of faculty appointments, and to some extent succeeded. It is noteworthy that for the remainder of the nineteenth century, no other Jews or Roman Catholics were named to the faculty of the University. Evangelical Protestantism prevailed.

During this same period the University was facing stiff criticism throughout the state and also in the General Assembly. One legislator wrote to the chairman of the faculty with the proposal that the Virginia Military Institute be merged with the University, so that the latter might benefit from the economy and good order of the former. The idea occurred to him

> when I consider some of the sources of the prejudices against the University, her real or apparent want of discipline and economy, or when I look only at the frequent abuse which has been of late unjustly heaped upon her, and the strong feeling of hostility manifested in the present legislature. . . . Some change in the organization of the University, if not its total destruction, seems to be meditated by its enemies, on the grounds or the pretext of its expense and disorder.[76]

Public criticism prompted a move in the legislature to repeal the state's annual $15,000 appropriation to the University. The University was popularly seen as an elitist institution that afforded access only to the wealthy, and the tumultuous misbehavior of students, which had been virtually irrepressible during the first two decades of the University's existence, was much resented. The disorder of the student body was closely associated in the public mind with the deficit of religion at the University, and the faculty looked to religion, along with other remedies, as a means of instilling greater virtue, sobriety, and discipline in the student body. A causal relationship cannot be proven, but a correlation is undeniable: as piety was promoted at the University, disorder diminished.

The Minutes of the Faculty for July 5, 1845, contain the following surprising resolution:

> Whereas, it is the intention of the Faculty, in extending the benefits of its gratuitous instruction to those students who propose to enter the Ministry, to limit the privilege to such individuals as shall produce decided evidence of their disposition and capacity, to reap the advantages of the institution—therefore

> Resolved, that every student designing to enter the Ministry and desiring of availing himself of the privilege of gratuitous instruction shall submit a request to that effect for the consideration of the Faculty accompanied by satisfactory testimonials relating to his intentions, his moral character, and capacity—and that no such applicant shall be permitted to matriculate without payment of his tuition fees, unless previously approved by the Faculty.

This alludes to a provision that is mentioned in the Minutes of the Faculty for September 6, 1837:

> Whereas it has been the practice of the Professors since the first establishment of the University to allow ministers of the Gospel and Students of Theology to attend the lectures of their respective Schools free of charge, but the faculty has hitherto adopted no formal resolution on the subject, Resolved, that hereafter it be considered the privilege of persons of either of the above classes to attend the lectures in any of the Schools without fee.[77]

This provision was probably conceived originally in connection with the invitation to theological schools to set up shop "on the confines" of the University, because it refers to "students of theology," whereas theology could not be studied in the University. It is not likely to have originated with Jefferson, however, because it is spoken of as "the practice of the Professors," presumably voluntary, and not as a matter of official University policy. Thus it reflects a positive disposition of the faculty toward clergymen. It is unclear how frequently students aiming to become ministers may have claimed this benefit. But some among them had taken unfair advantage of it by misrepresenting either their vocational intentions or their academic interests and aptitudes. Hence in 1845 the board thought it necessary to insist upon some formal certification if the benefit were to be claimed. This tuition-free provision would come up for discussion yet again in the antebellum period.

By the 1850s religion had been warmly embraced by the University, and although a chapel was still wanting, evangelical Protestantism was firmly ensconced. But there were some who found fault that religion (Christianity) could not be studied academically at the University. In an expansive essay entitled "The University: Its Character and Wants," which appeared in the *Southern Literary Messenger* in 1856, the author maintained, "There ought to be provision made at the University for the study of Christianity; its philosophy and literature." Sounding a note that would find resonance a century later, he elaborated:

> We are not speaking of introducing in the University schools the hortatory or didactic expositions of the Pulpit. That is with the clergy. We are speaking now of a pure matter of science. We are speaking of Theology as we would of Natural History. It is a subject of just as much extent, and just as many convictions, and of as philosophical pretensions as Metaphysics or Philology; and it cannot without fatality, be overlooked in any intelligent system of polite education.[78]

He acknowledges that the "main difficulty in the general scheme would arise from the danger of sectarian teachings," but considers that a risk worth taking and appeals for support to Jefferson and the 1822 report to the Directors of the Literary Fund. But he was wrong to invoke Jefferson, and his plea would go unheeded until the twentieth century.

It will be recalled that in the 1822 report of the Rector and Visitors to the Directors of the Literary Fund the possibility had been floated that various denominations would be welcome to establish seminaries adjacent to the University.[79] Over several decades that prospect had attracted no interest whatever from any religious groups. But at last, in 1859, the Board of Visitors received an inquiry about the possibility of locating near the University "a Theological Seminary under the control of the United Synod of the Presbyterian Church." The Presbyterian seminary in the South at the time was simply the theological department of the College of Hampden-Sydney, located in relative isolation in rural Prince Edward County. The seminary was interested in offering more rigorous training and achieving greater national recognition.[80] As it happened, the Presbyterians were enjoying a certain prominence at the University in the 1850s. During the 1850–51 session, the Presbyterian chaplain, William. H. Ruffner, arranged a series of fifteen lectures by as many Presbyterian clergymen on the evidences of Christianity. The lectures, strongly supportive of thoughtful piety, were well received and soon published.[81] Professor McGuffey, an influential Presbyterian, was a forceful clerical presence on the faculty. And Dabney Carr Harrison was the much-admired Presbyterian chaplain in the sessions of 1857–59. Perhaps feeling that they had a foot firmly planted in the door of Jefferson's University, the Presbyterians considered erecting their seminary adjacent to it.

Recalling and affirming the statement that had been made in 1822, the board appointed a committee to explore the prospect.[82] That committee, having met with representatives of the Presbyterian Church, brought to the board at its next meeting a series of resolutions that aimed not only to endorse and approve the establishment of the seminary near the University but also to set out the terms and conditions governing the relation of the seminary and its students to the University and its students.[83] These terms and conditions were vigorously debated within the board, and various amendments were proposed and acted upon. The principal issues were what facilities of the University students of the seminary might use, what fees they would be required to pay, if any, and the extent to which they would be subject to the laws and regulations of the University. These questions proved to be complicated, and the Visitors could not come to any agreement.

It was not as though the University was or had been unsympathetic to the task of preparing young men for the Christian ministry. On the contrary, and in spite of its ostensibly secular and public character, from an early time the faculty had extended special consideration to ministerial students by exempting them from tuition fees. This provision got caught up in the fractious discussion about the possible establishment of a Presbyterian seminary near the University. Would any and all students at such a seminary be permitted free access to any and all schools of the University? The board disliked such a prospect and decided to end the practice of giving free tuition to would-be clergy:

> Resolved, that the Faculty regulation now in force providing that "young men" preparing for "the ministry" shall be allowed to attend any of the schools of the University without the payment of the fees of the Professors, be and the same is hereby rescinded.[84]

But there were almost immediate second thoughts about this action, and the board quickly moved to reconsider it, perhaps for fear of confirming the view that the University was unsympathetic to religion. The resolution was tabled, so the provision remained in effect. Nevertheless, the Visitors were not able to come to any consensus about the larger issue of whether and on what terms a Presbyterian seminary might be located adjacent to the University, and the question remained undecided for another year. During that interim, whatever enthusiasm there had been for the proposal in 1859 seems to have dissipated. At its meeting of June 30, 1860, a fresh resolution was proposed, namely,

> That Students of the Theological Seminary of the United Synod of the Presbyterian Church be authorized to attend lectures in the University, without matriculation or payment of fees, but not otherwise to participate in the advantages of the University, except that Professors and Students in said Seminary be authorized to avail themselves of the Library of the University in accordance with established regulations.[85]

But even this revised resolution could not gain approval. The situation was later characterized in the *Old Dominion Magazine:* "Embarrassments and objections thus presented themselves which had not been foreseen, and which seem to have cooled the zeal of the applicants, whilst they generated a growing reluctance on the side of the Board of Visitors to embark in the untried experiment of such a connection."[86] The Presbyterians, sensing that they were not entirely welcome, or perhaps that they were entirely unwelcome, abandoned their idea of locating a seminary near the University.

It was an odd twist that several decades later, in 1893, it was rumored that the Presbyterian seminary at Hampden-Sydney was again intending to relocate. Upon being informed of this, the University's Board of Visitors adopted a resolution to "encourage the removal of said Seminary to the vicinity of the University of Virginia, granting it such privileges and benefits as may be in the power of the Visitors." But the Presbyterians had a long memory and may still have resented the rebuff of 1859–60. In 1898 they moved their seminary, which since 1812 had been a theological department of Hampden-Sydney College, to its own new campus in the city of Richmond, where it flourished as Union Theological Seminary.

Interestingly, the University catalogue continued to carry the following notice under the topic "Expenses":

> **Ministers of Religion and Candidates for the Ministry.** Ministers of religion may attend any of the Academic School of the University without payment of the tuition fee. The same privilege will be extended to any young man who submits testimonials that he is an approved candidate for the ministry, and unable to meet without aid the expense of an education.

This provision obtained for an entire century, not lapsing until 1937.[87] Remarkably, over so long a time no one was disposed to see in it a transgression of the boundary between church and state, and yet this was a clear if indirect subsidy of religion by a public institution.

From 1845 onward, a student at the University could, if he chose, be more or less fully occupied on Sundays by attending a Sunday school at the University, the worship service led by the University chaplain, a Bible lecture given morning or afternoon, or both, by a member of the faculty, and a prayer meeting supervised by a faculty member. The Bible lectures given on Sundays by members of the faculty were, of course, extracurricular and attendance was voluntary. Even so, at least some of these faculty members not only encouraged but expected their students to attend, and students often attended these events with either the knowledge or the hope that their presence would enhance their professors' estimate of their curricular work. In addition there were daily morning prayers, and other prayer services held in the evenings during the week. And there were some religious or quasi-religious organizations that met during the week: the Bible Society, the Society for Missionary Inquiry, Bible study groups, and a temperance association.

How things stood by midcentury can be judged from an article that appeared in the *Southern Literary Messenger* in 1854, with the title, "The Free Schools and the University of Virginia." The anonymous author acknowledges that originally the University "was constructed without a distinct provision for religious teaching," but claims that "this has been remedied *under the demand of a public sentiment*" (emphasis added). He goes on to say that what with "public prayers, public religious teaching, a department of Moral philosophy which in these days is religious philosophy," there is little or no difference to be seen between private denominational colleges and the state university. The author regards efforts, such as Jefferson's, to construct educational institutions without religion as "uniform failures," but claims that the University has been "re-vivified by the incorporation of the religious element." He comments, no doubt correctly: "Society demanded it—public opinion required it—discipline could not be maintained without it."[88] Only with great difficulty could the University, funded and maintained by a religious public, resist incorporating a piety reflective of its constituency. Indeed, the idea that as a public institution the University *should* reflect the religious complexion of the Commonwealth was widely endorsed. This point had been strongly stated by John Holt Rice already in 1819, well before the University even opened. He had written then that

> . . . **the University of Virginia belongs to the people of Virginia.** It is *their* money which has founded, and will endow the institution. It is *their* children who are to be educated there; it is they and their posterity, who are to partake of the good or

suffer the evil, which it will produce. The Visitors too are truly and properly the representatives of the people of Virginia. . . . We deliver it then as our solemn opinion, that these officers have no right to regulate this public institution or select its professors, in conformity to any private sentiments of their own. They are bound to bring the public feeling and intelligence in contact with theirs, and so to conduct public education, as to satisfy the just expectations of the wise and pious.—We say *pious,* because we know that there is a connection between the religion and the learning of a country. . . . It is in vain to think of excluding religion from the University. It cannot be done. And if it could, the very fact would raise the hostility, and call forth the decided opposition of all who take a lively interest in religion.[89]

And so it had come to be: under the varied but combined influences of chaplains, faculty members, members of the Board of Visitors, and public opinion, an interest in, respect for, and participation in religious life became firmly established at the University. As early as 1835, a mere decade after the University opened, Jefferson's reservations about the intrusion of religion into the institution had been set aside as faculty and students, with the compliance of the Board of Visitors, welcomed occasions and expressions of Christian piety.[90] This openness to religion continued and grew through the antebellum period. Indeed, it has been said that by 1861 "there was as much religion and religious activity in the University as in any distinctively religious institution, notwithstanding that the students were not all saints."[91] W. H. Ruffner wrote in 1852, "With a Chapel, a Chaplain, two services each Sabbath, a weekly prayer meeting, a Sabbath-school, daily morning prayers, together with entire cordiality and accessibility on the part of all concerned, Christianity is now established at the University of Virginia on a basis which secures to it as much purity and efficiency as could be expected in such an institution."[92] And Andrew Dickson White, who became the president of Cornell, remarked in his autobiography, "Up to that time [ca. 1858] the highest institutions of learning in the United States were almost entirely under sectarian control. Even the University of Virginia, which Thomas Jefferson had founded as a center of liberal thought, had fallen under the direction of sectarians."[93]

Jefferson had envisioned a public, secular institution of higher education in which religion would play no role. But he sought to implement that vision in the midst of the most powerful wave of religious fervor ever to sweep over the United States, the Great Revival or Second Great Awakening, which began about 1800 but persisted in its effects through the middle of the century, and which reshaped the landscape of American religion. It was not possible for a small island of secular thought to withstand the rising tide of popular religious enthusiasm that washed over it. More and more, the University absorbed the evangelical Protestant piety of the public until the University itself became an agency of religious interests. After the war, as we shall see, the role of religion within Jefferson's university was still further enlarged and more fully institutionalized.

4

From the Civil War to World War I

Religion Takes Over

The Civil War precipitated many religious questions and theological problems. The American experiment had invoked biblical themes almost from its beginning as the new nation presumed to think of itself as a "new Israel," a chosen people, and considered its destiny to lie in the hands of a beneficent divine Providence. But if this high calling was originally predicated of the United States as a whole, the growing sectional conflict leading up to the war caused each side to claim that privilege only for itself. The South considered itself a bastion of the Christian spirituality and agrarian values that had prospered the American project, and saw the industrial North as defecting from the faith and engaging in a godless pursuit of material wealth and mercantile power. Persuaded that it enjoyed divine favor and that its objective was righteous, the South experienced a profound crisis of faith after the Union's decisive victory. The Confederacy's defeat was all the more difficult to accommodate precisely because it had invested religious meaning in its cause. Defeat could only be interpreted as a divine chastisement upon the people of the South, although the reason for such a chastening remained an impenetrable mystery of providence, not to be accounted for by slavery or by secession. Southerners of faith struggled to integrate the war's material devastation and human loss into the Christian narrative of redemption through sacrifice, and even though redemption remained a remote and uncertain prospect, the Southern soul felt somehow sanctified and strengthened by the suffering of war. The endurance of common suffering and loss could be construed as a purification from which the region emerged with a sense of confirmed virtue, renewed righteousness, and deepened dignity. In this way the conservative evangelical faith of the South, rather than being repudiated or revised, was retained and reinforced, and the personal, privatized piety it fostered became an integral dimension of Southern social identity and a prominent element in the romantic nostalgia of the Lost Cause.[1] Denominational differences remained, but they were relativized within a widely shared conservative Protestant outlook. In the South, religion after the war was an even more potent force of social and cultural cohesion than it had been before the war.[2]

The University of Virginia had remained open during the war, although the war deprived it of most of its students and distracted the attention of the few who remained. Enrollment during the war years averaged only fifty-four students.[3] And even though Charlottesville and the University escaped the worst of the war's devastation, most of Virginia and much of the South lay in ruins. Postwar conditions were difficult. The Southern economy had been destroyed and its social structure dismantled, and many of the young men who survived the war had to give their interest and efforts to elemental necessities rather than to education. Higher education throughout the South was in a depressed state and near a standstill.[4] Lacking resources and students, the University was very slow to regain its prewar footing.[5]

This was all the more unfortunate because enormously important developments were taking place in American higher education during the decades following the Civil War. While the South languished, in the North and the Midwest there was a vigorous expansion and transformation of higher education, which resulted in the emergence of the modern American research university. With the patronage of private industrial fortunes or the stimulus of the Morrill Act of 1862 authorizing state land-grant institutions, new universities were established and older ones were reformed. Unlike antebellum colleges, which emphasized teaching, focused on the classics, and aimed to produce men fitted for service to church or state, the new universities emphasized research, offered a broad curriculum, and, by means of graduate and professional schools, aimed to produce scholars, specialists, and professionals in many disciplines. Drawing upon features of German universities, the American research university that came into being in the late nineteenth century took as its task not the transmission of a traditional body of knowledge but the production and dissemination of new knowledge, especially the scientific and technical knowledge that would have useful applications in a society that was rapidly becoming urbanized and industrialized. Pace-setting institutions of this sort were Johns Hopkins, Cornell, Harvard, MIT, the University of Michigan, the

University of Minnesota, and the University of Wisconsin.[6] Darwin's *Origin of the Species* (1859) had a powerful influence as a demonstration of the value of scientific method, and under that influence the developing research universities strongly emphasized science, empirical methods, inductive reason, and practical results. Crucial to their educational enterprise was academic freedom—the elective freedom of what to study, the methodological freedom of how to study it, and freedom from the constraints of received tradition, including religious doctrine.[7]

The emphasis on rationalist, naturalistic, and scientific thought was ultimately inhospitable to religion, and it was inevitable that research universities would acquire an increasingly secular character. It was not that the new institutions were hostile to religion, for many of their leaders were persuaded of the moral value of religion and wanted to retain it in the curriculum. But this required a conception of and approach to religion that was "scientific" and could command respect in an intellectual culture based on scientific inquiry. This could be achieved, however, only if theology and dogma, which were immune to empirical assessment, were eliminated from study.[8] The effort to fashion a "scientific" approach to religion was generally unsuccessful, at least in support of morality, and the effort to bring religion into some kind of alignment with the methods and results of science was, in the end, counterproductive.[9] The result was a default to institutional secularism. The secularization of universities did not happen all at once, or in the same way everywhere. Some of the new universities, especially the public ones, were established on a specifically secular basis, excluding both religious exercises and the teaching of religion. Other institutions maintained for a time traditional religious exercises, though often on a reduced schedule or a voluntary basis, and experimented with ostensibly "scientific" courses on religion.[10]

As the role of religion was eclipsed, these new or revamped universities were frequently criticized as godless and inimical to piety and morality—the same charges that had been laid against the University of Virginia in its early decades, and that continued to be made. "In the last third of the nineteenth century the religion that had nurtured the colleges appeared as one of the greatest antagonists of the universities."[11] As a result, leaders of the new or reformed universities usually found it prudent and expedient to make accommodations for religious worship and to provide for the religious nurture of their students, thus to defend themselves against religious critics.[12] But the impetus toward secularism was powerful. If in the antebellum collegiate system religion had held pride of place as worthy of study and practice and as the foundation of morality, in the research universities that emerged after the war religion had difficulty maintaining a foothold. The hegemony of religion in the sphere of public higher education had been decisively undercut, and would not be restored. In the new environment the development of both intellect and character was increasingly seen as independent of religious influence.

The University of Virginia had been conceived and established by Jefferson to embody many of the very features that later came to characterize the research universities that emerged in the last third of the nineteenth century: an elective system, specialization, advanced studies, an emphasis on the sciences and their useful application, free inquiry, and a secular orientation. It is a large irony that this did not make the University of Virginia even a participant, let alone a leader, in the postwar development of the modern research university.[13] On the contrary, given its depressed circumstances, its regional insularity, and its cultural conservatism, the University was slow to alter its antebellum orientation, emphases, and form of governance, and so lagged far behind the progressive reform movement.[14] As we have seen, by midcentury it had also left behind its pioneering secular charter and had gained a strong resemblance to a denominational college. In the postwar decades, when emerging research universities were becoming more and more secularized, the University of Virginia was embracing religion all the more warmly.

The Early Years of the YMCA

Shortly before the outbreak of the Civil War an event took place that would determine the role of religion in the University for the half century following the war. This was the establishment in the autumn of 1858 of the University of Virginia Chapter of the Young Men's Christian Association (YMCA), an organization that would become a powerful force in promoting religion at the University of Virginia.

The YMCA had come into being in London, England, in 1844 as a Christian evangelistic organization that aimed to meet the needs of young men who came to the city looking for work but encountered there the harsh economic and social conditions spawned by the Industrial Revolution. The YMCA aimed to provide for them a low-cost residence in a Christian environment—a place of refuge and support away from home with a strong religious orientation, promoted through Bible study, prayer, and active evangelistic outreach. The idea was extremely fertile: by 1851 YMCAs were to be found in cities of most European countries and in larger cities of North America. The various local and national agencies formed themselves into an international federation in 1855.[15]

From the outset the fundamental motive of the YMCA was religious. Originally, its principal purpose was to convert young men to evangelical piety and to motivate them to spread the gospel, giving testimony of personal salvation to other young men by preaching in the streets, missionizing in neighborhoods, or distributing religious literature. Although the YMCA was an urban agency and had no original connection with educational institutions, its focus on young men inevitably fostered constituencies in colleges and universities. The collegiate YMCA movement, however, was not initiated by the international YMCA. Rather, in the United States it began as an autonomous, grassroots manifestation of evangelistic enthusiasm among students at the University of Virginia and at the University of Michigan. These two student associations arose almost simultaneously, but independently of each other, in 1858. It has long been arguable, and argued, which of these groups could claim to be the first collegiate association in the world, but the precise sequence of these foundations has no importance for present purposes.[16]

It suffices to notice that the YMCA chapter at the University of Virginia had antebellum origins, and that it was not planted by the international organization but came into being at the initiative of a small group of students who were moved by a revivalist impulse that swept the United States in 1857–58 and had a strong impact in Charlottesville and at the University. Contributing local factors included an outbreak of typhoid fever in April and May of 1858 in which twenty students died, and the powerful preaching of John A. Broadus, pastor of the First Baptist Church of Charlottesville between 1853 and 1859, and chaplain to the University in 1855–57.[17] One participant in Broadus's revival meetings at the First Baptist Church reports that "they were largely attended by students of the University, and the result was the awakening of a deep, widespread interest in religion. This interest grew and manifested itself in local weekly prayer meetings in all of the boarding houses and was freely participated in by all denominations."[18] The University chaplain at the time (1857–59), Rev. Dabney Carr Harrison, sought to channel this enthusiasm for religion and proposed the creation of a student association for the pursuit of religious work. Harrison came to be called "the Father of the University Young Men's Christian Association."[19]

The constitution of the new group stated its purpose to be "the improvement of the spiritual condition of the students and the securing of religious advantages to the destitute points in the neighborhood of the University." The organization got off to a fast start: by its third year it had more than 160 members and had developed a careful plan for missionary work within the

University and in an eight-mile radius around the University, where some fifty students preached or taught Sunday schools and Bible study classes. All indications are that the fledgling YMCA had strong and positive effects on religious life in and around the University.[20] Although it was established with energetic purpose and had immediate impact, the activity of the organization was soon interrupted by the Civil War, during which it was essentially dormant. With the conclusion of hostilities, the chapter was quickly and effectively reactivated, and entered upon a long period of ever more extensive and successful work. Growing in numbers and influence through the 1870s and 1880s, the organization's heyday was in the years 1890–1915. It is interesting to trace the development and progress of its influence within the University by references to it in official University publications.

The first mention of the YMCA occurs just after the war in the University catalogue for 1865–66. Previous editions of the catalogue had carried, toward the end, a brief and perfunctory paragraph under the heading "Religious Exercises," announcing in general terms the availability of voluntary religious services. But in the 1865–66 catalogue, this heading was revised to "Morality and Religion," and the substance of the paragraph was enlarged in several ways, including the first allusion to the YMCA.

Morality and Religion

These are recognized as the foundation and indispensable concomitants of education. The discipline is sedulously administered with a view to confirm integrity, and to maintain a sacred regard for truth. Great efforts are made to surround the students with religious influences; but experience has proved that the best way to effect this result, is to forebear the employment of coercion to enforce attendance on religious exercises, which is entirely voluntary. Prayers are held every morning in the Chapel, and divine service is performed on Sunday morning by a Chaplain, selected, in turn, from the principal religious denominations. By means of a Young Men's Christian Association, new comers are shielded, as much as possible, from vicious connections, and the energies of those willing to engage in Christian enterprises of the neighborhood are called into active exercise.

The original interest of the international YMCA in protecting young men from corrupting influences ("vicious connections") and in pursuing evangelistic work ("Christian enterprises of the neighborhood") is evident here, but equally noteworthy is the University's desire to capitalize on the nascent YMCA, along with chapel services, in order "to surround the students with religious influences." Coercion is disavowed, of course, but it is clearly intended that the environment itself should be fully persuasive. The idea that religion and morality "are recognized as the foundation and indispensable concomitants of education" was widespread in eighteenth- and nineteenth-century educational thought, and had come to be tacitly acknowledged in establishing a chaplaincy and multiplying religious exercises. But importantly, in this statement about the YMCA the University explicitly embraced the promotion of piety as part of its fundamental mission, and in so doing moved beyond simply providing opportunities for the free exercise of religion. By means of its support for and cooperation with the YMCA the University from this point forward became an increasingly active sponsor of religious convictions, values, and activities.

This paragraph remained unchanged in University catalogues for more than a decade. But in the catalogue for 1878–79 it was divided into two discrete sections. The first, previously called "Morality and Religion," was now retitled "Discipline and Religious Worship." It included the same language, but omitted reference to the YMCA. Information about the YMCA was reserved for a new paragraph with its own heading and some new content. It read as follows:

YOUNG MEN'S CHRISTIAN ASSOCIATION

The Society seeks to bring new students under good influences, and furnishes opportunities for Christian work in the University and its neighborhood. It has been in active operation many years, but has recently established the

STUDENTS' UNIVERSITY READING ROOM

This is convenient of access, comfortably arranged and furnished, and supplied with a large selection of the best periodical literature. It is open to all members of the University upon the payment of a small fee to meet its current expenses.[21]

In subsequent editions of the catalogue these statements under "Discipline and Religious Worship" and on "Young Men's Christian Association" remained unchanged for another decade, although it is interesting to note that in the catalogue for 1887–88 the paragraph on "Discipline and Religious Worship" is followed by a new one, entitled "Conduct," which contained a requirement of "a decorous observance of Sunday" and forbad "all outdoor sports on that day." This Sabbatarian regulation remained in the catalogue for many years. We see some slight but significant enlargements of the descriptions of the YMCA and its reading room in the catalogue for 1888–89. It read as follows (italicized portions are the additions):

Young Men's Christian Association

The society seeks to guard new students from evil influences, and furnishes opportunities for Christian work in the University and its neighborhood. *It is the oldest of the College Associations, having been established in 1858, and has been in active operation ever since. It conducts several Sunday schools in the neighborhood of the University, co-operates with the Chaplain in the maintenance of Religious Services, secures periodical Public Lectures and Sermons, and directs the Students' Reading Room.*

Students' Reading Room

This is convenient of access, comfortably arranged and furnished, and supplied with a large selection of the best periodical literature. It is open to all members of the University upon the payment *of an annual fee of $4* to meet its current expenses. *In their hours of recreation the students are thus enabled to make themselves acquainted with the best expressions of current thought on various questions of letters and science which arise in their University work.*

These descriptions indicate an enlargement of the interests and activities of the organization in various directions, accompanied by a growing sense of its importance as the agency that cultivates students' religious life and sponsors their religious outreach.

A University Chapel—at Last

Concurrently with the early growth of the YMCA, aspirations for a chapel were reviving. No practical steps had been taken during the years following the war, but on November 13, 1883, the University chaplain, Rev. Otis Glazebrook, seized the initiative. Recognizing the interest of faculty wives and other female friends of the University community, he organized the Ladies' Chapel Aid Society. Reverend Glazebrook and members of this group were aware of a relatively small sum—about $500—that remained from prewar solicitations for the construction of a chapel. With this as seed money, Reverend Glazebrook and the Ladies' Chapel Aid Society created and energized a broad coalition of faculty members, students, the YMCA, and alumni of the University to raise funds for a chapel. Immediately, almost fifty years after the idea of a chapel had first been floated, the Board of Visitors abandoned its long-standing resistance to a separate chapel building, and at its meeting of November 15, 1883, the Visitors acted to approve the project:

Whereas, it is proposed to build by general subscription for the uses of the University a separate Chapel to be placed on such site of the grounds of this Institution as may be designated by this Board: Therefore

Resolved, That such Chapel may be erected on such site of said grounds as may be designated by the Committee on Grounds and Buildings and approved by the Executive Committee; but that its erection shall be made under the general supervision of the Proctor and the Chairman of the Faculty.[22]

A mass meeting of the student body was held on December 4. The crowd was exhorted by Chaplain Glazebrook, Professor Noah Davis, and Professor William Thornton, after which the assemblage unanimously adopted a resolution supporting the intention to build a chapel and pledging the earnest efforts of the students to help raise the funds. Soon after, the *Virginia University Magazine* reported,

The subject which now engrosses the attention of University residents more than all others is the University chapel *in prospectu*. It seemed to spring upon us all at once, without any warning. Whether the affair was preconcerted among a knowing few, the plans all laid, the details studied and perfected before allowing it to be brought to the light of public gaze, or whether a spontaneous feeling, of the necessity of the improvement in view, pervaded us all at once, we have no means of determining. We can only certify that wherever we go someone will introduce the project of the new chapel. It is heard in the lecture room, in the dormitory, in the dining hall, on the lawn, in the parlor, everywhere; and surely if talking would build a chapel we would have completed already an edifice more pretentious and imposing than the most enthusiastic friend dares hope ever to see in our midst.[23]

Amid such excitement the various constituencies set to work, and by May of 1884 they had raised $15,000.[24] It was a powerful proof of religious zeal that the money could be raised in a mere six months.

Construction funds had come into hand even before the site of the new chapel could be decided. The faculty preferred a location on Monroe Hill, the majority of students thought it should be placed in the field between the East Range and the Post Office near the Corner, but some favored the area just to the northwest of the Rotunda.[25] In June of 1884 the Committee on Grounds and Buildings recommended to the Board that the chapel be sited "north of the Garth boarding-house, and near the pond in the lawn" (that is, west of the Rotunda and north of the West Range), remarking that "this site is preferred by a large majority of those most deeply interested as the one most agreeable to the citizens, students and faculty. It is of easy access, and with ordinary care can be built without injury to any of the University property."[26] The decision to locate the chapel outside the Jeffersonian precincts, and not, as once proposed, at the foot of the lawn opposite the Rotunda, is and ought to be a cause of enduring gratitude, since the chapel's Gothic Revival style stands in jarring contrast to the classicism of the original buildings.

The chapel was designed by the Baltimore architect Charles E. Cassell, an alumnus of the University.[27] Construction began in October of 1884, and the cornerstone was laid on March 30, 1885, with an elaborate ceremony. The principal address on that occasion was offered by Maximilian Schele de Vere, professor of modern languages, and it is particularly interesting for our purposes. Professor Schele (as he was known) alluded at length to the long-standing infidel reputation of the University and its founder:

> The great founder himself, who had so brilliantly fought for the severance of Church and State, and who looked upon his Act Establishing Religious Freedom as a triumph well worthy of being engraven on his tombstone, could not but dread the idea of his beloved University being involved in sectarian strife or propaganda. This was the reason why he omitted religious teaching from the general plan of instruction—and not, as has often been recklessly and even maliciously asserted, a feeling of hostility to religion. . . . With like injustice infidel views were ascribed at random to Visitor or Professor, for how little does the world know of that mysterious life which is forever going on in the secret recesses of the heart of man!

As against its reputation for impiety, Professor Schele spoke of a powerful religious impulse within the University leading finally to the building of a chapel:

> But while envy and malice were thus whispering of Theism and Atheism, the heart of the people began to yearn and long for spiritual solace, until at last the needs of the little community became too pressing to endure any longer this stern denial of religious privileges. Soon the voice of prayer was daily heard in our halls; soon the Sabbath bell summoned old and young to worship in common, while our young men, full of fervent zeal, went out over hill and dale, to carry to the poor, neglected and forsaken mountaineers the glad tidings of the Gospel.
>
> One of the blessed results of this unforced and unasked activity was the steady growth of the desire to have a house of God in our midst, filling the minds of men and stirring the hearts of all. . . . And what countless appeals were

made from far and near, from anxious parents, from former students, from friendly well-wishers, and from conscientious servants of the Lord, all urging the one great, sacred duty of building Him a house in our midst, and thus setting at last the seal of the Almighty upon the great and good work that was going on here.

In his peroration Professor Schele proceeded to draw a sharp contrast between earthly wisdom and heavenly truth, which he found symbolized, respectively, by the Rotunda and the chapel—pagan temple and Christian church:

> And thus we stand here, at last in one of Nature's fairest scenes, and on a spot which seems to have been specially chosen, to symbolize most strikingly the contrast between earthly wisdom and heavenly truth, between the halls of worldly learning and the house of God.
>
> Behind us rise in cold though classic beauty the outlines of a pagan temple, flanked on either side by ornate structures in chaste perfection, and between them long, low colonnades, forever buried in dim twilight or dark shade. What so fit as this to typify the search after truth on earth?
>
> Before us and around us is spread out God's own fair nature: vast fields . . . the blue lake . . . the everlasting mountains. Within—the pointed window, the flying buttress, the pointed steeple, all lead the eye upward, and with the eye the heart also is lifted up, aspiring to heaven.[28]

Jefferson's firm confidence in the capacities of reason "in the search for truth on earth" is here represented as a futile groping about in the dark; it is, instead, Professor Schele suggests, revelation that enables a spacious comprehension of reality. Schele's exalted rhetoric, although tailored to the occasion, nevertheless represents a sharp qualification of Jefferson's secular conception of the University ("this stern denial of religious privileges"), if not its outright repudiation. The chapel's materials, style, and location all mark it as a Christian building that stands in contrast to the Academical Village and looks in a different direction for truth.

Although the chapel was originally expected to cost about $15,000 (or somewhat more),[29] an amount that had been pledged by the time construction began, costs soon began to mount, contributions fell off, and construction was delayed. Ultimately the chapel would cost in excess of $30,000, so that after the laying of the cornerstone much more money needed to be raised. From 1886 to 1889 the Ladies' Chapel Aid Society mounted a series of events to increase the chapel building fund. In April of 1886 it held a "Mikado Tea" in Washington Hall, which had been converted into a "bazaar embellished with Japanese ornaments" where tea and other dainties were served to paying patrons.[30] Next came a "Mother Goose Entertainment," a two-day affair in December of 1886, when the ladies, costumed as characters in nursery rhymes and playing their roles, sold fancy stitchery and baked goods.[31] This was followed by a yet more elaborate event in December of 1888 called "The Congress of Nations," when booths representing many different countries were constructed and occupied by ladies in typical national attire who offered for sale "all the novelties of the season at reasonable prices."[32] Between these major productions the ladies also held occasional smaller bazaars. Such efforts resulted in funds sufficient to proceed with finishing the building. The chapel was finally dedicated on Sunday, June 8, 1889, with the sermon of dedication preached by Reverend Glazebrook, who had been the principal figure in inspiring and organizing the fund-raising effort.[33] In its minutes of June 27, 1890, the Board of Visitors acknowledged receiving the following statement from Miss Mattie M. Minor, president of the Ladies' Chapel Aid Society:

> At a meeting of the Ladies' Chapel Aid Society of the University of Virginia, Monday, June 16, 1890, the following resolutions were unanimously adopted:
>
> Resolved, that the ladies of the Chapel Aid Society, respectfully notify the Honorable Board of Visitors of the University of Virginia of the completion and dedication to the worship of Almighty God of the Chapel, which they, aided by the liberality of many friends of the cause, and acting as an auxiliary to the Chapel Building Committee of the Faculty, have lately had the privilege of erecting on the University grounds.
>
> 2d, That as a society, they herewith transmit to you through the building Committee, their surrender into your care of the structure as it now stands, thus releasing themselves from all future responsibility connected therewith.
>
> In presenting to you their congratulations on the achievements of this enterprise, designed for the highest good of this noble institution of learning, and, in making surrender to you of this pet object of their devotion which, for six years, has never flagged in its zeal, the ladies beg to bespeak from the Honorable Board, in behalf of this sanctuary erected to the glory of God, the Eternal Father, and source of wisdom, its beneficent care and protection now, and for all time to come.

The board responded graciously, pledging to "accept the care and responsibility of the Chapel and the duty of preserving it, for the holy uses to which

University Chapel construction, J. T. Wampler, photographer, 1889. Facsimile reproduction

it has been dedicated," and resolving that "the new Chapel shall be devoted exclusively to the uses and purposes of religious worship."[34]

The chapel was not opened for use until 1890, and even then it lacked some of its intended accouterments—including the organ and memorial windows. Most of the memorial windows were put in place in May of 1890, and the organ was installed and dedicated in February of 1891.[35] It was not until 1897 that the chapel was provided with a bell. This was a 1,200-pound bronze bell, cast by the McShane Bell Foundry in Maryland and donated by the University's Drama Club (the VVV). It has chimed the hour ever since.[36]

With the opening of the chapel in 1890 the preexisting pattern of worship was continued, only now in a new setting: in the chapel the University chaplain conducted two services, morning and evening, on Sundays. This long tradition was interrupted when the newly appointed chaplain for the 1896–97 session, Rev. Lachlan C. Vass, died suddenly just after the term began. Vass was a well-experienced Presbyterian, already in his sixties. He had scarcely taken up his duties and had just preached his first sermon on September 20 when he fell ill with pneumonia. He died only a week later.[37] Because it was too late to name a new chaplain, a temporary scheme was devised whereby visiting preachers would be invited to fill the University pulpit each Sunday. A Committee on Religious Exercises was set up, consisting of three faculty members and three students, to schedule visiting preachers, who were to be "representative ministers of all evangelical denominations, invited from Virginia and adjacent states."[38] This plan worked so well that it was continued for the succeeding session, and then was made permanent beginning in 1898–99.[39] The chaplaincy, which had lasted through sixty-three years and thirty-nine chaplains, was now discontinued in favor of "Preachers to the University." In the University catalogue for 1896–97 the list of "Preachers to the University" follows immediately upon the list of "Officers of Instruction and Administration," suggesting their institutional importance. Among these preachers were many prominent clergymen, drawn from a broad geographical area. Their names and the dates of their preaching are listed in the University catalogues from 1897 to 1919. They were not, however, chosen from "all evangelical denominations" but only from the four traditionally recognized by the University.

The Ascendancy of the YMCA

The construction of the chapel gave a further boost to religious interest at the University, and the YMCA, as both a patron and a beneficiary of that interest, gained even greater prominence. This can be seen in the catalogue for 1894–95, where for the first time an entire page was devoted to the YMCA. It read as follows:

THE YOUNG MEN'S CHRISTIAN ASSOCIATION

This was founded in 1858, and is the oldest of the College Christian Associations. Its object is to promote the religious and moral welfare of the students by furnishing opportunities for religious work in and near the University, and facilities for various kinds of healthful recreation and instruction. Under the former head it conducts Sunday-schools at the University and among the poor of the neighboring mountains, carries on a system of central and district weekly prayer-meetings, and arranges for courses of Bible-study under the direction of competent and experienced teachers. Under the latter head it publishes a compact and useful Students' Hand-Book to the University, secures periodical public lectures and discourses, conducts the Students' Reading-Room, and has purchased and put into a high state of improvement a valuable field near the Fayerweather Gymnasium as a free campus for athletic sports. The Students' Reading-Room is convenient of access, comfortably arranged and furnished, and supplied with a large selection of the best periodical literature. It is open to all members of the University upon the payment of an annual fee of $2 to meet current expenses. The Visitors and the Faculty of the University heartily commend the good work of the Association to the students of the University, all of whom are invited to unite in its membership and privileges.

The description went on to list a series of lectures on the "evidences of Christianity" that were offered under YMCA auspices.

There are fresh and important points in this description. The operations of the YMCA had by now become very extensive. In addition to sponsoring Sunday schools, prayer meetings, and Bible study classes taught by its own student members, it was now arranging public lectures in proof of the truth of Christianity offered by distinguished clergymen and scholars. This new educational effort was aimed specifically at the student body, and at a higher level than the Sunday schools and Bible study classes. Further, as early as 1883 the YMCA had begun to publish and distribute a handbook for students. The content of this *vade mecum* was not confined to the religious interests of the YMCA, but provided much information and generous advice about student life at the University outside the classroom, and thus served as an important supplement to the University's official catalogue, which was limited to curricular information.[40] We also learn that the organization had obtained property adjacent to the University, namely, the several acres just east of Fayerweather Gymnasium (later to become known as "Madison Bowl"), which it made available for athletic activities. This property had been acquired by the YMCA in 1887–88 with the aid of the International Committee of the YMCA and through the personal agency of Professor Noah K. Davis, who was a strong supporter and benefactor of the organization.[41] But especially to be noticed is the commendation of the YMCA by the Board of Visitors and the faculty to the students, all of whom were encouraged to join the organization. Each of these aspects of the YMCA was destined for important development in the following years.

In the University catalogue for 1896–97, yet a further major shift can be seen. Previously the notices about the YMCA were brief and occurred in connection with the topic of "Discipline and Religious Worship." In the 1896–97 catalogue "Religious Worship" becomes the title of a discrete section, and beneath it there is, first, a very lengthy description of the purpose, work, equipment, facilities, membership, and support of the YMCA, and, second, a briefer statement about religious services at the University.[42] Several points of this entry signal a significant change in the status of the organization at the University.

First, it is claimed that the YMCA "is the largest student-organization in the University," and that it aims "for a higher spiritual life among the members, and for united effort to help others in the attempt to live consistent Christian lives." The "distinctive work" of the organization is described as sponsoring a midweek prayer service, conducting Sunday schools within the University and in the University's neighborhood, arranging Bible study classes, and inviting "eminent Christian workers" to address the student body on topics of religious interest. The financial support of "interested friends" enabled a series of thirty lectures to be given over a six-week period by Rev. H. L. Willett on the subjects "The Life of Christ," "Old Testament History," "Prophecy," and "Beginnings of Christianity." The "equipment" of the YMCA, according to this catalogue entry, consists of the "YMCA Campus" (the name given to the land east of Fayerweather Gymnasium), which is "fitted up for tennis, base ball, football, and with a graded and ballasted running track." Further, membership in the YMCA is now divided into two categories: "active" members are members in good standing of evangelical (i.e., Protestant) churches; "associate" members are persons of good moral character, upon payment of dues of $1.50 per session. But most notably, the commendation of the YMCA by the Board of Visitors and the faculty becomes even stronger. It is designated as their "indorsement" of the organization, with the arresting addendum that "it is earnestly desired that every parent or guardian see to it that the student under his care is encouraged to join the Association as soon as he reaches the University. An opportunity to do this is always given at the opening reception for new students." Thus the administration of the University gave its full support to the organization and wished all students to belong to it. It is hard to regard this as anything short of religious advocacy by the University.

Clearly, during the 1890s the YMCA assumed an ever more prominent and influential role in the life of the University. Two developments contributed to the growth of the organization and the proliferation of its activities.

The first was the establishment of the office of a "general secretary." This was a salaried position that gave to the University YMCA the benefit of local, full-time professional leadership and administration. It was an experiment when, in the 1893–94 session, J. I. Curtis, who had previously served as the student president of the YMCA, took on the role of general secretary, but the office was formalized in the 1894–95 session. It was held by a number of men between 1894 and 1902, but it was under the leadership of Hugh M. McIlhany, who served as general secretary from 1902 until 1908, that the YMCA at the University reached the height of its success.[43] McIlhany held a Ph.D. and had previously served as secretary of the International Committee of the

Young Men's Christian Association for the South, so he was well connected both with the larger YMCA organization and with the academic world.

Second, the acquisition of the several acres immediately north of the Rotunda enabled the YMCA to offer an entirely new form of activity and one highly attractive to young men, namely, athletics. Offering facilities for baseball, football, tennis, and track, the "athletic campus" of the YMCA proved to be highly popular. It also marked a change of emphasis insofar as the YMCA's Christian education programs now came to include Christian *physical* education. This was wholly in keeping with developments in the YMCA at large. From its broadly evangelical Protestant origins, the YMCA came to incorporate, during the last decades of the nineteenth century, a strain of piety known as "muscular Christianity."[44] This was a type of Christianity that emerged in England in the mid-nineteenth century as a means of instilling character in public-school boys, but it spread rapidly to other countries. In the United States it found its most congenial home in the YMCA, which, under the influence of muscular Christianity, began to emphasize health, physical exercise, and competitive athletics as important applied dimensions of religious commitment.[45] Muscular Christianity aimed to promote a healthful and vigorous "manliness" among young men as a means of combatting the debilitating sedentariness of urban life, countering the ostensibly feminizing aspects of religion, and meeting the challenges of modern society with strength, courage, and industriousness. The University YMCA's acquisition and development of its own athletic campus marked its full investment in muscular Christianity. Not only did this marriage of religion and sport broaden the appeal of the YMCA; it was also at the root of the emergence of collegiate athletics at the University of Virginia, as elsewhere. Although muscular Christianity has largely been forgotten, its influence persists even today in such organizations as the Fellowship of Christian Athletes and Athletes in Action.

In spite of the large role it had come to play, the YMCA as yet had no permanent physical headquarters of its own in the University, and this lack was felt as a hindrance to its objectives.[46] For a time the YMCA met on the upper floor of Temperance Hall, and then in the northwest wing of the Rotunda, but as early as 1886 there was interest in the possibility of a YMCA building at the University, and a promising prospect that the funds to build it could be raised.[47] A meeting held in the new chapel in March of 1890, attended by John R. Mott, then the college secretary of the International Committee of the YMCA, created a committee to raise money for a YMCA building. Subscriptions began to be gathered, and during the following decade students, faculty, alumni, and friends raised an endowment fund of some $20,000. When Hugh McIlhany became general secretary in 1902, he took a particular interest in finally securing a building for the association. His commitment, supported by the interest of John Mott, who had now become president of the World Student Christian Federation, induced Mrs. William E. Dodge of New York and her family to make a gift of $40,000 toward the construction of a building to house the YMCA at the University of Virginia. The land was already available, namely, the several acres north of the Rotunda that had earlier been purchased on behalf of the YMCA through the agency of Professor Davis. Here was constructed Madison Hall, named for President James Madison, the second Rector of the University. The handsome building in the Federal style was formally dedicated on October 18, 1905.[48] On the preceding evening a dedicatory address was delivered by John R. Mott with the theme "The Influence of the University of Virginia Association on the World-Wide Student Movement." The main address during the formal dedication was given by Woodrow Wilson, then president of Princeton University, on the topic "The Relation between the Religious and the Intellectual Life," a relation he described as inextricably close.

Upon its completion and dedication Madison Hall immediately became the center not only of religious activities but also of virtually all extracurricular student activities. The main floor contained a large reception area, a larger and a smaller auditorium, a well-furnished reading room, a ladies' parlor, and a secretarial office. The basement floor provided three offices for college publications, an office for the drama club, a kitchen, a game room, a smoking room, showers, a barbershop, and storage rooms. On the upper floor were

Madison Hall, headquarters of the YMCA, soon after its construction in 1905

bedrooms for YMCA officers, a guest room, and rooms for Bible study and missionary meetings. Behind the building, the athletic fields were converted to tennis courts. So many attractive amenities made the YMCA much more appealing and effective than it had ever been, and the decade following the construction of Madison Hall marked the apex of the organization's success. No other University office or organization was capable of addressing the many and various needs of students—social, spiritual, or recreational—that were met by the YMCA. By virtue of its services and its facilities Madison Hall and the YMCA became, to all intents and purposes, the student union of the University of Virginia.[49]

With the completion and occupation of Madison Hall in 1905 the YMCA began publishing a newsletter, *Madison Hall Notes*, which appeared every week during the session. Widely distributed and well supported by local advertisers, this newsletter provided information about the YMCA and its programs, carried a schedule of meetings and events sponsored by the YMCA, encouraged attendance at chapel, and contained summaries of sermons, religious lectures, and moralizing essays. By now the interests of the YMCA were no longer exclusively religious. Beyond the provision of athletic facilities (especially tennis courts), the YMCA sponsored what was called the Lyceum Course. This consisted of musical, dramatic, and literary entertainments by traveling artists or troupes several times during each session. These events were highly publicized in *Madison Hall Notes* as enrichments of local culture. *Madison Hall Notes* was published for more than a decade, until the 1916–17 session.

The University had subsidized the YMCA in a variety of ways, by providing it with an office, a well-furnished meeting room, and a reading room, by contributing labor and materials to the development of the YMCA athletic campus, by allowing it to have the rents from Temperance Hall and the parsonage, and by other appropriations from University funds.[50] With the 1904–5 session the University began collecting, as part of the "Contingent Deposit" portion of University fees, two dollars from each student "for the support of the Chapel Services and General Religious Work of the University, *unless within one month after matriculation the student shall request the Bursar not to deduct this contribution* [italics original]." This statement is followed by a justification:

> It will be observed that this amount also (which is less than the average contribution made by the students who have given toward the Chapel Fund in past years) is not a necessary expense, as the support of the religious work of the University is left entirely to the option of students and professors. This method

of collection is intended merely as a substitute for the canvass formerly made, and it is the desire of the Faculty that the students will thus unite with them in sustaining the religious work of the University.[51]

With this and other subsidies, the budgetary functions of the University became nearly indistinguishable from the promotion of religion. Although any student was free to opt out of this "contribution" by means of a formal notice to the bursar within thirty days, many, perhaps most, students would have either been ignorant of this provision or too tardy to make use of it. The student newspaper, *College Topics,* objected, pointing out that some students would inadvertently be paying a religious "tax" against their will.[52] Clearly, by exacting the fee and placing the burden on the students to demur, the University was favoring religion. Objections notwithstanding, this provision remained in effect until the 1918–19 session, when University religious services in the chapel were discontinued.[53]

Many faculty members of the University had been strong supporters of the YMCA, most notably William H. McGuffey and Noah K. Davis, professors of moral philosophy; John B. Minor, professor of law; Francis H. Smith, professor of natural philosophy; Francis Dunnington, professor of chemistry; and Charles Kent, professor of English. The deep involvement of the faculty is visible in many particulars, and is further evident from the fact that, when in 1888 the YMCA incorporated under a board of directors, virtually all the members of that board were members of the faculty.

The faculty member to whom the YMCA considered itself to owe the most was Noah K. Davis. Davis (1830–1906), the son of a Baptist clergyman, joined the University faculty in 1873 as professor of moral philosophy, succeeding Professor McGuffey. A graduate of Mercer University in Georgia, he went on to study chemistry, architecture, and music and then took up an academic career, first as professor of natural science at Howard College in Alabama, then as principal of Judson Female Institute, and, before coming to Virginia, as president of Bethel College in Kentucky. Professor Davis, though not a clergyman, was a deeply religious man and an enthusiastic student of the Bible. Almost from his arrival at the University in 1873, he lectured each Sunday afternoon from 3:30 to 4:30 on some biblical topic, a custom he maintained for twenty-five years.[54] Some of the substance of these popular talks is preserved in two of his books, *Juda's Jewels,* a study of the poetry of the Hebrew Bible, and *The Story of the Nazarene,* a meditative study of the career of Jesus. Professor Davis was one of the strongest and most reliable supporters among the faculty of the University chapter of the YMCA and was instrumental to its

Noah Knowles Davis, Professor
of Moral Philosophy, 1873–1906,
patron of the YMCA and its
agent in acquiring the land north
of the Rotunda to be occupied
by Madison Hall and the YMCA
athletic fields

most successful period of growth. Not the least of his contributions was his
successful work to obtain for the organization the very valuable land directly
north of the Rotunda. That parcel, together with the construction of Madison
Hall on it, gave to the YMCA a physical presence to match the imposing influence it had acquired within the University.

Over the years and in many ways the University had become increasingly
reliant on and intertwined with the YMCA. The YMCA *Student Hand Book,*
published since 1883, became and remained an indispensable authoritative
guide for student life, even though it was not an official publication of the
University and its content was determined entirely by the YMCA. The YMCA
was front and center at the opening of any session with its welcoming receptions and orientation meetings, which effectively constituted the University's
only orientation program for new students.[55] Final exercises always included a
formal address before the YMCA. Moreover, the YMCA had from its beginning stood in a cooperative working relationship with the University chaplain, and, when the chaplaincy was discontinued, the general secretary of the
YMCA became, in effect, the University pastor. He was responsible for
the spiritual welfare of the student body, assisted in the selection of visiting
preachers for Sundays, conducted a midweek service, and led daily morning
prayers. Further, the YMCA provided the principal venue of athletic activity
on its campus, and the facilities of Madison Hall were meeting places for student

extracurricular organizations and social gatherings. The YMCA served as a clearinghouse for employment opportunities and living situations for students, engaged in community service projects, and disseminated essential information. Briefly put, the YMCA had become a very important agency of the University administration. It had developed and deployed that broad range of student programs and services that, decades later, would be taken over by professional (and nonreligious) offices of "student affairs."[56]

The Bible Lectureship

In addition to Professor Davis, another faculty member who strongly supported the YMCA was Charles W. Kent (1860–1917). Kent had been a student at the University from 1878 to 1882, and graduated with an M.A. After pursuing further studies in German universities and receiving a Ph.D. from the University of Leipzig in 1887, he taught for five years at the University of Tennessee before being appointed in 1893 as professor of English literature at Virginia. Kent was brought up in the tradition of the Disciples of Christ and led

Charles W. Kent, Professor of English Literature, 1893–1917, promoter of the Bible lectureship and of the School of Biblical History and Literature

an earnest and active religious life. At Virginia he was enthusiastically engaged with the YMCA, chairing its executive committee and playing a leadership role both locally and in the larger collegiate YMCA movement. He was the longtime chair of the Faculty Committee on Religious Exercises, established in 1897, when the chaplaincy was discontinued, to coordinate religious activities in the University. Professor Kent also taught a regular Sunday morning Bible class; it was one of his favorite venues, and had an average attendance of more than a hundred students. The Board of Visitors' tribute to him noted that "his private not less than his public life was governed by temperance and reverence and piety. He loved his Church and gave himself without stint to her service in body, mind and spirit."[57] A brilliant lecturer and productive scholar, Kent was a man of broadly humanistic interests, including religion. He had, of course, a religious appreciation of the Bible, but he was also much interested in the literary influence of the English Bible, and he included study of the English Bible in his courses on English literature. It was with this interest that he initiated the effort to create a Bible lectureship at the University of Virginia, and saw it through, not merely as an adjunct to English literature, but to the larger end of establishing at the University a School of Biblical History and Literature. The ground for this was prepared through the YMCA.

Bible study had always been a basic part of the YMCA program, and so it was also at the University of Virginia. Study groups under the direction of students described as "competent and experienced teachers" met at least once weekly and aimed to derive spiritual edification and moral guidance from the English Bible. In addition to these small student-led gatherings, lectures that focused for the most part on the Bible, some of them in extended series amounting to "courses," were occasionally given by the University chaplain, by local or visiting clergymen, or by members of the University faculty. All such events were under the general aegis of the YMCA. These various classes, lectures, and courses were no part of the academic curriculum of the University and carried no credit toward the degree.

In its description of the YMCA, the University catalogue for 1893–94 announced six courses, all taught by faculty members of the University, as follows:

1. History and Teachings of the New Testament, especially as contained in the Gospels and the Acts of the Apostles. Prof. John B. Minor (Law).
2. Book of Job, as an independent production and in its relation to the Old and New Testaments. Prof. Francis H. Smith (Natural Philosophy).
3. Life and Times of Jesus our Lord. Prof. Noah K. Davis (Moral Philosophy).

4. Book of Jonah, in its poetical, historical and religious aspects, with side-lights from the Psalms. Prof. Schele de Vere (Modern Languages).

5. New Testament Greek; a critical study of one of the Gospels, with exegetical notes and comparison of parallel passages. Prof. James M. Garnett (English Language and Literature).

6. The Bible and Missions; outline studies of the commands, promises and declarations concerning the spread of Jehovah-worship through the Jews to the Heathen. Dr. A. Damer Drew (Medicine).

The catalogue for the next session (1894–95) listed another set of lectures sponsored by the YMCA that were delivered during 1894 by clergymen of various denominations and institutions, as follows:

1. "The Unity of the Old and New Testament Scriptures," by Bishop J. C. Granberry, D.D., of the Southern Methodist Episcopal Church.

2. "The Historic Christ," by Rt. Rev. Thomas U. Dudley, D. D., Bishop of Kentucky, Protestant Episcopal Church.

3. "Jesus Teaching Nicodemus," and "The Truth of the Old Testament Proven by the New," by Rev. John A. Broadus, D. D., President of the Baptist Theological Seminary, Louisville, Ky.

4. "Jesus the Supreme Teacher," and "The Sad Tone of Infidel Literature," by Rev. Moses D. Hoge, D. D., of the Southern Presbyterian Church.

5. Two discourses on the "Testimony of the Monuments to the Truth of Revelation," by Rev. Walter W. Moore, D. D., Professor in the Union Theological Seminary, H-S College, Va.

Instruction in the Bible under the sponsorship of the YMCA continues to be mentioned in the University catalogue until the issue for 1896–97, but with a difference. It is noted that "during the present year, through the kind liberality of interested friends, a six-weeks' series of lectures was given by Rev. H. L. Willett, Ph.D., of the University of Chicago, consisting of four parallel courses as follows: Life of Christ (twelve lectures); Old Testament History (six lectures); Prophecy (six lectures); Beginnings of Christianity (six lectures)." This series of lectures was given in the University Chapel in February and March of 1897. The "interested friends" whose "kind liberality" made them possible were members of the Disciples of Christ in Virginia, including John B. Cary of Richmond, who made a large contribution and promised continuing support.[58] This is the first indication of influence in the University by the Disciples of Christ, whose founder, Alexander Campbell, had been rebuffed by the University in 1838. It is also the first mention of John B. Cary, of whom more will be said below.

The groundwork for these lectures on the Bible had been laid in the preceding year, when in the spring of 1896 Rev. Charles Young had visited the University of Virginia. Young was a clergyman of the Disciples of Christ who had held a pastorate in Ann Arbor, Michigan. While in Ann Arbor, Young had conceived the idea of Bible chairs at state universities. In the late nineteenth and early twentieth centuries it was commonly supposed that the separation of church and state precluded public universities from teaching religion. Young thought this obstacle could be effectively circumvented if a denomination privately funded a teacher of the Bible who would offer courses outside of but collateral with the university's curriculum, and thus make the study of the Bible available to students in state universities. Young proposed such a strategy to the Christian Woman's Board of Missions (CWBM), an agency of his denomination, the Disciples of Christ. Interest in missionary activity was intense in the late nineteenth and early twentieth centuries, and there was a corresponding flourishing of "missionary societies" among American Protestant denominations, some being devoted to "foreign missions" and others to "home missions." Many of these societies were sponsored and administered by women, and the CWBM, founded in 1874 and headquartered in Indianapolis, Indiana, was one of these.[59] Reverend Young persuaded the CWBM to embrace his conception of Bible chairs as part of its work, and with the financial backing of the missionary agency he established the first Bible chair at the University of Michigan in 1893.[60]

Young's visit to Virginia was made to explore the possibility of establishing a Bible chair at the University. Professor Charles Kent, a fellow member of the Disciples of Christ, invited Young to explain the Bible chair project at a meeting of the faculty. Kent was reportedly "pleased with the consideration which some of his colleagues gave the Bible Chair idea."[61] At its annual convention in October 1896, the CWBM endorsed the effort to establish a Bible chair at Virginia "as the next point of enlargement," and committed itself to raising funds adequate to its permanent endowment. Reverend Young reported that Col. John B. Cary promised $500 per year toward the project.[62] Dr. Willett's report to the CWBM about his lectures at Virginia in the winter of 1897 was altogether positive. "The attitude of the university authorities toward the work is cordial," he wrote. "There was a disposition to give attention to it on the part of the instructors themselves, several of whom were frequent, and some constant, attendants."[63]

In the 1897–98 session Reverend Young, who had been working since 1896 to build support for a Bible chair at Virginia and to solicit funds, was himself sent with the support of the CWBM to serve as the instructor in Bible at the University. The catalogue for 1897–98 announced, under the heading of "Biblical Instruction," that "under the auspices of the Y.M.C.A. and through the generous support of the Christian Woman's Board of Missions, Rev. Charles A. Young, of Chicago, conducted Bible courses extending through six weeks and covering the following subjects: 1) The Life and Letters of St. Paul, 2) The Minor Prophets, and 3) Popular Lecture Course on Hebrew Poetry." The catalogue went on to indicate that for the 1898–99 session Reverend Young would offer four further courses, and that two additional courses would be offered by other teachers, one by Rev. Carl Grammer of the Episcopal Theological Seminary, and another by Rev. John Sampey of the Southern Baptist Theological Seminary.[64]

Charles Young remained the lecturer from 1898 to 1901 and during those sessions offered a large number of extracurricular courses, but he was also active in raising money to support the Bible lectureship. It was a surprising turn of events when in 1899 the Board of Visitors elected him to the faculty as "Instructor in Hebrew," with duties to include also some courses in the English Bible.[65] That appointment to the faculty lasted for only one session (1899–1900), however: the faculty recommended to the Board of Visitors that the position be discontinued at the end of that session, and Reverend Young submitted his resignation.[66] The Board commended Young for his teaching and thanked him "for contributing by his words in private and in public during his recent travels through the land in the interest of the Endowment of the Bible work here, to the better understanding by the people of what we are trying to do here *and to the removal of certain prejudices as to the moral status of the institution, which has been of long-standing*" (emphasis added).[67] This statement makes it perfectly clear that the Board of Visitors regarded the availability of instruction in the Bible as an important means of countering the persistently popular idea that the University was a haven of infidelity and immorality, a suspicion that had dogged the University since its founding.

An original sponsor and the most generous benefactor of the Bible lectureship was John Baytop Cary (1819–98) of Richmond. Cary, a native of the Hampton area, was educated at William and Mary. Upon graduating in 1839, he entered the teaching profession and taught at a "common" or "free" school for several years before moving to Hampton Academy, where he taught until 1852. He then established Hampton Military Academy and served as its principal until the outbreak of the Civil War. He was commissioned as major, was later promoted to Lt. Colonel, and commanded the 32nd Virginia Infantry until he was transferred to an administrative post in Richmond. After the war he remained in Richmond, where he built up a prosperous insurance agency. In 1886 he became Richmond's first superintendent of schools, and after his retirement he served with the Virginia Department of Education until his death in 1898. Because the family had long been active in the Disciples of Christ movement, and because Colonel Cary was a man of great piety who was devoted to biblical teachings, there is nothing surprising in his support of the Bible lectureship at the University.

After his death and in his memory, Colonel Cary's family made an additional gift of $10,000.[68] The gift, which was made to the CWBM as "independent trustees," was acknowledged with gratitude by the Board of Visitors in March of 1899, noting that it was intended "to provide for nonsectarian Biblical instruction without in any wise connecting this work organically with the University or without soliciting from the University any financial support or official recognition."[69] This defensive statement, reasserting the University's traditional insistence on a nonsectarian posture and emphasizing the principle of the separation of church and state, shows that the board regarded instruction in Bible as a tricky issue. The board went on to express the hope that a full sum of $25,000 needed to endow permanently the John B. Cary Bible Lectureship might be quickly raised, and it was. Thus the University catalogue for 1900–1901 refers to "The University of Virginia Bible Lectureship, Founded by John B. Cary,"[70] but the catalogue for 1901–2 and for subsequent years refers to "The John B. Cary Bible Lectureship."[71] The following description of the lectureship was given in the 1901–2 catalogue:

> The authority and divine inspiration of the Bible are emphasized, but the lectures are given purely from the standpoint of history and literature. All distinctively theological questions are ignored. . . . The endowment of this Lectureship now amounts to a little more than twenty-five thousand dollars, of which the interest is to be used in providing for regular and systematic instruction in the English Bible from the standpoint of history and literature and in procuring distinguished lecturers for special courses. The purpose of this Lectureship, which is not organically connected with the University but exists with its approval and sympathy, is to furnish instruction in every respect totally nonsectarian; and therefore in selecting the public lecturers care is had not to their denominational affiliation but to their evangelical relations.[72]

The close reader will find this statement remarkable, not least for its incoherence: the "authority and divine inspiration" of the Bible are entirely theological claims, presupposed as true and indeed "emphasized," yet it is asserted at the same time that "theological questions are ignored." It is further stated that under the lectureship "the best and most representative Christian scholars of evangelical denominations" are to be engaged, yet that "the lectures are entirely devoid of sectarian bias." Again, it is peculiar that while only Christian scholars, and of them only evangelical (that is, Protestant) ones are invited, it is nevertheless asserted that there is no sectarian bias. In the twenty-first century these statements are manifestly self-contradictory, but they seemed far less so in the early twentieth century, when it was taken for granted that the Bible is above all a Christian book, and when the constituency for Bible study at the University was not only almost exclusively Christian but also almost exclusively Protestant.

Even so, the relation of this lectureship to the University was a sensitive issue. This may be seen in the statement that the lectureship is "not organically connected with the University, but exists with its approval and sympathy," which signifies that some thought the lectureship was in danger of being conceived or represented as an instrument of the University, and thus as compromising the separation of church and state—a concern already reflected in the Board of Visitors' acknowledgment of the Cary gift. Another reservation about the character of the lectures themselves appears in the claim that the purpose of the lectureship is "to furnish instruction in every respect totally non-sectarian." The redundancy of this avowal suggests that some thought the lectureship might be biased in favor of one or another denomination's interests.[73] The University obviously wished to have its cake and eat it too: it welcomed the Bible lectureship and regarded it as beneficial to the University, but was anxious to stress that it was not actually part of ("organically connected with") the University.[74]

The Bible lectureship went unfilled for the 1902–3 session because no suitable candidate was available, but for the following session William M. Forrest was appointed. He would prove to be a key figure, and not only in the development of the lectureship. Forrest (1868–1956), a native of Baltimore and a graduate of Hiram College, was, like Reverend Young, an ordained minister of the Disciples of Christ. He had been associated with the Christian Woman's Board of Missions since 1896, when he went under its auspices to Ann Arbor, Michigan. There he held a pastorate and taught English Bible as holder of the Bible chair that had been established there, as Charles Young had done before him. After some further academic work at the University of Chicago, the CWBM sent Forrest to another of its evangelistic beachheads, the Calcutta

Bible Lectureship in India, but after two years he had to return to the United States because of his wife's poor health. He was then dispatched to Charlottesville to fill the Cary Bible Lectureship at the University of Virginia. This was only the beginning of Forrest's relation to the University, for he would remain at the University for thirty-six years—until 1939.[75]

Religion Finds an Academic Home: The School of Biblical History and Literature

William Forrest arrived in Charlottesville in 1903 and took up his duties in the lectureship. At first he found the work very disappointing. He began with a single course that drew only three students, and over three years he mounted a variety of courses on the Bible, but although competently taught, they attracted very few students. Forrest reasoned that Bible courses would draw more students only if they were not extracurricular but could be counted for academic credit toward the degree.[76]

To assist him in achieving that objective Forrest had a ready ally on the faculty in Charles W. Kent, whose interest in the Bible's influence on English literature had led him several years earlier to take a leading part in the effort to establish the Cary Bible Lectureship. Thus he "had stood sponsor for the Bible work [at Virginia] since its inception." Together, Forrest and Kent approached the administration about making Bible courses credit-eligible. They conferred with President Alderman and secured his approval of a modest proposal to make one Bible course per session an elective for credit. Alderman took the proposal to the Board of Visitors, but the board balked at some of the provisions and the plan was stymied. Forrest was discouraged and thought seriously about leaving the University and returning to India, but his wife's precarious health prevented that. Then in January of 1906 Alderman took the idea back to the board, this time successfully.[77] But there were still sticking points that had to be worked through.

The question of making Forrest's Bible courses credit-eligible was complicated because the instructor would have to be made a member of the faculty. Initially, the Christian Woman's Board of Missions wanted to designate the faculty member; after all, they had established the lectureship and they were paying the lecturer. But President Alderman objected to a faculty appointment being made by an outside agency.[78] Professor Kent then cobbled up a proposal that he hoped would resolve the impasse, namely, that William Forrest would be appointed as an "adjunct associate professor" for a trial period of three years, to teach one course per year to be credited toward the B.A.[79] The Board of Visitors also objected to the prospect of a faculty member being compensated by an agency outside the University, and authorized President Alderman to ask the CWBM to turn over the John B. Cary fund to the University on condition that its income be used to support "an Adjunct Professorship, for instruction in the history, literature, and interpretation of the Bible, upon a non-sectarian basis."[80] The CWBM, however, refused to surrender the money. Kent and Forrest then fashioned a compromise that enabled a way forward. Forrest would be appointed as an adjunct professor for a trial period of three years, during which courses taught under the Cary Bible Lectureship could be taken for degree credit. The CWBM would retain control of the Cary endowment, but would transfer the interest to the University, and the University would disburse the funds to Forrest.[81]

Thus in 1906 the Board of Visitors moved to "create for a period of three years an Associate Professorship of Biblical History and Literature to be known as the 'John B. Cary Chair of Biblical History and Literature.'" The board further resolved that the incumbent of this chair be authorized to offer a course of three hours a week for the whole session, and that this course "may be pursued by a candidate for the B.A. degree as an elective at large." Given the structure of the University, the creation of a professorship entailed also the creation of a "school" in which it functioned, in this case a "School of Biblical History and Literature." William Forrest was appointed to this temporary professorial chair, effective September 15, 1906, his salary and expenses paid *through* the University but *by* the Christian Woman's Board of Missions from the proceeds of the Cary fund. A final provision was that after three years the agreement would be reviewed, and continued, revised, or revoked by either of the contracting parties.[82]

Although the agreement was in many respects unconventional, reservations about it soon evaporated, and after only two years, instead of the allotted three, the arrangement was revisited and revised to secure "the perpetual maintenance" of the chair of biblical history and literature in the University, and a corresponding School of Biblical History and Literature among the other schools of the University. This was done by means of a detailed trust agreement drawn between the University and the Christian Woman's Board of Missions.[83] The agreement established an endowment for the chair, consisting of the funds previously raised by the Board of Missions for the support of the Cary chair, the money earlier donated for the Cary Lectureship, plus a gift of $20,000 contributed by Mr. T. A. Cary, son of John B. Cary. The total endowment came to $49,500, subsequently rounded up to $50,000, of which some $32,000 had come from members of the Cary family and their friends. The interest on this endowment (but not the principal) was to be turned over to the University bursar, who would use it to pay the professor's salary and expenses. An opt-out clause stated that if at any time the University became unable or unwilling to continue the chair for three consecutive years, all of the endowment for the chair would revert to the CWBM.

The agreement had other noteworthy provisions. It stipulated that, in appointing a professor to this chair, "recommendations from the Trustees of this Fund [the Cary Endowment] will be cordially considered, and *no appointment shall be made that meets with the expressed disapproval of said trustees*" (emphasis added). Since the trustees were the executive committee of the Christian Woman's Board of Missions, the University was here giving veto power over a faculty appointment to a religious organization. At a later time this would be unthinkable, but it shows how comfortable the University's relation to religion had become. This is also seen in another detail of the trust agreement.

If the School of Biblical History and Literature was to stand on the same footing and have the same prerogatives as the other schools, there was nevertheless an important difference. In setting out the qualifications of the professor, the agreement states that "not only his scholastic fitness must be considered, but also his Christian character. He must be *not only a scholar, but a distinctly Christian man, interested in men as well as in books, and able by his manly life to commend to students the teaching of the Book from which he instructs them*" (emphasis added). And in stating his duties it adds that, beyond his ordinary professorial responsibilities, "he shall cooperate with the YMCA, and other religious agencies at the University, deliver such open-lectures on the Bible, and conduct such volunteer Bible classes as time and occasion may permit, *and endeavor to make himself a positive religious factor in the religious life of the University*" (emphasis added). Put bluntly, what we find here is no less than a religious test for a professorship in Jefferson's university: the professor of biblical history and literature was not merely to teach about the Bible but also to profess, exemplify, and promote Christian piety within the institution. These provisions, uniquely applied to the professor of biblical history and literature, show all too well that the interests behind the establishment of this chair and its corresponding school were *not* strictly academic and scholarly, but were deeply enmeshed with religious motives and objectives. Nor should it be thought that these specifically religious aims were somehow forced upon the University by the Christian Woman's Board of Missions or the Cary family; they were warmly shared by most members of the Board of Visitors, by most members of the faculty, by President Alderman, and, one supposes, by many in the student body.

This is how far the University had now moved from the aims of its founder on the subject of religion. Jefferson had deliberately marginalized the study of religion and excluded a professor of divinity; he had opposed the appointment of any clergymen to the faculty; and he also had small regard for the Bible and could find value in it only by a highly selective reading of the Gospels alone. Now the Board of Visitors was adding a professor and a School of Biblical History and Literature to the schools originally intended by Jefferson, stipulating that the professor must be Christian, charging him with the responsibility of promoting piety, and appointing a clergyman. Given the parties and the presumptions involved, it is hard to imagine that Jefferson would have countenanced such a move.

There is yet another point of importance to observe here. When, beginning in 1906, courses offered by the professor of biblical history and literature were recognized as academic electives, the University of Virginia became the first state university in the nation to grant credit toward the degree for a course in religion, thus placing religion on the same curricular footing as other disciplines.[84]

In the University catalogue for 1906–7 there appears for the first time a listing of "The John B. Cary School of Biblical History and Literature" among the regular schools of the University, and hence there is no longer a listing of the Cary Lectureship under the "Religious Worship" rubric. William Forrest is accordingly now listed as the professor of this school (although initially he had the rank only of associate professor), and thus incorporated into the University faculty. Leaving aside the brief tenure of Reverend Young as instructor in Hebrew, Forrest was only the second clergyman to become a regular member of the faculty, the first having been William McGuffey.

Early in the twentieth century the academic study of religion was still in its infancy, in private as well as in public institutions. It was noted above that it had yet to be clarified whether, to what extent, and how religion could be, or ought to be, studied objectively and dispassionately, independently of confessional commitments or existential bias. Notwithstanding the manifestly religious aims that lay behind it, the establishment of a School of Biblical History and Literature within the curriculum of a public university, if it were to be legitimate, required an understanding of the distinction between the confessional and devotional study of the Bible on the one hand, and the objective, academic study of the Bible on the other. And that understanding was present, at least in the minds of some at the University, though it was not universally shared. Already in an essay entitled "Bible Study at the University," unsigned but certainly written by Forrest and published in the *Alumni Bulletin* of 1903, the two methods of Bible study were carefully distinguished: first, "critical, literary and historical study," and second, "devotional study." The former "is pursued almost exclusively in connection with the curriculum of the college in which it is undertaken" and should be done "under the direction of expert instructors." The devotional approach, on the other hand, "is practically everywhere left in the hands of the Young Men's Christian Associations." It is led by students, and has the aim of fostering daily Bible study and encouraging "each man to apply the facts to his life day by day."[85] Forrest was sympathetic toward personal, devotional study of the Bible, but in his teaching work he conceived of himself as a critical scholar, and was careful not to import theological doctrines or evangelistic aims into the courses he taught. In an article titled "The John B. Cary Memorial School of Biblical History and Literature," written several years after the school had been created, Forrest lamented that so little serious, scholarly study of the Bible—as distinct from merely inspirational and devotional study—was available to students in public universities, and that even where it had become available, as it now had at the University of Virginia, students took little advantage of it.[86] He remarked,

> It has been found, however, that no very general demand for biblical knowledge exists among the students. The classes have been small during the four years of work. While that is true of other classes in the University, it is somewhat surprising in this case. The students come very generally from Christian homes, and *there has always been a certain amount of criticism against the University from the churches because of alleged irreligion, or non-religion.* Yet it is quite certain that if the homes and churches of the students considered Bible study a vital matter they would be able to induce them to avail of instruction offered. Certainly the establishment of such courses *has shifted the responsibility for lack of biblical knowledge from the University to the students, their homes, and their churches.* (emphasis added)[87]

Although Forrest and other supporters of the Cary Bible Lectureship had argued that more students would take courses on the Bible if those courses could be counted for academic credit, that did not prove true: during the first several years of their availability Bible courses attracted pitifully few students.[88] Clearly, a devotional interest in the scriptures did not readily translate into an academic interest in the Bible. But even while conceding this, Forrest went on to make an important claim: *by virtue of offering these courses and making them credit-worthy the University had freed itself from all allegations of irreligion.* The blame for low enrollments, he said, now rested entirely upon "the students, their homes, and their churches." Here again we see that the University's willingness, indeed eagerness, to embrace Bible study, like its other alliances with religious professionals, agencies, and projects, was motivated in large part by the desire to counter the long-standing public perception that the University was antagonistic to religion.

A Religious Institution?

By 1910 the YMCA had become an imposing organization with enormous influence in the University. Its salaried general secretary oversaw the religious life of the University; its commodious new building was headquarters for most student activities; its numerous Bible study groups, prayer meetings, Sunday schools, and lecture series expressed and instilled piety; its student handbook was an indispensable guide to University life; and its athletic facilities were popular recreational venues. The University faculty and the Board of Visitors were happy to embrace the YMCA and to represent it to parents and guardians as a guarantor that the University provided an environment that not only offered opportunities for religious worship and study but also strongly encouraged them. From the YMCA's Bible lectureship there had emerged a School of Biblical History and Literature. In addition, the University subsidized the YMCA in various ways, early on allocating space for YMCA meetings and activities, allowing it to keep the rent from the parsonage and Temperance Hall, later paying part of the salary of the general secretary, and making annual appropriations for the maintenance of Madison Hall, the payment of its utility bills, and program support.

In short, over several decades and by degrees the University increasingly entered into a relationship of codependence with the YMCA. However desirable or useful the activities and programs of the YMCA may have been, the University's heavy reliance upon them made it complicit in that organization's aims, which were fundamentally religious. By the beginning of World War I it was very difficult to see any daylight between the University and the YMCA. It was symptomatic of this circumstance that the president of the University, Edwin Alderman, was also the president of the Board of Trustees of the YMCA.

Thus, almost from the beginning, throughout the nineteenth century, and into the early twentieth century, there was a gradual and steady increase in the University's emphasis upon religion, and hence of interest in religion, and hence also of resources by which to satisfy that interest. First there were religious services on Sundays, then came the establishment of the chaplaincy, followed by a proliferation of daily and weekly religious occasions, then a parsonage was constructed, and soon thereafter the YMCA was founded. After the war, a chapel, long desired, was finally built, and the YMCA flourished, gaining its own fine building and sponsoring many religiously motivated programs and events. None of this was accidental. On the contrary, throughout this long series of religious innovations, the faculty and the Board of Visitors were uncomfortably aware that the University had a standing public relations problem: it was widely viewed and frequently criticized as a godless institution, hostile to religion and corrosive of morality. The faculty and the Visitors believed that it was important for the welfare of the institution to overcome that reputation, and so they took steps toward that end when relevant opportunities arose, although this was sometimes done with hesitancy and uncertainty about its legitimacy. Still, as a rule, anything that promoted piety was welcomed.

Near the end of the University's first century, then, it could fairly be said that Jefferson's vision of a secular institution had been set aside as an inhibiting liability. In fact, as much *was* said, and by no less a figure than the University's first president, Edwin Alderman. In a speech entitled "The Religious Ideals of the University," delivered in 1910, he remarked,

> An irreligious university would be a monstrosity, the existence of which men would not tolerate, for the purpose of a university is to make men. The essence of manhood is character, and the deepest purpose of religion is to guarantee the training that issues in character and moral strength. *The University of Virginia, therefore, is a religious institution.* . . . [There is] a persistent and constant effort to surround the student with religious opportunities and privileges. A singularly vital religion informs the life of a forceful fraction of the student body. The religious home of the University is a noble building, worthy of its great function. The religious man, however bold and outspoken in his faith, if he be a real man, wins the respect and admiration of his fellows here. *The very genius and spirit of the place, I dare to claim, contrary to some rather widespread but ignorant misapprehensions, is essentially religious.* (emphasis added)[89]

This entire statement throws into sharp relief how far the University had moved away from Jefferson's conception of the University. To be sure, Alderman's definition of religion was broad, his logic questionable, and his rhetoric, which echoes themes of muscular Christianity, overblown. Nevertheless, he clearly believed that it was important for the University to cultivate a religious atmosphere, encourage religious conviction, and provide rich opportunities for religious engagement and activity. It is equally important to notice that, nearly a century after the University's founding, it was still felt necessary to counter the persistent perception, "widespread but ignorant," that the University was an antireligious institution. That perception seems to have been nearly as strong in 1910 as it had been in 1825, notwithstanding the University's steady investment in religious arrangements throughout the nineteenth century.

Because of its cultural orientation, its cumbersome administrative structure, and its lack of adequate financial resources, the University of Virginia entered the twentieth century as an institution lacking in academic distinction. The innovative features that Jefferson had sought to establish in the University by way of reforming higher education in the United States had for the most part faded away over the course of the nineteenth century. Jefferson's University had become unremarkable, lying outside the circle of the nation's foremost institutions of learning. The University was better known as a finishing school for southern gentlemen than as a seat of strong scholarship. The hiring of Edwin Alderman in 1904 as the University's first president was a departure from Jefferson's plan for University governance, but it signaled an institutional ambition for a higher reputation.

Alderman wished for the University of Virginia to become more like the University of Wisconsin, one of the newer American research universities, rather than more like Oxford. He was especially keen to put the University at the service of the Commonwealth and its needs, and in order to do so he created in 1913 the Extension Division of the University, which he called "the most daring and beautiful and moving movement of advance in the whole history of the university." Its purpose was to make the University's expertise available to all areas of the state, rural and urban. This was done in various ways: by sending out members of the faculty to lecture around the state, by holding conferences at the University, and by publishing bulletins on various subjects. Unsurprisingly, this effort often included the promotion of religion. The very first bulletin published was on "rural life" and was entitled "The Country Church." Its various essays discussed the importance of the country church, ways of invigorating it, and means of increasing its influence. In 1915 another bulletin described at length "religious activities and advantages at the University of Virginia," and a 1916 bulletin provided a "program for the use of Sunday schools and churches in the observance of country church day," replete with suggested scripture readings, sermon themes, prayers, hymns, and poems. Yet another 1916 bulletin carried an "official syllabus of Bible study for high school pupils," which laid out ninety lessons covering the Old and New Testaments. Nor was Judaism entirely neglected: a bulletin for 1917 entitled "The Jewish Chautauqua Society and the University of Virginia" included a lengthy address given by Professor Charles Maphis to the society, favorably comparing its educational aims with those of Thomas Jefferson, and concluding with an appeal for gifts to the University from the Jewish community.[90] Alderman was a staunch Presbyterian, strong in his support of religious life at the University, and persuaded of religion's civic importance. Hence it is not surprising that his Extension Division showed frequent interest in the subject. Although Alderman made a number of reforms in the University and secured better funding for it, his tenure as president (1904–31) did not move the University into the upper echelons of higher education.[91]

It is a telling fact that at the University's Centennial Celebration (held in 1921 instead of 1919 because of the war), the first public session convened "in commemoration of the religious contributions of the University."[92] In this session the first public address carried the title "Religion at the University of Virginia" and was delivered by Rev. William Alexander Barr, an Episcopal minister and dean of the Episcopal cathedral in New Orleans. In it Barr maintained that the true aims of education could be attained only by Christianity, which provided "the loftiest idea of scholarship because of its inherently progressive spirit." Further, he claimed that "the University of Virginia could never have been anti-Christian or even non-Christian. It was essentially Virginian, and Virginia has been a Christian commonwealth. Indeed, the whole Southern people were practically a Christian people and out of Christian homes and Christian churches came the men who thronged its halls." Barr went on to rehearse something of the history of religion in the University, noting that "throughout the whole career of this university, if a student has wanted no contact with religion, he has been compelled to go a long way around in order to avoid it."[93] Indeed, so religious had the University been that "Surprise has sometimes been expressed that there should have existed at any time, among the people, the impression that the University of Virginia was irreligious or even non-religious in its character. . . . Let us believe, however, that it was through no vicious motive that such charges became current, but through a misunderstanding of the freedom and toleration which were contemplated [by Jefferson] in all matters of religion."[94] It took an entire century, but the University seemed finally to have thought, with Reverend Barr, that the Jeffersonian legacy of impiety had been put behind it, and that the institution was as religiously respectable as any might wish.

It has been shown thus far that the University of Virginia, despite being a public institution, and despite having been established on an explicitly secular basis, nevertheless made ample room for religion within its institutional life during the nineteenth century. It must now be said that in this regard the

University of Virginia had done nothing fundamentally different from many other state institutions of higher education. Those public institutions, while acknowledging the principle of the separation of church and state, did not think that it precluded the support of religion so long as that support was nonsectarian. What this really meant was that they did not think that the separation of church and state prevented the support of *Christianity,* so long as that support was *nondenominational.* Since, on this construal, nonsectarian did not mean nonreligious, some state universities readily and generously accommodated themselves to the culturally dominant Protestant Christian establishment, and often took an explicitly Christian stance.[95] And so, for example, in the late nineteenth century there were other state universities that had regular chapel services and daily prayers, and in some state universities these were even compulsory.

In relation to religion, the difference between the University of Virginia and other public universities was twofold. First, thanks to Jefferson, Virginia had begun with an absolutely strict interpretation of the separation of church and state that deprived religion of institutional presence. It was a legacy of the Revolutionary and early post-Revolutionary periods that the Commonwealth had a more sharply defined and deeply ingrained conception of the separation of church and state than any other state. Even so, the originally secular character of the University was lost during its first several decades. Second, having absorbed strong religious influences during much of the nineteenth century, the University of Virginia responded more slowly than other state institutions to the secularization of higher education in the decades following the Civil War. While other public universities gradually distanced themselves from religious entanglements, and were largely free of them by the end of the nineteenth century, Virginia persisted with its interests in and incentives to religion well into the twentieth century, perhaps not surprisingly, given its cultural attachment to the Old South.[96] But its (re-)secularization would occur, if somewhat later than that of other institutions. That process is the subject of the following chapter.

5

The Twentieth Century

Retreat from Religion

World War I, known as the "Great War" on account of its scope, length, and human toll, marks a turning point in the place of religion at Jefferson's University. The war brought major changes to American life and thought in general. Among other things, it dealt a blow to religion, especially to the liberal Protestantism that had prevailed in Europe and America. Although the war was opposed by some leading religious figures, popular sentiment, combining Christian idealism and patriotic enthusiasm, crystalized in support of the war effort. Impelled by religious and martial fervor, the struggle against "German aggression" produced enormous casualties, unimagined suffering, and terrible destruction, but all for very little measurable gain. In the aftermath many became disillusioned with religion and lost confidence in its capacity to provide moral guidance. Consequently, the postwar years witnessed an upsurge of cynicism and skepticism and a corresponding decline in religious interest and activity.[1] This distancing from religion was evident also in the University. During the decades following the war two trends are evident: student interest in and engagement with religion went into decline, and the University became increasingly wary about its relationship to religion and religious organizations. These trends had many particular manifestations.

The Chapel and Local Churches

The University Chapel, built in 1888–90, hosted Sunday services for almost three decades. Those services were initially conducted by the University chaplain, but, as recounted earlier, with the sudden death of Rev. L. C. Vass, who had been appointed chaplain for the 1896–97 session, the chaplaincy was discontinued. In its stead the University instituted a system of inviting visiting preachers to officiate at Sunday services in the University Chapel.[2] That system remained in place for two decades, but it was difficult to arrange for so many visiting clergy, and attendance at the services gradually dwindled. In May of 1918 President Alderman reported to the Board of Visitors that Sunday services in the University Chapel had been very difficult to keep up in the preceding session, and that the Committee on Religious Exercises, which was charged with arranging and administering them, recommended that they be discontinued in the future.[3] Thus beginning with the fall semester of 1919, Sunday services were no longer held on the Grounds. The Chapel became thereafter a venue for infrequent worship services, for weddings of students and alumni, and for memorial services of faculty and staff members, but since 1919 the Chapel's principal function has been for its bell to toll the hour.

Beyond the war's depression of religious interest, the decline in attendance at the Chapel was in part also a result of the construction nearby of St. Paul's Memorial Episcopal Church. When the University was established, there were no churches at all in Charlottesville or within easy reach. This is why it was permitted for a University classroom to be used for religious worship. But soon after the opening of the University, churches began to be built in Charlottesville: Christ Episcopal Church in 1828, a Baptist Church in 1831, First Presbyterian Church in 1840; later were First Methodist Church (1860), Immanuel Lutheran Church (1868), and the Church of the Paraclete (Catholic) (1880). Still, these churches were a little too distant for students on foot. Only in the twentieth century did churches begin to be built in the immediate environs of the University. The earliest, closest, and most influential of these was Saint Paul's Memorial Episcopal Church.

The plan to establish St. Paul's was approved by the Episcopal Diocese of Virginia in 1907, and its implementation was put in the hands of Rev. Hugh McIlhany, who had been so successful as the general secretary of the YMCA at the University. From the beginning St. Paul's was intended as a mission church, with its mission field being the students of the University, the majority of whom were Episcopalian, and hence at first it was called St. Paul's Chapel. Land for the church was acquired on 12th Street, but that was given up when in 1909 a much more convenient lot became available at the corner of University Avenue and Chancellor Street, immediately adjacent to the University. Reverend McIlhany initially raised money for the construction of a temporary wooden church building, in which the first service was held in September of 1910.[4] Sadly, only a few weeks later the well-known and well-liked McIlhany died suddenly. He was succeeded by Rev. Beverly D. Tucker, who served the church until 1920. Immediately upon its establishment St. Paul's became, to all intents and purposes, the "university church" and remained such for the next several decades.[5] The presence of St. Paul's in such close proximity to the University made the University's chapel largely redundant and contributed to the decline and eventual cessation of religious services there.

Other churches in the immediate vicinity of the University came later: University Baptist Church (1929), Westminster Presbyterian Church (1939), The Newman Club and Center (Catholic, 1947), Wesley Memorial Methodist (1954, meeting in the University Chapel until 1957), and later still, St. Mark's Lutheran Church, The Thomas Jefferson Unitarian Universalist Church and St. Thomas Aquinas Catholic Church. Each of these churches aimed especially to serve the University community—faculty, staff, and students. Each of them also formed its own denominational student fellowship, and most of them also added to their staffs a "campus minister" or chaplain who was specifically charged with serving the religious needs of the students of its denomination. One effect of these near-by churches and their outreach to students was to resolve the constituency of the nondenominational YMCA into its various denominational components and draw them to the churches. The attraction of these denominational student fellowships led to a steady dropping off of the membership of the YMCA and a decrease of its influence within the University.

The Decline of the YMCA

Given the very large role that the YMCA had come to play in the University, it is perhaps not surprising to find in the minutes of a meeting of the Board of Visitors in 1925 that "the question of the status of the Young Men's Christian Association of the University of Virginia in its relation to the University was brought up and after some discussion was referred to a special committee consisting of Messrs. Rinehart, Dillard and the President, to take into consideration and report back."[6] Some members of the board, at least, perceived that the relationship was problematic. The YMCA had become so expansive, so influential within the University, and so closely identified with its aims that the University could easily be seen as complicit in the religious character and

purposes of the YMCA, and thus in violation of its obligation as a public institution to steer clear of promoting religion.

The record does not preserve any report of that committee, but the issue
was mooted by subsequent events. A crisis arose in the YMCA itself in 1927–28
when the general secretary, Brooks Anderson, and the student leadership fell
into sharp disagreement over the aims and programs of the organization. At
bottom, the issue was whether the organization's purpose was religious or social. By this time most students wished it to be simply social, but the general
secretary considered it to be principally and necessarily religious.[7] One might
say that the diverse and extensive nonreligious programs that had been developed by the YMCA had come not merely to obscure but virtually to displace its
original religious purposes. Indeed, by this period the whole range of YMCA
programs was commonly referred to under the designation "Madison Hall"
rather than "YMCA," and Madison Hall was functioning, albeit unofficially,
as the student activities center of the University of Virginia. In the larger context, what may also be seen here is an effect of the progressive secularization
and moral laxity of society (and hence of the student body) following World
War I and during the Roaring Twenties.[8] The conflict in the YMCA between a
social agenda and a religious agenda resulted in a temporary discontinuance of
the office of general secretary of the YMCA and a de-emphasizing of its religious programs.

Thus began in the late 1920s a slow but steady decline in the prominence
of the YMCA in the University. The onset of the Great Depression weakened
the organization yet further, reducing its endowment funds and limiting its
operations. In 1931 the group asked the University to assume the expense and
responsibility for publishing the handbook and student directory, which had
been in the hands of the YMCA for almost fifty years. Although the University
depended heavily on the handbook, President Newcomb refused the request.[9]
The financial condition of the YMCA became so dire that it began to discuss
with the Board of Visitors the possible sale of Madison Hall to the University.
The proposed price was $90,000, but the offer was not accepted because the
University itself was under great financial duress.[10] Subsequent discussions
produced in 1933 a different arrangement, namely, that the University would
lease from the YMCA the basement and main floor of Madison Hall as accommodation for student activities, while the YMCA would retain use of the upper
floor. Correspondingly, social programs and other functions that served the
student body generally, all of which were previously sponsored by the YMCA,
would now be administered by the University through a newly established Student Union, whereas religious programs and activities would be left entirely to

the YMCA.[11] This arrangement aimed both to meet the University's need for a student social center and to mitigate the financial straits of the YMCA, but at the same time it had the important result of segregating student activities from the religious organization that had generated them and supervised them. Practically, then, it represented a sharp reduction in the scope of activities sponsored by the YMCA, all of which, save the specifically religious, were taken over by the University. Henceforth Madison Hall would be a venue of social activity and social service, while the YMCA itself would continue to lose membership and influence as student interest in religion diminished.[12]

The agreement of 1933 implicitly addressed and resolved the question that had been raised by the Board of Visitors in 1925 about the relationship between the University and the YMCA. If the University had become so entangled with and dependent upon the YMCA that clear distinctions could not be drawn between them, with the new agreement the University effectively withdrew from that relationship, took responsibility for nonreligious student activities, and left the YMCA to fend for itself in religious activities. It seems clear that in thus divorcing itself from the YMCA the University was motivated at least in part by legal concerns, although financial and administrative concerns were also at work.

From then on the YMCA came to be known also and alternatively as the University Christian Association. The latter designation came into use because increasingly the YMCA lost its traditional role as the chief promoter of religious activities and provider of religious resources and became instead an agency for coordinating religious activities and resources that were now being furnished by denominational groups, and for negotiating relationships among those groups and between them and the University. Deprived of centrality and of close cooperation with and subsidization by the University, the organization continued to exist, although with declining membership and diminishing influence. Its decline was furthered by the increasing religious diversity of the student body. Not all students were Christians, and even among them the number of Roman Catholics had grown steadily since the 1920s and '30s. Jewish students had also become much more numerous. Accordingly, given its coordinating role, in 1950 the University Christian Association was renamed the University Religious Council.[13] The University Religious Council comprised the campus ministers or chaplains of the various denominational student groups and was overseen by the general secretary of the YMCA.

Despite its more limited role, in the years following World War II the YMCA continued to sponsor a variety of religious events. It arranged a weekly vesper service on Tuesday evenings and mounted a Religious Emphasis Week each year through 1950. That week, heavily scheduled with worship services, lectures, seminars, luncheons, receptions, and discussions, was intended "to present the relevance of the Christian faith to the needs of all sorts and conditions of people—and specifically to the needs of the University community."[14] Beyond the Religious Emphasis Week, the YMCA sponsored a University Address in Religion, offered during orientation, and a University Preaching Series, which arranged for prominent preachers to hold forth in the chapel several times a year.

Incorporating Protestant, Catholic, and Jewish groups into a University Religious Council enlarged the number of students whose interests could be addressed, but it also complicated the task, for their interests were not identical. Thus, under supervision and coordination by the YMCA, the University Religious Council planned different series of lectures for different religious groups. In 1957, for example, there was a University Religious Series, broken down into Protestant, Catholic, and Jewish segments. For a brief period the council even sponsored lectures for specific schools of the University, designed to show the relevance or importance of religion to particular fields, such as engineering, education, or law. But the combination of growing religious diversity and declining student interest in religious events made for an unwieldy situation.

In these challenging circumstances, the YMCA mounted in 1958 a centennial celebration, commemorating its founding at the University of Virginia in October of 1858. At intervals during the 1958–59 session four prominent religious figures—two Protestant, one Catholic, and one Jewish—each gave several lectures, accompanied by other events.[15] But this celebration of the long life of the University YMCA was held in its dying days. Although the organization still liked to think of itself as the patron and arbiter of the University's religious life, and was sometimes invoked as such by the administration, the YMCA/University Christian Association/University Religious Council was a pale shadow of its former self. It was symptomatic and symbolic that in 1959 the new lease agreement for the University's use of Madison Hall relegated the YMCA to a single room in the building's basement. Reports of the YMCA's Program and Planning Committee show that by 1964 the organization was experiencing an acute crisis of identity and mission and was casting about for ways to recover some relevance and effectiveness.[16] None was to be found, however. Finally, a little more than a century after its founding, the YMCA/University Christian Association recognized that it had outlived its purpose and lost its constituency. The organization was reincorporated as the Master and Fellows of Madison Hall, a nonprofit social service organization without any explicit religious identity or agenda. Its charter was accordingly revised to eliminate any relation to the international YMCA. The building, Madison Hall, which had been the proud possession of the YMCA since its construction in 1905, together with its grounds ("Mad Bowl"), was finally sold to the University in 1971 for $721,000. Proceeds from this sale were used in 1975 to construct a smaller building, called Madison House, and to establish an endowment fund to support the group's work. Thereafter Madison Hall would house the offices of the University's central administration.

It is worth both notice and emphasis that, in addition to the extensive community service work that continues under the auspices of Madison House, many services and programs that the YMCA initiated and for many years managed for the benefit of students were eventually taken over by the University. These new agencies include the University Office of Student Affairs, the Counseling Service, Career Planning and Placement, and Student Housing. Thus the YMCA left an enormous though mostly unrecognized legacy.

Religious Subsidies, Scholarships, and Lectures

The long-standing practice of the faculty to permit ministers or candidates for the ministry to attend the University without the payment of tuition fees was mentioned earlier. Although this provision occasionally came up for review, it was maintained until 1936, when it was finally discontinued in the recognition that it was a direct subsidy to religion and inappropriate for a public institution. By that time, however, the subsidy had decreased in importance because the University had acquired two private endowments that were designated for the support of students who intended to enter the ministry. One of these was given by James H. Skinner, who was an alumnus of 1846, a veteran of the Civil War, a prominent lawyer in Staunton, and a member of the Virginia legislature. His will, drawn up in 1877, provided that after the decease of his sister the proceeds of his estate were to fund scholarships at the University for "white male persons who purpose to become ministers of the Protestant Episcopal Church." The Skinner scholarships were established in 1914.[17] Another bequest was received in 1935 from the estate of Fanny B. Marchant in memory of her husband. Henry C. Marchant (1838–1910) had been the owner of the Charlottesville Woolen Mills, and a prominent and progressive contributor to the economic, civic, educational, and religious life of the town of Charlottesville. Most of his estate went to the University, and part of it was to support fellowships for students, "regardless of religious denomination, who are preparing to become medical missionaries or to enter the ministry."[18] These private bequests enabled the University to provide financial support for ministerial students without offering a blanket waiver of fees, thereby avoiding for the future a public subsidy of religion.

Encouragement of interest in religion was also provided by a lectureship endowed in 1923 by the will of Este Coffinberry, of San Francisco. This was the James W. Richard Lectures. The will stipulated that the lectures must be on "the Christian religion," and that "the lecturer shall be a man of evangelic faith and of international reputation as a scholar." He was to be free to choose his subject so long as it "pertains to the advancement and application of the principles of the gospel." Secondarily, Coffinberry intended that, should the funds of her estate prove sufficient, another lectureship might be established that would "treat comparatively and exhaustively some period of history," and thus be called the James W. Richard Lectureship of Comparative History. Both lectureships came into being. The Richard lectures in religion, the first of which was offered in 1931, were to bring many distinguished scholars to the University, but their lectures were not always in full accordance with the terms of the bequest.

The Development and Growth of a
Department of Religious Studies

While the University was gradually reducing its problematic relationships with religious organizations, it maintained its School of Biblical History and Literature, but there too changes would be called for. Although the partnership of the University with the Christian Woman's Board of Missions to create the John B. Cary Professorship had at first seemed unproblematic, it was not long before tensions arose. In 1915, less than a decade after the professorship had been established and occupied by Professor Forrest, Anna Atwater, director of the Christian Woman's Board of Missions, wrote to President Alderman that "we are not satisfied with the results being reached through this work." She complained of not receiving regular reports of expenditures and results, said that the money might be better spent elsewhere, and posed to the president a series of implicitly critical questions.[19] The president responded apologetically, and advised her to get in touch with Professor Forrest directly. There followed an acerbic exchange between Atwater and Forrest, which revealed their widely divergent agendas. The Christian Woman's Board of Missions clearly thought that the professorship should be evangelistic, producing both converts to Christianity and candidates for the ministry; Professor Forrest, however, had a thoroughly academic objective and insisted that his Bible teaching at the University "is scholastic, and not evangelistic or pastoral," and went on to say, emphatically, "I am employed by the University and not by you."[20] Atwater was much dissatisfied and wrote again to President Alderman to say that the Christian Woman's Board of Missions would proceed with "the legal investigation of our privileges," and to Professor Kent to reiterate that the CWBM was not getting its money's worth. But no more was said, and the contractual arrangement remained uneasily intact.

There was another dustup in 1929–30. The Christian Woman's Board of Missions, which in the meantime had changed its name to the United Christian Missionary Society, had decided to abandon altogether its work of promoting Bible instruction in state universities, including the University of Virginia. Thus it intended to withdraw the money with which it had endowed the Cary chair and divert those funds to "something more distinctly evangelical and denominational."[21] This proposal met with immediate and stiff resistance both from the University, whose views were communicated to the society through Professor Forrest, and from the surviving children of John B. Cary, namely, Gillie Cary McCabe and Lizzie Cary Daniel. Professor Forrest wrote a strong remonstrance to the president of the society, reminding him of the generosity of the Cary family to causes of the Disciples of Christ, and disputing the justice of redirecting funds contrary to the intentions of their donors.[22] Gillie Cary McCabe, writing to the society's vice president and speaking for the family, also stressed that the Cary family had long been generous benefactors of the Disciples of Christ and of the missionary agency, and suggested that any withdrawal of support from the Cary chair at the University would be utterly contrary to the wishes of the family and to the intentions of other donors to the Cary fund.[23] At the same time, the University's legal advisers suggested that the terms of the 1908 trust agreement seemed to preclude any such diversion of funds as the society now contemplated. Faced with such staunch opposition, the society decided not to withdraw its support, and so the 1908 agreement continued in force.[24]

During his long tenure Professor Forrest was well respected by his faculty colleagues and, in addition to his teaching, took a prominent part both in University life and in the affairs of his denomination. He was not a very productive scholar in terms of research and publication, but he understood, appreciated, and applied academic biblical criticism, and in his teaching and research he took a descriptive and analytical approach, avoiding theological claims and controversies, not to mention proselytism.[25] The 1920s witnessed a great controversy in American Protestantism, which was sharply divided between fundamentalists and modernists.[26] The fundamentalists championed the authority of the Bible and its literal interpretation, along with other doctrines they regarded as "fundamental," whereas the modernists were responsive to the advances of modern science, disavowed biblical literalism, and sought an accommodation between religious convictions and intellectual rigor. Forrest, while perhaps not a full-fledged modernist liberal, was a moderate who kept up with biblical scholarship and practiced so-called higher criticism. He had no patience with fundamentalism and during his career was frequently attacked by theological conservatives, even of his own denomination.[27] Although he maintained his affiliation with the Disciples throughout his life, his position in the University gave him security against theological complaints and recriminations from outsiders. Having integrated the study of the Bible into the University's curriculum, one of his chief projects was to promote the teaching of courses on the Bible in the public high schools of Virginia. He succeeded in doing this under the auspices of the Virginia State Board of Education, and he developed a curriculum for the purpose, "The Official Syllabus of Bible Study for High School Pupils," which was used for many years in high school courses. Forrest served as the examiner for all Virginia high school courses until his retirement in 1939. Throughout his tenure Forrest seems to have fulfilled the terms of the appointment, that he be "not only a scholar, but a distinctly Christian man, interested in men as well as in books, and able by his manly life to commend to students the teaching of the Book from which he instructs them." At the same time, he also seems to have been careful not to evangelize.

Forrest's successor as professor of biblical history and literature was Selby Vernon McCasland (1896–1970), who would occupy the chair until his retirement in 1967. A Texan by birth, McCasland received his undergraduate education at Abilene Christian College and Simmons College. After graduating from Simmons (1918), he returned to Abilene Christian, where he was the football coach for the 1919 season, winning two games and losing two. From that brief detour into college athletics he went on to the Southern Baptist Theological Seminary, where he took a theological degree in 1922. From there he proceeded to the University of Chicago, where he earned an M.A. and Ph.D. under the prominent biblical scholar E. J. Goodspeed, with a concentration on the New Testament and early Christian literature. After a year of further research at German universities and the University of Chicago, he was appointed professor of religion at Goucher College in 1928, and in the same year was ordained as a clergyman of the Disciples of Christ.

Upon his appointment in 1939 to the faculty at Virginia, McCasland made some important changes. He proposed that the John B. Cary Memorial School of Biblical History and Literature be renamed the John B. Cary Memorial School of Religion. The Board of Visitors, with the concurrence of the United

Christian Missionary Society, acquiesced in the suggestion.[28] The intention was to bring the name of the school into line with a more contemporary conception of the field of study. "Religion" is a far broader subject than "the Bible," and "religion" permits and requires more approaches and perspectives than "history and literature." Accordingly, McCasland enlarged and diversified the course offerings of the school. Courses on biblical topics continued to be offered, but they were supplemented by such courses as Religion in American Life and Religions of the World. Thus the notion of "religion" was no longer construed entirely in Christian, let alone Protestant, terms, and a comparative point of view was encouraged. Then, in 1952, the University conformed its nomenclature to more common usage in higher education by redesignating some of its "schools" as "departments," and reserving the name "school" to the professional units of the University. Thus the John B. Cary Memorial School of Religion became the John B. Cary Memorial Department of Religion.

Unlike William Forrest, McCasland was an active scholar in research and publication, producing five scholarly monographs and many articles in refereed journals.[29] He became a well-known and respected figure in the national guilds of biblical scholarship and of religion, and served a term as president of each of the two national scholarly societies, the American Academy of Religion (1949) and the Society of Biblical Literature (1953). In addition, McCasland continued Forrest's project of promoting the study of the Bible in high schools, writing a text for high school students and also producing an extensive syllabus for home study.[30]

For most of their teaching careers at the University of Virginia, Professor Forrest and Professor McCasland single-handedly sustained the School of Biblical History and Literature/Religion. Forrest occasionally, and McCasland more regularly after 1947, had assistance from young adjunct instructors, who, however, would teach only a single course.[31] For a few years in the early 1960s Professor McCasland gained a regular colleague, Anthony Wu, who offered courses in Eastern religious traditions, which were doubly challenging because of Wu's limited command of the English language. But as a rule, a single professor had responsibility for six courses per session.

Both William Forrest and Vernon McCasland were members of the Disciples of Christ/Christian Church, and the School of Biblical History and Literature/Department of Religion had grown out of an extracurricular lectureship initiated and funded by a missionary agency of the Disciples of Christ. The long, unbroken connection between the University and the Disciples bears some reflection. It was recounted earlier that in 1838 permission was sought for Alexander Campbell, one of the founders of the Disciples movement, to speak at the University, but the request was refused on the grounds that the Disciples were reputed to provoke religious controversy, which the University wanted to avoid. But, ironically, it was the Disciples who were ultimately able to exert the most influence over the study of religion in the University. There were reasons for this result.

Jefferson, it will be recalled, had a deep-seated dislike of sectarianism, which was his term for the fractious diversities of religion. He regarded the numerous varieties of Christianity as sponsors of petty and pointless controversies over their theological differences, and, as such, threats to the cohesion of civil society. Further, Jefferson intended that the University be secular, which meant that it should be indifferent to religion and not favor any one sect against others. As we have seen, in the post-Jefferson era, when it came to religion, the University made nonsectarianism its watchword, but applied the concept only to Christian denominations. As it happened, the principal objective of the Disciples movement was precisely to transcend Christian sectarianism and restore the (presumed) primitive unity of Christianity. The Disciples grew out of the so-called Stone-Campbell movement, which had its origins in the Great Revival of the beginning of the nineteenth century.[32] Thomas Campbell and his son, Alexander, began as Presbyterian clergymen in western Pennsylvania, but soon came to value closer relationships with other Christians than Presbyterianism condoned. They maintained that no creed should stand as a condition of fellowship among professing Christians, rejected all ecclesiastic authority—whether synod or bishop or priest—and appealed instead to the Bible and its explicit teachings as the proper authority and common basis of all Christian belief and practice. In 1809 they withdrew from Presbyterian fellowship and established "the Christian Association" of Washington, Pennsylvania. Its charter was Thomas Campbell's "Declaration and Address," in which he set out the basic principles of the movement. What the Campbells intended was a restoration of the form and substance of Christianity as it appears in the New Testament, that is (as they imagined), without schisms or divisions of any kind, and depending on teachings "expressly revealed and enjoined in the Word of God." They called themselves Disciples of Christ. The Campbells became acquainted with Barton W. Stone and his followers in 1823. Stone was originally a Kentucky Presbyterian, but, motivated by a desire to unite all believers, he had withdrawn from his original presbytery and established another. But he soon came to reject the Presbyterian label altogether and to adopt the simple designation "Christian." The principles of Stone and other like-minded ministers had been declared in the "Last Will and Testament of Springfield Presbytery," issued in 1804. The extensive (though not complete) agreement between the views of the Campbells and those of Stone led in 1832 to a merger of their followers (Disciples of Christ and Christians). The very last thing that the Stone-Campbell movement intended was the creation of yet another denomination, for its whole objective was to restore unity to Christianity on the basis of biblical teaching. Yet a denomination is what it became, albeit a broad-minded one of open fellowship, acknowledging no authority for faith and practice beyond the scriptures, particularly the New Testament.

The Disciples were successful in Virginia from about 1830 onward and had a relatively strong presence in Charlottesville and the surrounding area.[33] Their antisectarian emphasis would have appealed to Jefferson, but they would otherwise have been subject to his disdain, for they cherished many Christian convictions that he did not. In their early days, as they sought to "reform" sects, the Disciples were occasionally engaged in debates and controversies, especially with Presbyterians and Baptists, over doctrine and polity, and even though "Campbellites" were early rebuffed by the University for this reason, the inclusiveness of the Disciples melded nicely both with the nonsectarian principle of the University and with the generic Protestantism that the University had progressively embraced over the course of the nineteenth century. Such compatibility was not, however, the basis for the relationship between the University and the Disciples. The basis was, rather, that the Disciples had put up the money for the Bible lectureship.

In April of 1966 Professor McCasland wrote to President Edgar Shannon, stating his intention to retire at the end of the next session (June 1967). With that letter he enclosed a copy of the original 1908 trust agreement between the University and the Christian Woman's Board of Missions and offered some comments on its provisions. While recommending that a faculty committee be appointed to name his successor, he called the president's attention to the article of the agreement that gave the missionary agency veto power over appointments to the Cary chair. And, noting that both he and his predecessor, Dr. Forrest, had been members of the Disciples of Christ, McCasland proposed that in making a new appointment the University should seek out the best-qualified candidate, without regard to denominational affiliation.[34]

The prospect of McCasland's imminent retirement drew attention to the terms of the 1908 endowment agreement, which had been largely forgotten during the lengthy tenures of Professors Forrest and McCasland, together spanning sixty years. Suddenly, the University discovered itself party to a contract that mortgaged to an outside body, and a religious one at that, the power to second-guess and frustrate an appointment to the University faculty. While the University had apparently seen no difficulty in such an arrangement in 1908, by 1966 it was entirely at odds with the its policies and procedures. Robert Harris, professor of political science who was then dean of the faculty, referred to this provision as "unfortunate" and "perhaps illegal." In addition, he recommended to the provost and the president that they consider the possibility—and in his view the desirability—of discontinuing religion as a separate department. In Harris's judgment, religion did not merit the investment of University resources in an academic department.[35]

While looking into its awkward and legally questionable partnership with a religious agency, the University had to decide how to proceed. The initial impulse was simply to find a successor to McCasland, without undertaking to rethink the whole issue of whether and on what terms the study of religion ought to be part of the University's curriculum. Thus in June of 1966 Provost Frank Hereford appointed a search committee in the faculty of arts and sciences for a new Cary Professor. The committee consisted of Lewis Hammond (philosophy), Julian Bishko (history), and Lester Beaurlein (English), with Beaurlein as chair, and it was charged to seek "a scholar of substantial eminence" in the field of biblical studies. So the old presumption that the Bible should be the focal point remained intact.[36] After several months of surveying a broad field of candidates, the committee reported to Dean Harris and unanimously recommended the hiring of Harry M. Buck, an associate professor at Wilson College in Chambersburg, Pennsylvania, whom they regarded as "by far the best choice." Buck was also the managing editor of the *Journal of Bible and Religion,* one of the two most important journals of the scholarly guild (later to be renamed the *Journal of the American Academy of Religion*). The committee thought that bringing both Buck and the journal to Charlottesville would immediately enhance the University's stature in the field of religion and make Charlottesville "a center of religious publications."[37] Buck, however, declined the overture, apparently because he lacked confidence in the University's commitment to building a department.

At this point the principals stepped back to consider the larger issues. It was obvious that the trust agreement of 1908 establishing the Cary Professorship was illegal and would have to be discontinued. Negotiations to that end with the Missionary Society resulted in the endowment being divided: $29,500 was retained by the Missionary Society, while $20,000 given by the Cary family for support of the lectureship remained with the University.[38] All connections between the Missionary Society and the University were thereby severed, and the University gained a free hand: a regular faculty appointment could be made without any influence of the long-standing trust agreement and also without being limited to the area of Biblical history and literature. After all, the department was now a department of religion, not merely of Bible. And there were other considerations too. To have a single faculty position in the subject of religion was hardly satisfactory. The University's enrollment was approaching 10,000, and President Shannon had been working energetically to upgrade the faculty and the academic programs of the University. So a decision was required: whether to discontinue instruction in religion altogether or to establish a regular department of religion with an adequate faculty and a more extensive curriculum. It was President Shannon's firm opinion that the study of religion ought to be put on a regular basis within the College of Arts and Sciences, and that the department of religion should be freshly established. In that view the president was fully abreast of developments elsewhere among public institutions.

Since the colonial period the study of religion in American higher education had been confined almost entirely to private institutions, and indeed many of the oldest and most prestigious private colleges and universities were founded for the theological education of Christian ministers. That aim did not, of course, belong to public institutions, and certainly least of all to the University of Virginia. On the contrary, state institutions of higher education, which proliferated with the Morrill Act of 1862, routinely excluded the study of religion on the grounds of the separation of church and state. But this point of principle, itself legitimate and proper, was fast becoming moot, first because of developments in the study of religion, and second because of relevant decisions by federal courts.

In early American colleges and universities, the study of religion was pursued in the interest of religion, that is, in the presumption of its truth and authority and in furtherance of its influence in society and culture. And in these educational contexts "religion" had always meant Christianity. But with the European Enlightenment, in consequence of fresh acquaintance with and interest in other religions than Christianity, and in consequence of the emergence of the scientific method, this approach to the study of religion began to change. It was recognized that Christianity was only one among other religious systems, which varied among societies and cultures, even if Christianity nevertheless tended to be regarded as a "higher" or superior religion. In addition, Christianity itself—its sources, its history, its teachings—began to be subjected to critical scrutiny and comparison with other religions. In colonial America, however, the Enlightenment had made only limited inroads on religion or on the study of religion. The population in general was fervent in its religious enthusiasm, and evangelistic competition among various denominational forms of Christianity was energetic. The study of religion was confined to institutions that were founded by Christian denominations, and in that setting the study of religion (Christianity) was done from a committed and confessional point of view. But gradually, with the emergence of the modern university in the late nineteenth century, the study of religion, traditionally a humanistic field with normative aims, began to aspire to "scientific" standing and to be understood as an impartial, objective, analytical, and descriptive inquiry. Beginning in the late nineteenth century and continuing through the first half of the twentieth century, the study of religion, although still located mainly in denominational institutions, was gradually disengaged from confessionalism, invested with theory and methods, and pursued in accordance with the canons of inquiry that obtained in other academic disciplines.[39] By the 1960s the study of religion had acquired sufficient academic respectability and disciplinary status to be classed among the liberal arts. Still, the discipline continued to be under-represented in public institutions, which were reluctant to run afoul of the Establishment Clause.

These developments in the academic study of religion found a positive legal correlative in a Supreme Court Case of 1963, *School District of Abington Township, Pennsylvania, et al. v. Schempp et al.*[40] This case had nothing directly to do with the academic study of religion in public colleges and universities, and in fact no Supreme Court ruling has ever addressed the question whether departments of religion in public institutions are constitutional. The *Schempp* case had to do, instead, with devotional Bible reading and prayer in public schools. In its ruling the Court banned prayers and religious exercises in public schools as a violation of the First Amendment. Nevertheless, among the dicta of its lengthy ruling the Court drew a clear distinction between "teaching religion," in the sense of indoctrinating students with the tenets and values of a particular religion, religious sect, or denomination, and "teaching about religion" in an objective and descriptive manner, and the Court effectively foreclosed the former while permitting the latter.[41] The distinction, although it seems simple and straightforward, conceals a host of philosophical and pedagogical issues. Nevertheless, it has become the mantra of the academic study of religion. Perhaps beyond the intention of the Court, this decision was widely taken to give a green flag to departments of religion/religious studies in public university settings.[42]

Ten programs in Bible, religion, or religious studies existed in public universities by 1930, many of them in southern institutions, but the trend toward establishing such enterprises escalated sharply in the decade between 1960 and 1970: the number of programs in public colleges and universities rose meteorically from 36 to 96.[43] Hence when President Shannon was considering whether to establish a regular department of religion at the University of Virginia, the prospect was entirely in keeping with contemporary developments in American higher education.

There were, nevertheless, issues to be considered. One was opposition within the faculty. Some did not support the inclusion of religion in the University's curriculum on principle, because such a department seemed either a contradiction of Jefferson's vision of the University or a violation of the Establishment Clause of the Constitution, notwithstanding the *Schempp* decision. Other faculty objected on more practical grounds, either because they did not regard religion as a legitimate subject for academic study, or because they thought the funding of a department of religion would consume resources needed in other areas. For such reasons there was limited enthusiasm among the faculty for the prospect of a department of religion. Moreover, a department of religion in the University could no longer function, nor could it command attention or respect, if staffed by a single faculty member, as it had been historically. A number of new faculty members would be required, and, with McCasland's retirement, a department would have to be created from the ground up.

The effort to hire Harry Buck having failed, and the need to hire a specialist in Bible having been obviated, it was decided to invite David. B. Harned.[44] Harned was a young professor at Smith College who held a doctorate from Yale in Christian thought. He accepted the offer and came to Virginia as the founding chair of what would effectively be a new department of religion but still to be known as the John B. Cary Memorial Department of Religion, perpetuating the name of the old endowed lectureship and chair. Harned was well aware of the circumstances in which he was working at Virginia, and he immediately sought to do two things: first, to make cordial personal connections in the University community with both the administration and the faculty, and second, to begin putting together a departmental faculty. For the 1967–68 session he was able to bring along only one other person, Seshagiri Rao, an acquaintance from India who had gotten his doctorate at Harvard, to teach Hinduism. But major steps were taken over the next several years. For the 1968–69 session, when Rao was on leave, Harned was joined by Dan O. Via, a specialist in biblical studies who was on the faculty at Wake Forest College, and by two young scholars just completing their doctorates, Glen Chesnut (history of Christianity) and James Childress (religious ethics). For the 1969–70 session two more young scholars, Walter Neeval (Asian religions) and Allen Lettofsky (Judaism), were brought on, and Rao returned, so that very quickly the department had seven faculty members, a critical mass. Neeval and Chesnut departed at the end of the 1969–70 session, but for the 1970–71 session three additional assistant professors were hired, one in the philosophy of religion, one in the psychology of religion, and one in American religious history. In the same year, Joseph Washington, who came to the University as the chair of the African-American Studies program, was also named to the Department of Religion. This remarkably rapid early growth of the faculty, which numbered nine regular members by 1970, signaled not only the University's commitment to building a solid department but also Harned's ambitious drive and his sense of the appropriate breadth of religious studies. In fact, he requested and received approval for the department no longer to be named the John B. Cary Memorial Department of Religion, but simply the Department of Religious Studies. Apart from dropping the reference to Cary as not only "clumsy" but suggesting a "privately supported special program in religion, rather than a normal department of full academic standing," Harned thought that "religious studies" better connoted the dynamic and interdisciplinary character of the academic study of religion.[45]

Harned knew the politics and economics of the University well enough to realize that what fundamentally counted in the viability of the new department was the number of students enrolling in its courses, so he pressed upon his faculty the importance of interesting courses and engaging classroom teaching. Under those stimuli, departmental enrollments began to grow rapidly, creating a need for yet more faculty members. Over the next several years, additional faculty positions were authorized and filled, some with distinguished scholars, others with young assistant professors. Three appointments in the early to mid-1970s called wide attention to what was happening at the University of Virginia: David Little, a bright and dynamic Harvard-trained specialist in religious ethics, then on the faculty of Yale Divinity School; Julian Hartt, a nationally prominent theologian who had been on the Yale faculty for many years and had chaired its department; and, perhaps even more eye-opening, Nathan Scott, a distinguished, longtime member of the University of Chicago faculty who had trained a generation of scholars in the field of religion and literature and had served as the dean of the University Chapel at Chicago.[46] With Scott's appointment it could be fairly said that the Department of Religious Studies at Virginia had come of age. Other hires were made in the areas of Chinese and Japanese religions, Islam, and Tibetan Buddhism. Despite a few voluntary and involuntary departures, by the late1970s, barely ten years after it began, the department had sixteen faculty members—large by national standards—who covered most aspects of the subject.

Beyond promoting the popularity of the department among undergraduates, Harned recognized that the full flowering of the enterprise depended on the establishment of a graduate program. A modest beginning was made in 1972 by offering an M.A. degree. In 1975 the department successfully proposed, first to the University and then to the State Council on Higher Education, the creation of a program of graduate studies empowered to confer the Ph.D. degree as well. Initially, the department sought to play to its greatest areas of strength—at that time Christianity and Buddhism—and to capitalize on collateral resources in other departments. But it was not long before areas of specialization multiplied, and by the early eighties a broad-based program was well underway in a variety of subdisciplinary areas: religious ethics, religion and literature, philosophical theology and philosophy of religion, the history of religions (i.e., comparative religions), New Testament studies, and American religious history. Graduate enrollments were at first modest but grew steadily, and by the mid-1980s the department had about seventy-five graduate students, most working toward doctorates. As the only public university in the southeastern region of the United States to offer doctoral studies in the field of religion, Virginia drew large numbers of graduate applicants and matriculants from other states.[47]

A Yale product himself, Harned had naturally tended to look to Yale for prospective faculty members. The Yale connection continued to be strengthened as the department grew, and by the early 1980s roughly 80 percent of the departmental faculty had either earned their degrees at Yale or had taught there. Some in the guild began to speak wryly of the Department of Religious Studies at Virginia as "Yale South." This was not exactly a cause for embarrassment—Yale was, after all, one of the foremost institutions in training scholars of religion—but it was clearly time to look elsewhere also. Additional faculty members would soon come from Chicago, Harvard, Hopkins, Princeton, Brown, and other institutions, balancing the scales. Only a dozen years after its founding, the department counted among its faculty numerous scholars of international stature and many promising younger people.

Harned left the University of Virginia in 1980 to become president of Allegheny College in Meadville, Pennsylvania. The strong, well-populated department he left behind was in large measure the legacy of his personal vision, energetic efforts, and inventive (and occasionally Machiavellian) schemes. In his absence the chairmanship passed to Nathan Scott, whose persuasive eloquence on behalf of the department continued to advance its fortunes.

By the mid-1980s the Department of Religious Studies at Virginia had become the largest and most prominent such department in a public university in the United States—an astonishing result in less than two decades—and it was rapidly moving toward becoming one of the most highly regarded departments in public or private institutions in the world, counting among its faculty many nationally and internationally known scholars. When, in 1994, the National Research Council ranked religious studies graduate programs in the United States, the department at Virginia was well up in the top ten in the nation in both teaching and research, and it has retained that rating into the twenty-first century. With a faculty of more than thirty, it remains the largest department of religious studies in any public university in the United States and is larger than any in private institutions that do not also have divinity schools. What began as occasional lectures on the Bible sponsored by the YMCA and a denominational missionary group had come to a very large but unforeseen result.

The strength of any academic department lies in its faculty and the faculty's productivity in teaching and research. Excellence of classroom teaching was a hallmark of the department from its beginning and remained the major driver of departmental growth. The curriculum is very broad, and hardly any dimension of the subject escapes attention. Some courses have routinely enrolled as many as 350 students in any given semester, and the department as a whole has been known to have as many as 5,000 enrollees in a single semester. The subjects and the religious traditions that attract student interest have varied somewhat over time. Early on, courses in Christianity were especially popular, 9/11 spurred a strong interest in Islam, Buddhism has come to have strong appeal. Courses in religious ethics, biblical studies, and religion and literature have been steadily subscribed. It can be plausibly supposed that student interest in the study of religion is a function not only of attractive and well-taught courses but also to some extent of the University's cultural location in the Bible belt, where religion continues to be an important dimension of personal and social life and to command respect as a subject of study.

Although the study of religion is today a well-established field in higher education, and in public as well as private institutions, it has not altogether escaped suspicions about its legitimacy. At Virginia, as at other institutions, some faculty members in other departments, both humanists and scientists, do not think that religion is a fit subject of academic inquiry. There are both faculty members who are religious skeptics and regard religion as hardly more than childish superstition, and faculty members who are theologically very conservative and believe that the academic study of religion actively undermines the faith of students. Further, University administrators do not always understand or appreciate departments of religious studies, wrongly assuming that they aim to promote religious faith. For such reasons, departments of religion in some institutions are marginalized as second-class operations.[48] The department at Virginia has sometimes been subject to such negative perceptions but has managed to avoid their serious effects, partly because it has worked closely with supportive and well-informed administrators, partly because it has emphasized the interdisciplinary character of the study of religion, and partly because it has cultivated constructive relationships—personal, professional, and institutional—with other departments in arts and sciences, especially English, history, classics, and philosophy, and with other schools of the University, especially medicine and law, thus avoiding the gheottoization suffered by some departments of religious studies in other universities. Early in the twenty-first century, its foundation seems secure and its future promising.

It is a question, of course, whether Jefferson, who excluded from the University a professorship of divinity, would have condoned a department of religious studies as it evolved in the twentieth century. Any answer must be hypothetical guesswork. When it came to religion as a curricular matter, Jefferson was staunchly opposed to the advocacy of any particular religious perspective, and since he believed that any professor of divinity would necessarily be of some sectarian identity and espouse sectarian views, he could not countenance such a professorship. But if it were possible to teach *about* religion, without at the same time advocating or inculcating particular religious convictions, and if multiple traditions were impartially represented, Jefferson may not have objected. (He himself studied and thought a good deal *about* religion, even though he was not very religiously inclined.) The principal issue for him remained freedom of thought, prominently including the freedom to hold one's own religious opinions. So long as there was no limitation on that liberty, he would probably have found acceptable the dispassionate and descriptive study of religion. Whether he would have thought it as valuable as "the useful sciences" is another question.

Negotiating Relationships with Student Religious Groups

Notwithstanding its commitment to an academic Department of Religious Studies, the University struggled throughout the twentieth century to determine how, as a public institution, it could or should accommodate religion as practice. This challenge had various dimensions because religious groups could be problematical in different ways. Further, the University's administration was consistently confronted with the need both to deal with contemporary events and to refer to its founding principles. There were many opportunities for misjudgments.

A small but interesting case in point has already been referred to, namely, the very long standing practice of waiving fees for students who were ministers or candidates for the ministry. That provision was in effect virtually from the beginning of the University up until 1936. During that long time it seems not to have occurred to anyone that this practice amounted to state support of religion, and hence was unconstitutional. As the University became more sensitive to its legal obligations as a public institution, it recognized the necessity of dispensing with this clerical exemption from fees.

When, after World War I, the nondenominational, generically Protestant YMCA entered a long but steady decline, denominational interests began to assert themselves. Protestant denominations had realized at the beginning of the twentieth century that very many of their student members were attending public, tax-supported institutions or private, nondenominational colleges where there was little religious support and no reinforcement of denominational identity. To address that situation, denominations began to develop a new form of ministry to students—the university pastorate or the campus minister. "Campus ministry"—the phrase most commonly used to designate denominationally sponsored religious outreach and activity on college and university campuses—intended to sustain and nurture the faith of their young student adherents, especially in public, secular institutions. Although it began in the early twentieth century, the most successful period of this kind of work, and the flourishing of denominational student groups, was between the end of World War II and the mid-1960s.[49] This was the period of their prominence at Virginia. Denominational campus ministers were not active at the University of Virginia early in the twentieth century because such ministers were usually based in and supported by a nearby church, but churches near the University were few until World War II.

Since early in the nineteenth century the University had been sensitive to the denominational affiliations of its students and had kept track of the numbers of students who belonged to each of the various denominations. This had been a consideration, for example, in setting up a chaplaincy that rotated among the major denominational groups, and even after the nondenominational YMCA was established at Virginia, the numbers continued to be tallied and published in the University Record. After the demise of the YMCA, it remained part of the official registration process for the College to ask students to fill out a religious preference card, indicating their religious or denominational affiliations. The information thus gathered was then distributed by the University to the various local churches or the denominational Protestant ministries, which proceeded to draw those students into the corresponding student religious group—whether the Canterbury Club (Episcopal), the Wesley Foundation (Methodist), the Westminster Fellowship (Presbyterian), the Baptist Student

Union, the Newman Club (Roman Catholic), Hillel (Jewish), or some other. This routine religious census-taking by the University, and its collaboration with local churches, persisted into the late 1970s, when it was belatedly recognized as inappropriate and was discontinued.

Whether or not student religious groups had meeting space in local churches, they sometimes desired to meet in University spaces. This became a controversial issue in June of 1966 when the president of the Student Council, Josh Fletcher, wrote to President Edgar Shannon asking that student religious organizations be allowed to meet in and otherwise make use of University buildings. The Student Council had previously extended recognition to student religious organizations, and now wished to extend to religious organizations the same sorts of privileges that were enjoyed by other recognized student groups. The petition from Student Council was soon supported by a letter to President Shannon from John Witech, chairman of the Middle Atlantic province of the Newman Movement, a Roman Catholic student organization. That organization had sponsored a local effort called TRIALOG to coordinate several student religious groups and had prompted the Student Council initiative.

The formal recognition of student religious groups as bona fide student organizations, and the desire of those groups to use University facilities, posed yet again for the University the question to what extent and in what ways the representation of religious interests could be accommodated in a public, secular institution. President Shannon's response to Student Council provides some interesting insights into the problem and into the thinking of the administration.[50]

First, Shannon expressed respect for the various student religious organizations and for local churches, but emphasized that none of them is an organization of the University of Virginia, and, accordingly, none of them is permitted to use meeting rooms or other University facilities except on the specific authorization of the president. Second, he spoke of the longstanding and fruitful presence at the University of the YMCA, which he regarded as the principal coordinating agency of denominational religious groups and activities, and one effectively committed to "interdenominational fair play"—this in spite of the fact that the YMCA was by this time very nearly defunct. Finally, and of greatest interest, was the appeal Shannon made to the founding intentions of Thomas Jefferson, particularly as expressed in his letter to Thomas Cooper (November 2, 1822). There Jefferson referred to the recent report to the Directors of the Literary Fund in which appeared the suggestion of "the expediency of encouraging the different religious sects to establish, each for itself, a professorship of their own tenets, on the confines of the university, so near that the students may attend the lectures there, and have the free use of our library, and every other accommodation we can give them."[51] Fletcher, the president of Student Council, had also appealed to the same source in his letter to Shannon.

But Fletcher and Shannon had radically different interpretations of Jefferson's intentions. Fletcher thought that Jefferson intended for the various denominations to have full representation *within* the University and expected that by mixing together students of different beliefs the "asperities" of denominational conflicts would be moderated. Shannon reformulated Fletcher's interpretation and imputed to him the view that Jefferson "was recommending official sanction [of denominational groups] by and within the University." Shannon asserted that Jefferson's intent was precisely the opposite of this, namely, that religious organizations and establishments should be located "outside the Grounds" and that this would preserve, in Jefferson's words, "their independence of us and of each other." Shannon additionally called attention to the fact that although no denominational seminaries had been established near the University, churches of all major denominations had by now been built in the near environs of the University, and that these had their own "parish houses, hospitable meeting rooms, and social halls" and were well able to accommodate meetings of student religious organizations. Therefore, Shannon averred, "Never in the history of the University has there been a less appropriate time for denominational demands upon the University's overtaxed facilities." For additional support, he cited the 1819 report of the Rockfish Gap Commission, which he called the effective "constitution" of the University, saying that "it establishes the secular character of the University." Acknowledging that over the years there had been "errors and inconsistencies" in the University's efforts to preserve its secular character, he asserted that the University wished "to preserve the secular tradition" but at the same time to give "all possible encouragement to student and faculty religious activities."

President Shannon proposed that these two goals could be accomplished by means of a plan then being worked up by the YMCA's director, Daniel Gibbes. The plan consisted of four elements: (1) that any proposed educational program or presentation on a religious subject would be planned by the YMCA when four or more student denominational groups requested it, (2) that a representative number of interested parties (presumably denominational student ministers) would be consulted for suggestions, (3) that the proposed program or presentation would be reviewed by various University officials and, when approved by them, (4) that the YMCA would request the use of University facilities. This very cumbersome, multistage process that still left decisions entirely in the hands of University administrators was obviously a barrier to the use of University space by student religious groups. Although the plan appears never to have been put into effect, the University's stance was clear: it opposed the use of University facilities by student religious groups. This was a very far cry, of course, from the circumstances and practices that prevailed in the University at least up until World War I, when the YMCA was enjoying vast influence in and many indulgences from the University. Of course, the YMCA had been a professedly nonsectarian or nondenominational organization, whereas now it was a matter of specific and diverse denominational groups. But whether that should have made a difference is arguable, since the YMCA, for all its nondenominationalism, was a thoroughly evangelical Protestant Christian organization, and thus sectarian in the larger sense of being biased against other forms of Christianity and other religions than Christianity. But however that may be, the University administration was now intent on keeping religious activity outside University spaces and asserting the secular nature of the institution.

The issue arose again in 1972–73, when an evangelical student group, Action Ministries, sought to hold a meeting in University space. The University permitted the meeting, but emphasized that this was a one-time exception, and that the policy prohibiting religious groups from meeting on the Grounds would remain in force. The University's wobbling on the question indicates that there was a growing institutional awareness of the historical inconsistencies in its dealings with religious groups and a persistent uncertainty about what position to take. Two students decided to challenge the policy of excluding student religious organizations, and after doing some legal and historical research, they presented their case to Ralph Eisenberg, who was chair of the Calendar and Scheduling Committee. On the recommendation of Eisenberg and the committee, President Shannon directed in March of 1973 that the policy be changed, and henceforth religious groups were permitted to meet in University facilities, with the proviso only that there be no discrimination by race, gender, or creed.[52]

In that decision Shannon anticipated a ruling made by the Supreme Court in 1981, in a case that was brought against the University of Missouri at Kansas City. That public, tax-supported institution had for several years permitted a recognized student religious group, Cornerstone, to meet in university buildings. Concerned that its practice was in violation of the establishment clause, the university rescinded its policy and enacted a new regulation stating that university facilities could not be used "for purposes of religious worship or religious teaching." Denied use of university space, the student group sued, alleging that its First Amendment right to the free exercise of religion and to free speech was being abridged. While the district court found in favor of the university, the appeals court reversed that decision, holding that "a content based discrimination against religious speech" was not justified by deference to the establishment clause. In this case, *Widmar v. Vincent, 454 U.S. 263 (1981)*, the Supreme Court ruled that public universities were *not* required by the First Amendment to deny the use of their facilities to religious organizations. Because it had created an "open forum" for student groups, the university could not abridge the students' right of free speech by "viewpoint discrimination." Applying the "Lemon test," the court judged that the use of the institution's facilities by a student religious group would be only an "incidental benefit" to that group and would not amount to a "primary advancement" of religion.[53] As a result of the *Widmar* decision, student religious groups gained greater access to the use of space in public institutions, including the University of Virginia, although institutions are not required to approve such use by all groups and are not assumed to endorse all messages or activities that occur in their facilities.

Yet another conflict between the University and student religious groups occurred some years later. This time the issue was not the use of University facilities, but the availability of University funding to student religious groups, and it was carried all the way to the Supreme Court in a case of national notoriety: *Rosenberger v. Rector and Visitors of the University of Virginia, 515 U.S. 819 (1995)*. In 1991 a student publication entitled *Wide Awake* applied to Student Council for financial support from funds accumulated through the University's student activities fees. Student Council denied the request on the grounds that *Wide Awake* was a religious publication that promoted a particular religious viewpoint. And indeed it did: its purpose was "to challenge Christians to live, in word and deed, according to the faith they proclaim and to encourage students to consider what a personal relationship with Jesus Christ means."[54] With the assistance of the Center for Individual Rights, Ronald Rosenberger, the student editor of the magazine, filed suit against the University in the U.S. District Court for the Western District of Virginia. That court ruled in favor of the University, and the ruling was sustained on appeal to the Fourth Circuit Court. The case was then appealed to the Supreme Court, which reversed the decisions of the lower courts by a 5–4 margin.[55] But the particulars are important.

The University funds the activities of student organizations by means of a mandatory student activities fee collected along with other fees from the student body. Registered student organizations may request money from the student activities fund to cover some of their expenses. The fund excluded certain activities, specifically "religious activities, philanthropic activities, political activities, activities that would jeopardize the University's tax-exempt status, those that involve payment of honoraria or similar fees, or social or entertainment-related expenses." Although *Wide Awake* was a registered student organization, its request was denied because the publication of the magazine was deemed a "religious activity" and thus ineligible under the funding provisions. The University's principal concern was, of course, to comply with the establishment clause of the Constitution, which it took to mean, in this case, that public monies (the student activities fees) could not be used to support religion.

The Supreme Court ruled 5–4 that by funding speech-related student activities, such as student publications, speakers, conferences, symposia, and the like, the University had created a "limited purpose public forum," and that to exclude groups from that forum on the basis of their viewpoint was a violation of the First Amendment guarantee of free speech. Further, the Court indicated that the establishment clause of the First Amendment does not preclude the funding of religious speech in the present case, because by permitting *Wide Awake* to draw on the student activities fee funds the University *itself* would not be promoting a particular religious viewpoint, but merely allowing participation in a "public forum" by an independent organization. To prohibit *Wide Awake* from participation would be to discriminate against a religious viewpoint, and thus to violate the First Amendment guarantee of free speech.

The Court's ruling, although very specific to the facts of the case, raised more questions than it answered.[56] It was clear only that the use of student activities fees was not to be denied to religious publications. Beyond that, the Court provided no real guidance. It fell, then, to the president and more especially to the Board of Visitors to revise existing policies to bring them into compliance.[57] This was done by listing "religious organizations" among those eligible for funding, by stipulating that no funding would be provided for "religious ceremonies," and by carefully defining "religious activity," as follows:

> The organized worship of a deity, divine power, or supernatural entity, whether or not such activity is consistent with the precepts of an organized denomination. No student news, information, opinion, entertainment or academic communications media group shall be considered to be engaging in religious activity merely because it expresses ideas or viewpoints that are religious in nature [nor shall it be] deemed ineligible for funding on the grounds that the

ideas or viewpoints expressed or advocated by such group are religious in nature or because such group primarily promotes or manifests a particular belief(s) in or about a deity or an ultimate reality.[58]

Conflicts between the University and student religious groups are almost bound to arise, partly because the precise application of the First Amendment to the postures and policies of public universities will continue to be tested and adjudicated, partly because student religious groups and their activities have multiplied, and partly because precisely what constitutes "religion" and "religious activity" is often arguable. Student Council lists no fewer than thirty-two student groups that it classifies as "religious and spiritual organizations," but there are many more religious or quasi-religious groups not found in that list. Collectively, these organizations represent not only the Christian, Jewish, Muslim, Hindu, and Buddhist traditions in their respective varieties, but also less prominent religions and groups that embrace general spiritualist ideas and practices. By the late twentieth century a broad and globally representative religious pluralism had come to characterize the student body of the University, which was once almost uniformly of an evangelical Protestant persuasion.

Jewish students were a small minority at the University for a long time. The first Jewish student, Gratz Cohen, matriculated in 1862, but few Jews enrolled in the University for the remainder of the nineteenth century, and although their numbers increased significantly in the first half of the twentieth century, they remained a small minority. The evangelical Christian culture of the Commonwealth fostered an anti-Semitism that infected the University from its early days, even though it remained largely latent.[59] As noted previously, in 1841 evangelical religious interests lodged complaints against the hiring of the University's first Jewish professor, J. J. Sylvester, who had a very brief tenure at the University. There was not another Jewish member of the faculty until the twentieth century. In 1920 Linwood Lehman, a graduate of the University, joined the faculty to teach Latin, and he remained at the University until his death in 1953. Another Jewish faculty member, Ben-Zion Linfield, a Russian immigrant who earned his Ph.D. from Harvard, was hired to teach mathematics in 1927 and remained until 1967. But notably, these two were the only Jewish members of the faculty during the first half of the twentieth century.

The University also felt some hesitations regarding Jewish students. Because of the immigration of several million Jews from Eastern Europe in the late nineteenth and early twentieth centuries, the number of Jewish students grew dramatically at many eastern colleges and universities in the early decades of the twentieth century, including the University of Virginia. Some administrators worried that they were becoming too numerous and recommended limitations on their admission. J. M. Page, the dean of the College, wrote in his 1926–27 annual report to the University president, that "[although] I have not made an accurate estimate of the number of applications received from Jews, I feel sure that 80% at least of the applications received were of that race—nearly all of whom live in New York." He went on to note that about 11 percent of all students in the College were Jews, a figure he expected to grow since "Jews are beginning to find out that they are well-treated here." He concluded, however, that "the University will have to set some limit to the number of Jews to be admitted, giving the preference, of course, to those who are citizens of Virginia."[60] Both racial and regional prejudices seem to underlie these comments, notwithstanding the claim that Jews were "well-treated" at the University. A quota on Jewish students was by no means unique to the University of Virginia. During the same period private schools in the Northeast were also moving to set quotas limiting the number of Jewish students.[61] It may be that their diminished prospects of admission at Harvard, Yale, Princeton, and Columbia pushed the issue southward and caused more Jewish students to apply to Virginia.

By the end of World War II prejudice against Jewish faculty or students had largely disappeared. The faculty began to be enriched with many outstanding Jewish professors in all fields, beginning with the appointment in 1955 of Marvin Rosenblum in mathematics. Religious identity also receded as a factor in student admissions. By the end of the twentieth century the University had many Jewish students. Already in 1939 Rabbi Albert Lewis had organized Jewish student life at the University by establishing the Jewish Student Union. That group became affiliated in 1941 with the national Hillel organization, and Hillel at the University of Virginia, now known as the Brody Jewish Center, has prospered enormously in membership, activities, and facilities. Further, although the study of Judaism had been part of the curriculum of the Department of Religious Studies since its reconstitution in 1967, in 2001 the University took advantage of the presence of resources on Judaism in many departments by inaugurating an expansive interdisciplinary program in Jewish studies.

The predominance of Christianity persisted, but was greatly diversified. The number of Roman Catholic students increased markedly after the middle of the twentieth century. By the mid-1970s more than one-fifth of the student body was Catholic, and the proportion was much larger by the end of the century, close to parity with Protestants. And while Protestant students, taken together, continued to be a slight majority, their denominational identities were much more numerous than the four that were historically privileged by the University. But more important, the tripartite taxonomy of American religion—Protestant, Catholic, and Jew—that had pertained in the 1950s and '60s soon lost applicability. Enriching the mix yet more, especially after 1980, were increasing numbers of Islamic, Buddhist, and Hindu students, not to mention yet other traditions. This rich diversity of faiths manifests the unbounded proliferation of religious opinions that Jefferson's Statute of Religious Freedom was intended to permit, and it appears not only to be readily tolerated but also welcomed and celebrated. The University may have been late in coming around to it, but it came.

Despite the growth of religious pluralism on the Grounds, evangelical Protestant activity by no means disappeared from the University. In the mid-1970s the so-called Jesus movement, a Pentecostalism-inspired amalgam of hippie culture and evangelical Christianity, made its presence felt on the Grounds. Born in California in the late sixties, it swept across the country in the seventies before dying out. For a year or two in the mid-1970s some professors of religious studies found themselves being interrupted and shouted down in their classrooms by "Jesus people" (not necessarily students) who disapproved of their teaching. In the 1980s it became a dependable expectation that at least a few times during the academic year an itinerant preacher would appear in a now-traditional location, the amphitheater, and for a day or two would harangue student passersby about their sinful ways and fearsome destinies, urging them to repentance. Although these events are mildly entertaining to some, they do not appear to have had much, if any, religious impact.

More serious and effective Christian evangelism has, however, found a continuing presence at the University. In addition to the student groups sponsored by mainline denominations and hosted by local churches, since about 1970 there have arisen within the University many parachurch organizations (that is, "alongside the church" and without denominational connections), which attract large numbers of students. Among the larger of these voluntary, nondenominational, religiously conservative Christian groups are Campus Crusade for Christ (now known as Cru), InterVarsity Christian Fellowship, Fellowship of Christian Athletes, Navigators, and Young Life. Such parachurch groups engage a considerable number of students and appear to be the most populous religious organizations on the Grounds. They have effectively taken the place in student religious life that was occupied for a century by the YMCA, since they perpetuate aims and activities that were once sponsored within the University by the YMCA. And although most denominational campus ministries have had only limited appeal since the 1970s, there are some conservative evangelical denominations that have been more energetic and successful. These include Chi Alpha, an organization sponsored by the Assemblies of God, and the Reformed University Fellowship, sponsored by the evangelical Presbyterian Church in America. Although the number of Roman Catholic students has increased greatly since midcentury, the larger Christian environment of the University has remained predominantly Protestant, and Protestant of an evangelical more than mainline sort.

In 1968 a freelance evangelist, Daryl Richman, began work around the University. He organized what he called Action Ministries and in a few years succeeded in enlisting some enthusiastic students. Some of these students went on to graduate school at Regent College, an evangelical school of theology in Vancouver, B.C., or spent time at L'Abri, a conservative Christian study center in Switzerland run by Francis Schaeffer. Returning to Charlottesville, they set about creating an analogous theologically conservative study center close to the University. Such a center came into being in 1976 as University Christian Ministries, which has since thrived as the Center for Christian Study, a nondenominational enterprise that sponsors programs for the theological education of laypersons (both students and community members), promotes fellowship groups in the professional schools, and supports a residential program for a limited number of students. The Center for Christian Study maintains a conservative evangelical Protestant theological stance, but differs from fundamentalism by fostering theological inquiry that remains engaged with contemporary culture. With its various functions the center has served as a religious "safe house" or retreat for evangelical University students who seek religious support in a secular environment. The center maintains that an orthodox Protestant faith is not incompatible with rigorous intellectual inquiry. Originally, the Center for Christian Study aimed to provide an alternative to the study of religion as conducted in the University's Department of Religious Studies, which was thought to be not merely neutral and dispassionate but skeptical and subversive of faith. (Indeed, for some years students and faculty of that persuasion mounted a Christian Orientation Program for entering students, who were warned against taking courses in the Department of Religious Studies, among other threats to their well-being.) Although this negative view of the Department of Religious Studies has softened over the years, it has not wholly disappeared.[62] In addition to the residential program of the Center for Christian Study, there are numerous "Christian houses" around the University where committed Christian students live together and nurture their faith.

The religious reality of the modern University is one of broad and diffuse pluralism. In the second half of the twentieth century the population of the University—both faculty and student—became religiously diverse to an extent and in ways that would have been unimaginable even in the first half of the twentieth century, let alone in the nineteenth. Virtually every posture within and beyond the five major world religions and their subsets finds both representation and organization on the Grounds. An obvious and important reason for this is the globalization of the educational marketplace that has affected most institutions of higher education in the United States. Students come from all over the world to attend highly regarded American colleges and universities, bringing with them their cultural and religious traditions. But other factors have also been at work.

The Resecularization of the University

A correlative condition for religious pluralism, perhaps less important but still demonstrable, has been the University's deliberate and steady retreat from religious emphases and entanglements since midcentury, or, in a word, its institutional resecularization. Up to about 1950 the University remained remarkably naive about its relationship to religion. Neither members of the administration nor members of the faculty seem to have given much thought to the question, and the ethos of white, southern Protestant piety that had taken hold in the nineteenth century continued to pervade the Grounds, no longer aggressively after World War I, but still with predisposing influence. But when, in 1947, the Supreme Court ruled in the *Everson* case that the establishment clause of the First Amendment applied to state and local governments as well as to the federal government, the University had to begin to consider its position regarding religion and to distance itself from any identification with or sponsorship of religious activities.[63] In the following decades the University drew back from its customarily unreflective relations with religious interests. The creation in 1967 of a full-blown Department of Religious Studies can be thought of as a means of domesticating the subject of religion and bringing it under academic auspices, thus maintaining an institutional interest in religion, while at the same time reducing and limiting the institution's engagement with the practice of religion. This more circumspect posture toward religion was undoubtedly needed, even though the judicial system was still working through delicate issues in the separation of church and state.

In other ways too the University was gradually brought to a more acute awareness of its legal obligations as a public institution of the Commonwealth. Racial desegregation made only grudging progress at the University in the 1950s, and real integration did not occur until the 1960s. The first undergraduate class that included women was not admitted until 1970. Both of these changes required judicial compulsion. Thus amid broad-based developments in society that supported cultural diversity, inclusion, and tolerance, the University moved steadily toward a pluralistic inclusiveness in matters of race, gender, and religion.

There is no reliable way to measure the scope or strength of religious interest and activity at the University today. Various recent studies have argued, and some have lamented, that by the late twentieth century colleges and universities in the United States had become more or less completely secularized, such that religion, including Christianity, had become peripheral or even alien to the enterprise of higher education.[64] Generally, this seems to be a valid observation. But if secularization means an *institutional* indifference to religion, it is hard to argue that contemporary *students* are less interested in religion than in previous periods. Religion seems as significant as ever, not to all students, of course, and perhaps not to the majority, but to a substantial minority. At Virginia in the early twenty-first century, student religious groups are more numerous than ever and more diverse than ever, and collectively probably involve more students than ever.[65]

Recently there has been much discussion in academic circles of the idea of postsecularism, and whether and in what sense we have entered a postsecular era. If secularism means indifference to religion, and secularization points to an ever-declining significance of religion, then postsecularism signals that we are leaving behind the era of secularism and witnessing instead a recrudescence of religion. Cited in support of this idea is the persistence of religious interest and activity (including among students) and, beyond the continuing vitality of departments of religious studies, the increasing attention being given to religion in other academic disciplines, both humanistic and social scientific. The literature on postsecularism is already very large, and the concept continues to be tested and contested.[66] But it is unquestionable that religion is today a subject of broader interest in the academy, and studied in more disciplinary contexts, than during most of the twentieth century. What the results of this will be is as yet uncertain: whether it will confer great legitimacy on the study of religion, or bring about a better understanding of just what religion is and what its functions are (for good or ill), or perhaps promote greater interest in the large questions of meaning and value, or even restore to higher education a dimension of moral formation or religious sensibility that has been diminished or even lost altogether. All this is yet to be seen. But it is unlikely that public universities will ever again be institutional sponsors or agents of religion, even if they liberally accommodate its free expression.

The University of Virginia enjoyed the distinction of being the first institution of higher learning in America to have an explicit and deliberately secular character. But as I have shown, it very early gave way to the pressure of the religious culture. As the nineteenth century wore on, the University incorporated more and more religious elements and sought to cultivate an ever more enveloping atmosphere of piety. Indeed, the speed and the scope of that development are remarkable in retrospect. This embrace of religion is explicable: Jefferson's legacy of alleged irreligion was a heavy liability to the University, and one that seemed to require countermeasures if the institution were to make any headway. In an odd way, the institution's custodians believed that it could survive and flourish only by compromising one of its founder's most basic convictions.

Other American colleges and universities began to adopt a secular stance in the late nineteenth century as the progress of science and the interest in applied knowledge reshaped the aims and emphases of higher education. That process was largely complete, at least in leading institutions, by the end of the nineteenth century or very soon thereafter. Ironically, the University that had pioneered the secular principle in American education was among the last to return to it. In the early twentieth century its own conservatism and its religious environment, little changed since the mid-nineteenth century, held it back. But by the end of the twentieth century the University had reclaimed its birthright as a secular public institution and had taken its place among the leading public universities of the nation. It could no longer be characterized as "a religious institution," as President Alderman had claimed in 1910, nor did

Old Cabell Hall: The Greek inscription of John 8:32 on the pediment reads, "And you shall know the truth, and the truth shall make you free"

it wish to be. Freedom of religion was underscored, as Jefferson had thought necessary, by institutional indifference to religion. That indifference was not intended to promote ignorance of religion, or hostility toward religion, but to assure complete freedom of religious opinion and expression, and to prevent any intrusion of the state upon the rights of conscience. In that case, it could be said that a basic Jeffersonian principle has finally come to full effect.

It is a notable, albeit local, curiosity that the pediment of Old Cabell Hall prominently carries a quotation, in Greek, from the Gospel according to John: "And you shall know the truth, and the truth shall make you free" (John 8:32). Not all may know that Old Cabell Hall is not a Jeffersonian building, and that Jefferson did not commission this inscription. Indeed, in its original context in the Gospel, the quotation represents much that Jefferson repudiated about religion, for the truth it speaks of is a revealed truth mediated by a divine Christ, and the freedom it promises is a freedom from sin and has nothing to do with government or civil society. Old Cabell Hall was designed by Stanford White and erected in 1898, and the quotation was proposed by Armistead Gordon, then Rector of the University.[67] In 1898 hardly anyone associated with the University would have thought a quotation from the Gospel of John, so prominently displayed in a public institution, was at all objectionable, because the religious impulse of the University was then near its height. Fortunately, given the secular character of the modern University, the quotation, taken by itself, is susceptible of a different exegesis, and even a Jeffersonian one. Although it is a politically hackneyed appropriation, it stands as a useful reminder, along with the chapel, that religion has, indeed, had a history at Jefferson's University.

Appendix A

Professor Bonnycastle's Plea for a Chapel

A Petition for a Chapel at the University of Virginia to the Visitors, Drawn up by Professor Charles Bonnycastle in 1837

We, the undersigned, students of the University of Virginia, urged by regard for an institution whence we have received so large a part of our education, respectfully direct the attention of your Board to the want of a sufficiently spacious and becoming place of public worship; and, in behalf of our successors, petition that a defect which lessens the benefits afforded by the institution may be removed by such means as you may deem appropriate.

Impressed with the important relations which the subject bears, not only to the institution but also to the interests of a still higher nature, we respectfully lay before you a brief representation of the extent to which the evil in question affects the students.

It will be unnecessary for us to dwell upon the admitted truth, that the most important object of education is to form those habits of thought and action which lead to undeviating and awful respect for the commands of the Supreme Being and to just and elevated notions of His attributes. This fact, recognized throughout the plan of government and instruction in the University, has caused the authorities to establish, in conformity with the views of the venerable founder, a system of religious service harmonizing, as far as possible, with all the chief persuasions authorized by the State. But in the same proportion that we are pleased with this liberal arrangement and convinced of the salutary influences which it has already exerted, we must regret that its efficiency should be impaired by the omission among the buildings of the University of a structure dedicated to the worship of the Deity.

The magnitude and importance of the institution and the fact that among its alumni there will probably be some whose opinions may have an influence on the future destinies of the State, seem to render such a building appropriate and even necessary, and to require that the respect paid to God should be marked by the decent separation of His temple from the halls devoted to other purposes.

In all ages the feeling which renders the institution of the Sabbath so appropriate to man has caused the scene of self-examination and communion with our Maker to be removed from the busy theatre of earthly vocations and passions. If, in those solemn and chastened thoughts which scenes of solitude or unexpected acts of Divine Power never fail to call forth, we see evidence of the force which place and occasion exert over the strongest intellects, can we esteem it of little moment that the youthful minds hereafter to be formed at this seat of learning shall be led to honor the Deity by observance which others pay, or be invited to worship the author of their being in a temple bearing decent and visible impress of the respect paid to His holy name, rather than in halls associated with the avocations and toils of the week, where no solemnity of preparation leads the mind to commune with itself; but the walls and benches are defaced with impure or trifling inscriptions, and every recollection attached to the place is calculated to awaken the idle and thoughtless feelings of restraint and weariness?

Were no other considerations urged but these, we feel confident they would induce your Board to add a chapel to the buildings of this extensive institution. But the argument which we have yet to make is of so much stronger and pressing a nature that we cannot doubt its obtaining your speedy and serious deliberation. The inappropriate character of the lecture-room, at present used for divine worship, is of less moment than its want of size. When we state that on those occasions on which the attendance of the students is most to be desired, scarcely one half of them can find accommodation in the room, and that from this fact many who could have heard instruction designed for their improvement are deterred from seeking it; and that the arrangement of the benches is so incommodious that it subjects to much inconvenience those who do attend; and that the other purposes to which the room is applied prevent any permanent alteration being made, we become convinced that your Board will regard our application as of pressing moment, and that you will either take such steps, or grant such facilities for removing the deficiency complained of, as you may deem best adapted to your power and the interest of the University.

The foregoing, drafted by Professor Bonnycastle on behalf of the students of the University, was not presented to the Board of Visitors, because there was no time enough before the end of the session to obtain a large number of signatories. The Board was, however, made aware of the existence of the petition. The petition came to light and was published in the *Alumni Bulletin* 3, no. 4, for February of 1897, from which it is reproduced here.

Appendix B

The Teaching of Hebrew at the University

Thomas Jefferson stipulated that three languages should be taught in the School of Ancient Languages: Greek, Latin, and Hebrew. The addition of Hebrew to the usual classical curriculum was part of Jefferson's concession to the sectarian critics of the absence of a professor of divinity.[1] In lieu of instruction in religion, Jefferson proposed that sectarian schools might locate in proximity to the University so that their students could complement their theological studies with University instruction in other disciplines and take advantage of its library.[2] The University, for its part, would make available instruction in Greek and Hebrew, so that adherents of any sect might acquire those basic linguistic tools for the study of scripture. This was a small gesture, for Greek and Latin would have been offered in any case. And so, when Jefferson commissioned Francis Gilmer to seek out European professors, he desired that the professor of ancient languages should be competent to teach Hebrew as well as Greek and Latin, not to mention rhetoric, belles lettres, ancient history, and ancient geography.

But this was a very tall order. Gilmer took his commission seriously and tried to find a classics scholar who had knowledge of Hebrew. In the end, however, he satisfied himself with George Long, a Fellow of Trinity College, of the University of Cambridge, who did not know Hebrew. In recommending Long to Jefferson and the Board of Visitors, Gilmer wrote:

> I have had the good fortune to enlist with us for the ancient languages, a learned and highly respectable Cantab. but there have been two obstacles, that have made me pause long, before I conclude with him. He has no knowledge of Hebrew, which is to be taught at the university. This I easily reconciled to my duty, from the absolute necessity of the case. Oriental literature is very little esteemed in England, and we might seek a whole year, & perhaps not at last find a real scholar in Latin & Greek, who understands Hebrew.

Gilmer confided to Long (August 21, 1824) that Hebrew "is also included, but there will be no occasion for it, I think, and you could easily learn enough for what may be required." In a follow-on letter Gilmer reiterated in a postscript: "The Hebrew I think of no importance as we have no clergy and you need not mind whether you know anything of it. The Rhetoric and belles lettres will be easily attained."[3] Consequently, Jefferson's proviso that Hebrew be taught at the University initially went unfulfilled.

It can be presumed that Professor Long, knowing no Hebrew, taught no Hebrew during his relatively brief tenure in Charlottesville. When Long departed for the University of London in 1828, he was succeeded by his young student, Gessner Harrison. Harrison, as noted earlier, was a devout Methodist, but it is unclear whether or how far he had any knowledge of the Hebrew language. He surely did not learn Hebrew from George Long, and yet he seems somehow to have acquired some knowledge of that language. But the question is provocative. One of Harrison's students was Francis S. Sampson (1814–54), who was a student at the University of Virginia from 1831 to 1836, graduating with an M.A. in ancient languages. Sampson was described as "a distinguished classical scholar in the University of Virginia, unsurpassed in his aptness to teach, and in a thorough knowledge of the Hebrew language he was probably excelled by no man of his age in America." After graduating from the University, Sampson went on to enroll in the theological department of Hampden-Sydney College, where he became a teacher of Hebrew in 1838, and was named the professor of Oriental languages and literature in 1848. It seems likely that during his student days at Virginia Sampson gained at least some knowledge of Hebrew. If so, and if he was not simply self-taught, he must have learned it from Gessner Harrison. This is made more likely by the testimony of two other Virginia students, Crawford H. Toy and Charles A. Briggs.

Crawford Howell Toy (1836–1919) was a student at the University from 1852 to 1856. He would go on to become a nationally prominent scholar of Hebrew and of the Hebrew Bible and be appointed a professor of Oriental languages at Harvard, the first non-Unitarian professor in Harvard's Divinity School.[4] Although as a student at Virginia he took a variety of courses—ancient languages, law, and physiology and surgery—and was a man of many interests and aptitudes, he eventually settled on a theological career. After teaching for three years at the Albemarle Female Institute, he proceeded from Charlottesville to the Southern Baptist Seminary in Greenville, South Carolina, and was ordained a Baptist minister in Charlottesville in 1860 by none other than John A. Broadus, with whom Toy had developed a close friendship. He intended a missionary career, but was deflected by the Civil War, during which he was a chaplain with the Confederate forces. After the war he went to Germany and studied for two years at the University of Berlin. On returning to the States, he became a professor of Old Testament interpretation and Oriental languages at the Southern Baptist Seminary. Toy resigned this position in 1879 because he could no longer accept the view of the Bible maintained by Southern Baptists. He promptly accepted a appointment at Harvard as the Hancock Professor of Hebrew and Semitic Languages. Like Sampson, Toy studied with Gessner Harrison, and Toy makes it clear that Hebrew was one of the languages he studied with Harrison. In an essay, "A Student's View of the University of Virginia, 1852–1856," Toy comments,

> Though Dr. Harrison did not pretend to be a specialist in Hebrew, he conducted a class or conference in that language which was attended by John A. Broadus and myself and another student (Williams of Norfolk, I think). Dr. Harrison and Broadus (recently tutor in Greek) brought to bear on our study the principles of grammatical interpretation familiar to them in other fields, and I thought it a great privilege to be thus associated with them.[5]

In his study of Hebrew with Harrison Toy may have been building on a foundation laid by his father, a Norfolk businessman, who is reported to have had a strong linguistic aptitude and to have known some Hebrew.[6] It is also possible that Toy did some additional study of Hebrew at the University with Basil Gildersleeve, for although Toy had graduated in 1856, before Gildersleeve's arrival, he remained in Charlottesville for the next several years, and after the war he was actually an instructor (licentiate) in Greek, assisting Gildersleeve, at the University during the 1865–66 session.[7]

In 1856 the Board of Visitors decided to divide the professorship in ancient languages into two professorships, one responsible for Greek and Hebrew, the other for Latin.[8] Gessner Harrison chose to hold the chair in Latin, and the chair in Greek and Hebrew was filled in 1858 by Basil Gildersleeve. Gildersleeve was entirely expert in Greek, but at the time of his appointment he apparently knew little or no Hebrew. He wrote to his friend Emil Huebner in 1858,

> My spare moments are devoted to Hebrew—which I tacked on to my department because–forsooth—the charter of the University requires that Hebrew is to be taught—and the number of students does not warrant the appointment of a separate professor! Every four or five years two or three stony theological students learn the alphabet—and some of the forms–become disgusted and give it up–and to satisfy this pressing necessity I have to devote to a study interesting enough in itself—the little time that I might spend more profitably on Roman Antiquity. Of course my own Hebrew is of the most elementary description. . . . Do mention to Bernays that I am a Professor of Hebrew.[9]

Several things are readily evident in these remarks. The University still affected to take seriously a commitment to offer instruction in Hebrew. It had appointed Gildersleeve professor of Greek *and* Hebrew, even though he was little acquainted with Hebrew. Gildersleeve felt obliged to bone up on Hebrew, though it was a largely thankless task, since so few students had any interest in it. We do not know who or how many were the "stony theological students" to whom he may have taught some rudimentary Hebrew, but they may well have included Charles Augustus Briggs, and perhaps Crawford Howell Toy.

Briggs (1841–1913) was a student at the University from 1857 to 1860, Gildersleeve's earliest years at the University, and during this period Briggs apparently underwent a conversion experience and felt a call to the ministry.[10] This must have awakened in him a special interest in the Bible and in biblical languages. What is certain is that he went on from the University to Union Theological Seminary at Hampden-Sydney, and from there to the University of Berlin (1866–69). It is interesting to find that Briggs and Toy, two University of Virginia graduates, were at the University of Berlin at the same time (1866–68), both studying Hebrew and other Semitic languages. After a brief stint as a pastor in New Jersey, Briggs was appointed in 1874 as professor of Hebrew at Union Theological Seminary in New York. Briggs was recognized as perhaps the most prominent Hebraist in the nation.[11] He championed the study of biblical Hebrew, saying that "we cannot afford to wait until all the colleges follow the noble lead of the University of Virginia, Lafayette, and others in giving their students the option of Hebrew instruction."[12] The implication is that Briggs exercised this option during his undergraduate days at Virginia, and if so, he most probably was instructed by Gildersleeve.

There is no evidence that Thomas Randolph Price, Gildersleeve's successor (1876–82), was acquainted with Hebrew, or taught any Hebrew at the University, even though he too, like Gildersleeve, had been appointed as professor of Greek and Hebrew.[13] The possibility cannot be excluded, however, because Price, more than a classicist, was above all a philologist and comparative linguist, interested and able in many languages. Still, University catalogues during his tenure do not mention the availability of any instruction in Hebrew.

Price's successor was John H. Wheeler (1882–87) who, like Gildersleeve and Price, was appointed as professor of Greek and Hebrew. After him came Milton W. Humphreys, who was listed, however, only as professor of Greek (1887–1915). Yet under both Wheeler and Humphreys, University catalogues, at the end of the listing of regular courses in Greek, give an additional heading for Hebrew, which is followed by a brief statement: "The Professor will also give instruction in Hebrew," or later, "Elementary instruction in Hebrew will be given when the demand for such instruction is sufficient." In two instances a specific instructor in Hebrew, other than the professor of Greek, is mentioned. In the 1887–88 catalogue, reiterating that instruction in Hebrew will be given when demand is sufficient, goes on to say that "during the present session such instruction is given by Rev. James M. Rawlings, the licentiate in Hebrew"; and in the catalogue for 1898–99 and again for 1899–1900 there is mention of a course in Hebrew to be taught by Rev. Charles Young.[14] An article appearing in the *Alumni Bulletin* of 1898 describes Sunday schools run by the YMCA some dozen years previously, and mentions in passing "a number of preachers, who were studying in a summer school of Hebrew."[15] Unfortunately, there is no other information about this summer program or who may have taught it.

After 1900, however, the University catalogue no longer makes any mention of instruction in Hebrew, which apparently lapsed altogether at the beginning of the twentieth century. It appears, then, that throughout the nineteenth century, Hebrew was offered only "on demand"—when there was a faculty member capable of teaching it and a sufficient number of students wished to study that language. Nowhere is it indicated what a sufficient number of students might be. Gildersleeve's comment, quoted above, mentions two or three students every four or five years—hardly enough to justify a regular course. Only twice is there an indication of a regular course, and in both cases it was taught by clerical adjuncts, not by the professor of Greek. In all this there is nothing strange. Biblical Hebrew was and is a language of interest only to Jews, to Christians who want to study the Hebrew Bible/Old Testament in its original language, and to scholars of Semitic languages. It has never been closely associated, let alone wedded, to the study of Greek and Latin. What Francis Gilmer found to be true in England—that one would have to look a long time to find "a real scholar in Latin & Greek, who understands Hebrew"—has remained largely true, save for biblical scholars who have learned both Greek and Hebrew. For that reason Jefferson's triad of ancient languages was never a viable prospect.

Instruction in Hebrew was revived at the University of Virginia only in the 1980s, and not in the Department of Classics, where it was originally to be housed, but in the Department of Religious Studies. There it was important for graduate students working in the area of biblical studies, and it has been offered as a two-year sequence up to the present. Only later, in the 1990s, did instruction begin to be offered also in modern Hebrew, which is taught in the Department of Middle Eastern and South Asian Languages.

Thus Jefferson's wish that Hebrew be taught at the University has come to full fruition, only much later than he had anticipated, in a different context, and for a different reason. But it had the remarkable consequence of helping to foster the two most prominent American authorities on the Hebrew language and the Hebrew scriptures of the late nineteenth and early twentieth centuries, Crawford Toy and Charles Briggs. The two of them did more than any scholars of the Hebrew Bible to advance in America the claims of the higher criticism of the Bible developed in Germany. In doing so, Toy, a Baptist, had to give up his post in that conservative denomination's seminary, and Briggs, a Presbyterian, was tried and condemned for heresy by his denomination. But both men were ahead of their times in biblical scholarship and made monumental contributions to that discipline.

Notes

1. Jefferson and Religion

1. Jefferson, *Notes on the State of Virginia*, Query XVII, in *Thomas Jefferson: Writings*, ed. Peterson, 286 (hereafter *Writings*, ed. Peterson).).

2. On Jefferson and Islam, see Spellberg, *Thomas Jefferson's Qur'an*. Such Muslims as were in America in Jefferson's time were slaves of North African origin, religiously unrecognized. Thus, as Spellberoter notes, "the first American Muslims may have numbered in the tens of thousands, a population certainly greater than the resident Jews and possibly even the Catholics" (6). See also Hayes, "How Thomas Jefferson Read the Qur'an."

3. On Jefferson's view of Judaism, see Healey, "Jefferson on Judaism and the Jews." There were, in fact, very few Jews in America in Jefferson's time: the first federal census (1790) counted only 1,243 out of a total population of 2,810,248. By 1820 this number had grown to only 4,000. See Gaustad, *Historical Atlas of Religion in America*, 144–45.

4. *Autobiography*, in *Writings*, ed. Peterson, 40.

5. All quotations of Jefferson's correspondence are taken from the National Archives website Founders Online: Jefferson Papers, https:/founders.archives.gov/?q= Project: "Jefferson Papers."

6. On the varying conceptions of "religion" that factored into the debates in Virginia about religious freedom, see Jon Butler, *Awash in a Sea of Faith*, 262–66.

7. As David Little has observed, "Contrary to the conventional impression, the original spirit of the American doctrine of the separation of church and state was heavily informed by a condescending attitude toward religious belief, rather than by an attitude of deep respect for the importance and centrality of religious convictions, or by a concern for the agony of those involved in resolving dilemmas caused by conflicts between religious faith and civic responsibility" ("The Origins of Perplexity," 192). See also now Porterfield, *Conceived in Doubt*, esp. chap. 2; and Grasso, *Skepticism and American Faith*.

8. *Notes on the State of Virginia*, Query XVII, in *Writings*, ed. Peterson, 286. There were, of course, pragmatic as well as principled reasons why Jefferson advocated religious freedom. Dissenters were reluctant to participate in the Revolution, and thus threatened its success, unless they were granted religious freedom. The Virginia Statute

for Religious Freedom probably would not have passed the General Assembly had the legislature not been inundated with petitions from thousands of Virginia dissenters, mainly Baptists and Presbyterians.

9. Among very many studies, the best informed and most useful are Buckley, "The Political Theology of Thomas Jefferson"; Conkin, "The Religious Pilgrimage of Thomas Jefferson" and "Priestley and Jefferson"; Gaustad, *Sworn on the Altar of God;* Healey, *Jefferson on Religion in Public Education;* Onuf, *The Mind of Thomas Jefferson,* 139–68 ("Jefferson's Religion: Priestcraft, Enlightenment, and the Republican Revolution"); Ragosta, "Thomas Jefferson's Religion and Religious Liberty," in his *Religious Freedom,* 7–39; Sanford, *The Religious Life of Thomas Jefferson;* Sheridan, "Jefferson and Religion," initially published as an introduction to Adams and Lester, eds., *Jefferson's Extracts from the Gospels,* subsequently published separately as *Jefferson and Religion;* Scherr, "Thomas Jefferson versus the Historians"; and Vicchio, *Jefferson's Religion.*

10. Among those anxious to make Jefferson a Christian, perhaps the most indefatigable is Mark A. Beliles in various publications, most recently *Doubting Thomas?* (with Jerry Newcombe). But see also Barton, *The Jefferson Lies.* Not to be relied on, these are special-pleading efforts in service of a modern agenda to diminish the separation of church and state and enlarge the access of conservative Christianity to the public square.

11. Jefferson frequently expressed a similar reluctance to others. Writing to Benjamin Rush (April 21, 1803) he said that he was "averse to the communication of my religious tenets to the public, because it would countenance the presumption of those who have endeavored to draw them before that tribunal, and to seduce public opinion to erect itself into that inquisition over the rights of conscience, which the laws have so justly proscribed." Writing to a would-be biographer, Joseph Delaplaine (December 25, 1816), Jefferson admonished: "Say nothing of my religion. It is known to my god and myself alone," a statement that he later quoted in a letter to John Adams (January 11, 1817). He wrote to Charles Clay (January 29, 1815), "I not only write nothing on religion, but rarely permit myself to speak on it, and never but in a reasonable society." To Mrs. Samuel H. Smith he wrote (August 6, 1816), "I never told my own religion." These comments reflect Jefferson's bitter experience of having been vilified by his political opponents for his alleged religious opinions. But one of Jefferson's grandsons, Thomas Jefferson Randolph, said that Jefferson would not reveal his religious views even to members of his own family and at their request (Randall, *Life of Jefferson,* 3:672). Jefferson implicitly acknowledged as much when he wrote to his daughter Martha (1803) and enclosed a copy of his "Syllabus" on the merits of Jesus' teaching, saying, "A promise made to a friend some years ago, but executed only lately, has placed my religious creed on paper. I have thought it just that my family should be enabled to estimate the libels published against me on this, as on every other possible subject."

12. For surveys, see Beliles, "The Christian Communities"; Richard B. Davis, *Intellectual Life in Jefferson's Virginia,* 119–46 (chap. 4, "Religion, Organized and

Individual"); and Bond, "Religion in Colonial Virginia: A Brief Overview," in his *Spreading the Gospel in Colonial Virginia,* 1–64.

13. With its disestablishment in Virginia in 1784, the Church of England, as reorganized in 1789, became known as the Episcopal Church of Virginia, and Jefferson retained his (nominal) connection with it: he was married in it, his children were baptized in it, and his own funeral was conducted according to its rites. But, as will be seen, Jefferson was unsympathetic to its doctrines.

14. Jefferson's lifelong devotion to the classics is examined in Lehmann, *Thomas Jefferson: American Humanist;* and in Onuf and Cole, eds., *Thomas Jefferson, the Classical World, and Early America.*

15. The theological orientation of William and Mary was latitudinarian, that is, somewhat relaxed in its attitude toward the doctrinal and liturgical tradition of Anglicanism, and focused more on the moral relevance of Christianity, the cultivation of Christian virtue, and tolerance in religious matters. Although latitudinarianism was not deistic, it could be a jumping-off point in the direction of deism. See further below, in n. 22. Latitudinarianism is well characterized by Cragg, *The Church in the Age of Reason,* 157–59.

16. Jefferson briefly sketched his educational experience in his *Autobiography,* written in 1821. See *Writings,* ed. Peterson, 4. On Small and his influence, see Hull, "William Small 1734–1775"; Cynthia L. Miller, "William Small and the Making of Thomas Jefferson's Mind"; and very fully, Clagett, "William Small, Teacher, Mentor, Scientist."

17. *Autobiography,* in *Writings,* ed. Peterson, 4; and Jefferson to L. H. Girardin, January 15, 1815.

18. For the forms and phases of the Enlightenment and their American appropriations, see esp. May, *The Enlightenment in America.*

19. This view was promoted especially by Gay, *The Rise of Modern Paganism.*

20. Recent reconsiderations of the relations between religion and the Enlightenment are surveyed by Sheehan, "Enlightenment, Religion and the Enigma of Secularization"; R. Robertson, "Religion and Enlightenment"; Caron and Wulf, "American Enlightenments," esp. 1082–88; and Grote, "Religion and Enlightenment." See also the earlier essay of Gilley, "Christianity and Enlightenment." Expansive discussions may be found in Sorkin, *The Religious Enlightenment;* and Bulman and Ingram, eds., *God in the Enlightenment.*

21. On the various connotations of this phrase, see Pailin, "The Confused and Confusing Story."

22. The so-called father of deism was Herbert of Cherbury (1583–1648), who argued in his *De Veritate* (1624) for a "natural religion" based on five innate and fundamental truths common to all religion: that God exists, that God should be worshipped, that the proper worship of God consists in morality, that humans should repent of evil, and that there are postmortem rewards and punishments. Still more important for the development of deism was John Locke, who argued in his *The Reasonableness of Christianity* (1695) that reason itself was the only appropriate and common basis for Christianity, and although he allowed that revelation might provide some knowledge that is

"above reason," it can never be "contrary to reason." Various English thinkers of the late seventeenth and early eighteenth century carried these ideas forward. John Toland (1670–1722), esp. in *Christianity Not Mysterious* (1696), argued similarly that "reason is not less from God than revelation," and indeed that revelation, which consists of elements that are not among one's own experience or observation, is nevertheless entirely rational and must be judged by reason. Anthony Collins's *Discourse on Freethinking* (1713) regarded free thought as fully capable of determining truth, and Matthew Tindal (1655–1733), in *Christianity as Old as the Creation* (1730), urged that the essential elements of Christianity have been present from the beginning (albeit without the name "Christianity"), and all human beings have always had the capacity to know and practice this true religion, namely, reason. Virtually all deist thinkers discounted the veracity and authority of scripture, were skeptical about miracles, and considered the real point of religion to be not metaphysics but morality. Useful recent studies of deism in England include Hudson, *The English Deists;* Wigelsworth, *Deism in Enlightenment England;* and Herrick, *The Radical Rhetoric of the English Deists.* To some extent, deism played off of latitudinarian thought in the English church. Latitudinarian thinkers in England repudiated the divisions and hostilities fostered by sectarian dogmatisms arising from the Reformation. They attached relatively little importance to particulars of doctrine, polity, and liturgy and emphasized as essential the convictions on which all Christians agreed and the moral relevance of Christianity. But latitudinarian Anglicans were not deists. See Emerson, "Latitudinarianism and the English Deists."

23. Jefferson did, however, use the term "deism" positively, and it clearly signified for him a strict and straightforward monotheism, which he affirmed. See the letters to Benjamin Rush (April 21, 1803) and Joseph Priestley (April 9, 1803). Some would deny that Jefferson was a deist, thus recently, e.g., William Wilson, "The Myth of Jefferson's Deism"; and Frazer, *The Religious Beliefs of America's Founders.* Their reason is that Jefferson occasionally made statements that suggest divine intervention or guidance in human affairs. But it is hard to make a strong case that Jefferson believed in divine interventions or special providence any more than he believed in miracles or credited revelation, written or otherwise, outside the natural order itself.

24. Bolingbroke (1678–1751), a Whig statesman and philosopher, was a prolific writer and a relatively minor English deist who had major influence on the young Jefferson's religious ideas. During the 1760s Jefferson kept a Commonplace Book in which he copied out from various authors passages that impressed him. His extracts from the works of Bolingbroke, which deal mainly with religion and morality, are far more copious than those from any other writer, making up almost half the contents (some 60 pages) of the Commonplace Book. See Douglas L. Wilson, ed., *Jefferson's Literary Commonplace Book,* who comments that "the entries from Bolingbroke, made when Jefferson was 22 or 23, record the unfolding of a momentous event in his intellectual development, the awakening of a skeptical and rationalistic deism in matters of religion" (11). Bolingbroke's writings were mostly published posthumously as *The Works of Henry St. John, Lord Viscount Bolingbroke* (5 vols., 1752). He was widely studied in the American colonies and influenced Adams and Madison, among others. The

Letters on the Study and Use of History contains an especially strong attack on traditional Christianity. On Bolingbroke and his religious ideas, see esp. Merrill, *From Statesman to Philosopher.*

25. The first of these revival movements is well described by Kidd, *The Great Awakening;* the second by Hatch, *The Democratization of American Christianity;* and Boles, *The Great Revival.* Eighteenth- and early nineteenth-century revivalism in America was a distant manifestation of the pietistic movement in Europe, which emphasized personal religious experience, critical self-examination, and renewed commitment to Christianity.

26. Among numerous studies, standard general treatments are G. A. Koch, *Republican Religion;* and Morais, *Deism in Eighteenth Century America.* But see also and more recently Walters, *Rational Infidels,* and *The American Deists.* Walters comments, "Although not a systematic philosopher, Jefferson was the most sophisticated American proponent of the deistic worldview" (*American Deists,* 110). Stewart, in *Nature's God,* wrongly construes early American deism as atheism. However qualified, deism was theistic.

27. On deistic personalities, societies, and journals, see Schlereth, *An Age of Infidels;* and Grasso, *Skepticism and American Faith,* part 1.

28. Paine's *Age of Reason* was published in three parts: Part 1 in 1794, Part 2 in 1795, but Part 3, which was ready for publication in 1802, was delayed until 1807 at the urging of Jefferson. The initial publication went through twenty-one editions between 1794 and 1800. Jefferson was a great admirer of Paine and was closely associated with him in the public mind.

29. On the role of the Enlightenment in the emergence of modern biblical criticism, see Reventlow, *The History of Biblical Interpretation,* vol. 4: *From the Enlightenment to the Twentieth Century;* Alan J. Hauser and Duane F. Watson, eds., *A History of Biblical Interpretation,* vol. 3: *The Enlightenment Through the Nineteenth Century;* and Sheehan, *The Enlightenment Bible.* For deistic approaches to the Bible, see Lucci, *Scripture and Deism.* J. W. Brown shows that the critical study of the Bible, as distinct from purely rationalistic demurrers, only found an American foothold in the nineteenth century, and then in New England. See *The Rise of Biblical Criticism in America.*

30. To Van der Kemp (July 30, 1816) Jefferson wrote, "Ridicule is the only weapon which can be used against unintelligible propositions. Ideas must be distinct before reason can act upon them; and no man ever had a distinct idea of the trinity. It is mere Abracadabra of the mountebanks calling themselves priests of Jesus." He thanked the publishers Wells and Lilly (April 1, 1818) for a sermon on the unity of God, which he hopes will help toward "the disbandment of the unintelligible Athanasian jargon of 3. being 1. and 1. being 3." To Jared Sparks (November 4, 1820) Jefferson opined, "The metaphysical insanities of Athanasius, of Loyola, and of Calvin are, to my understanding, mere relapses into polytheism, differing from paganism only by being more unintelligible." To James Smith (December 8, 1822) Jefferson wrote that the doctrine of the Trinity was a product "of the fanatic Athanasius. The hocus-pocus phantasm of a god like another Cerberus, with one body and three heads, had its birth and growth in the blood of thousands and thousands of martyrs. . . . The Athanasian paradox that one

is three, and three but one, is so incomprehensible to the human mind, that no candid man can say he has any idea of it, and how can he believe in what presents no idea? He who thinks he does only deceives himself."

31. Priestley's influence is discussed in Conkin, "Priestley and Jefferson." Jefferson was introduced to Priestley's work by Richard Price, a liberal London clergyman who, at Jefferson's request (letter of July 12, 1789) for some literature on Socinianism, supplied him with a few of Priestley's essays.

32. Among many other theological works of Priestley, the most important were *Institutes of Natural and Revealed Religion*, 3 vols. (1772–74); *Disquisitions Relating to Matter and Spirit* (1777); *A Harmony of the Evangelists* (1777); and *An History of Early Opinions Concerning Jesus Christ* (1786).

33. For Priestley's biography and the various dimensions of his thought, see now (in addition to Holt, *A Life of Joseph Priestley*) Schofield, *The Enlightenment of Joseph Priestley*, and *The Enlightened Joseph Priestley*. Also useful is Wykes and Rivers, eds., *Joseph Priestley, Scientist, Philosopher, and Theologian*.

34. Jefferson variously attests to the book's importance for his thinking. In a letter to Martha Jefferson (April 25, 1803) he said, "I have written to Philadelphia for Doctor Priestley's *History of the Corruptions of Christianity*, which I will send to you, and recommend to an attentive perusal, because it establishes the groundwork of my view of this subject." He wrote to Henry Fry (June 17, 1803), "The work of Dr. Priestley which I sent you has always been a favorite of mine. I consider the doctrines of Jesus as delivered by himself to contain the outlines of the sublimest system of morality that has ever been taught but I hold in the most profound detestation and execration the corruptions of it which have been invented by priestcraft and established by kingcraft constituting a conspiracy of church and state against the civil and religious liberties of mankind." And to John Adams (August 22, 1813) he wrote, "I have read *Corruptions of Christianity and Early Opinions of Jesus* over and over again; and I rest on them as the basis of my own faith. These writings have never been answered, nor can be answered, by quoting historical proofs, as they have done. For these facts therefore I cling to their learning, so much superior to my own."

35. According to Priestley, the essence of Christianity is that "the Universal Parent of mankind commissioned Jesus Christ to invite men to the practice of virtue, by the assurance of his mercy to the penitent, and of his purpose to raise to immortal life and happiness the virtuous and good, but to inflict adequate punishment on the wicked" (*History of the Corruptions of Christianity*, 480).

36. Jefferson to Benjamin Waterhouse, June 26, 1822.

37. Whether and how strongly Jefferson entertained an idea of life after death is highly debatable. For recent discussion, see Scherr, "Thomas Jefferson versus the Historians," 94–101.

38. Some role in Jefferson's developing perspective on Christianity was probably also played by Benjamin Rush, with whom Jefferson was in close conversation in 1798–99. Rush, a devout evangelical Christian, was persistent in his effort to convert Jefferson and toward that end recommended various books to him. Although he failed in the

attempt, Rush may have helped persuade Jefferson of the moral and political importance of the Christian concept of love. In the "Syllabus" he sent to Rush (April 21, 1803)
Jefferson acknowledged that Jesus' "moral doctrines, relating to kindred & friends,
were more pure and perfect than those of the most correct of the philosophers, and
greatly more so than those of the Jews; and they went far beyond both in inculcating
universal philanthropy, not only to kindred and friends, to neighbors and countrymen,
but to all mankind, gathering all into one family, under the bonds of love, charity,
peace, common wants and common aids." Their philosophical and religious differences
are discussed in D'Elia, "Jefferson, Rush."

39. Some years later, writing to William Short (October 31, 1819), Jefferson alluded
to that effort as "the work of two or three nights only, at Washington," which was
"attempted too hastily."

40. For the history of these epitomes of the Gospels, see Adams and Lester, eds.,
Jefferson's Extracts from the Gospels.

41. Priestley's letter to Jefferson of May 7, 1803, makes clear his deep misgivings
about Jefferson's view of Jesus. See also Bowers, *Joseph Priestley and English Unitarianism,* 35.

42. On the role of religion in the election of 1800 and the attacks on Jefferson, see
(among other studies) Gaustad, *Sworn on the Altar of God,* esp. 90–96; Lerche, "Jefferson and the Election of 1800"; O'Brien, "The Religious Issue in the Election of 1800";
Schultz, "'Of Bigotry in Politics and Religion'"; Lambert, "'God—And a Religious
President'"; McDonald, "Was There a Religious Revolution of 1800?"

43. For the history of the idea, see Barnett, *Idol Temples and Crafty Priests;* and for its
elaboration within deism, Harrison, *"Religion" and the Religions in the English Enlightenment,* esp. chap. 3, "The Religious Instinct and Priestly Corruptions: Lord Herbert
and Deism," 61–98; and Champion, *The Pillars of Priestcraft Shaken.*

44. There was in colonial Virginia a long-standing strain of anticlericalism, on which
see Isaac, *The Transformation of Virginia,* 146–57. Jefferson had an especially strong
contempt for Presbyterian clergy and the Calvinist theology they espoused. In writing
to William Short (April 13, 1820) he described them as "the most intolerant of all sects,
the most tyrannical and ambitious; ready at the word of the lawgiver, if such a word
could now be obtained, to put the torch to the pile" (that is, to burn heretics). But
he held in equal disdain, though for different reasons, the federalist clergy of New
England, who were mostly Congregationalists.

45. Thus Luebke, "The Origins of Thomas Jefferson's Anti-Clericalism." But Jefferson held the theory early on: in his *Notes on Religion,* written in 1776, he speaks of
"Christian priests following their ambition and avarice combining with the magistrate
to divide the spoils of the people."

46. On the long-standing role of the Disciples at the University of Virginia, see
chaps. 4–5 below.

47. Jefferson made a simple equation between his own deism and Unitarianism, but
they were by no means the same: Unitarianism still maintained a number of traditional Christian positions that Jefferson rejected. Furthermore, there were important

theological differences between the English Unitarianism of Priestley and the American Unitarianism emerging in Massachusetts, but Jefferson seemed unaware of these and focused only on what Unitarians had in common with deism, namely, the oneness of God. In fact, all American Unitarians were anxious to dissociate themselves from deism. On Jefferson's conception of Unitarianism, see Conkin, "Priestley and Jefferson." For the early history of Unitarianism, see Wright, *The Beginnings of Unitarianism;* and for a concise but lucid overview of American Unitarianism, see Conkin, *American Originals,* 57–109.

48. Jefferson to Thomas Cooper (November 2, 1822). In the same letter he went on to remark, "In our Richmond there is much fanaticism, but chiefly among the women. They have their night meetings and praying parties where, attended by their priests, and sometimes by a hen-pecked husband, they pour forth the effusions of their love to Jesus, in terms as amatory and carnal, as their modesty would permit them to use to a mere earthly lover." The sarcasm conveys a deep distaste.

49. For example, Jefferson's letters to Benjamin Waterhouse (June 20, 1822), to William Short (October 31, 1819; August 4, 1820), and to John Adams (October 12, 1813; April 11, 1823).

50. Thus to William Short he wrote (April 13, 1820), "It is not to be understood that I am with him [Jesus] in all his doctrines. I am a Materialist; he takes the side of Spiritualism; he preaches the efficacy of repentance towards forgiveness of sin; I require a counterpoise of good works to redeem it, etc." And further, "I read [Jesus' teachings] as I do those of other ancient and modern moralists, with a mixture of approbation and dissent."

51. Adrienne Koch, *The Philosophy of Thomas Jefferson,* characterizes Jefferson's materialism, esp. 94–104 (not mechanistic materialism of a metaphysical sort), and 34–36 (conservative materialist). But she judges that "his understanding of materialism was not profound" (36). On Jefferson's sensationism, see Holifield, *The Gentlemen Theologians,* 57–62.

52. Jefferson's definition of religion or religious conviction as "opinion" was fully operative already in his 1779 Bill for Establishing Religious Freedom.

53. Jefferson's letter to Adams of April 8, 1816, also invokes the argument from design (also known as the teleological argument). The argument seeks to prove the existence of God by reference to the appearance of design or purpose in the natural world. It appeals directly to facts of experience and maintains that because many features of the natural world (both objects and processes) seem to be designed for particular purposes, it may be inferred that the natural world is the product of a powerful, intelligent supernatural reality (God). This is not to be confused with the cosmological argument, which simply moves from effect to cause. In addition to the argument from design, Jefferson occasionally appeals to the *consensus gentium,* that is, that the (near) universality of belief in the existence of God proves the existence of God. Thus in writing to Adams (April 11, 1823) he says, "So irresistible are these evidences of an intelligent and powerful Agent, that, of the infinite numbers of men who have existed through all time, they have believed, in the proportion of a million at least to unit, in the

hypothesis of an eternal pre-existence of a Creator, rather than in that of a self-existent universe. Surely this unanimous sentiment renders this more probable, than that of the few in the other hypothesis."

54. See esp. Jefferson's letter to Thomas Law (June 13, 1814) and his letter to John Adams (October 14, 1816) but also his advice to Peter Carr (August 10, 1787) and to Martha Jefferson (December 10, 1783). In his view, atheists were as capable of virtue as the religious. The point is usefully discussed by Scherr, "Thomas Jefferson versus the Historians," 79–88. Little, "The Origins of Perplexity," points up the incoherencies of Jefferson's thought about morality.

55. Similarly, in his letter to John Adams, May 5, 1817: "[Religion] is more than an inner conviction of the existence of the creator; true religion is morality . . . the sublime doctrines of philanthropism and deism taught by Jesus of Nazareth, in which we all agree, constitute one religion."

56. See Bellah, "Civil Religion in America."

57. As noted earlier, even Jefferson's family remained largely ignorant of his religious posture, which suggests that his private life was not marked by religious features. Allusion is sometimes made to Jefferson's monetary contributions to religious causes, to his occasional attendance at church services, and to the religious rhetoric (invariably abstract) found in his public and political addresses, which are taken as evidence that Jefferson was a man of faith. These things should not be neglected, but they must also be considered in the context, on the one hand, of the political value of pro forma religious gestures and, on the other, of the many opportunities Jefferson had, but did not use, to exhibit religious conviction.

58. Healey, *Jefferson on Religion*, 114–15, 175–76, 225–26, suggests that for all of Jefferson's blandishments against "sectarianism," he himself was sectarian insofar as he was a dogmatic rationalist who believed all others were wrong and sought to bring them over to his point of view. The charge is not entirely fair. Jefferson assumed that reason, freely exercised, would lead to the truth even of religion.

2. Jefferson's Vision

1. The terms "secular," "secularism," and "secularity" and their proper meaning and application have been subjected to much recent discussion. A major stimulus has been Charles Taylor's expansive study *A Secular Age*. For discussion among American historians, see Grasso, "The Religious and the Secular." For the conflation and differentiation of "secularism," "neutrality," and "nonsectarianism" in the legal context, see Steven D. Smith, "Nonestablishment 'Under God'?" In the following discussion "secular" carries the sense of "apart from religion" or "absence of religion." Those who would dispute that Jefferson intended the University to be secular in this sense are few and misinterpret the evidence. On "nonsectarianism," see further below, chap. 3.

2. Kohlbrenner, "Religion and Higher Education." Nord, in *Religion and American Education*, remarks that in the eighteenth and early nineteenth centuries "the Bible, prayer, compulsory chapel, and revivals were a fact of life in most colleges, state

sponsored as well as private. Before the Civil War, nine out of ten college presidents were ministers, as were a third of the faculty. Throughout much of the nineteenth century, there were more or less formal religious tests for hiring, and teachers were expected to defend religion in the classroom" (263).

3. For the early years of these southern public institutions, see Knight, ed., *Documentary History of Education in the South*, vol. 3: *Rise of the State University;* Tewksbury, *The Founding of American Colleges and Universities;* Godbold, *The Church College of the Old South;* and Bratt, "Southern Souls and State Schools."

4. The characterization is offered by Johnson, "Sharper Than a Serpent's Tooth." See also Wenger, "Thomas Jefferson, the College of William and Mary, and the University of Virginia."

5. For the bill, see *Papers of Thomas Jefferson*, ed. Boyd, 2:535–43. A thorough discussion is given by Thomson, "The Reform of the College of William and Mary."

6. In addition, the bill would disband the Indian school in favor of simply hiring a missionary to Indians, although the bill itself gives far less emphasis to evangelism than to what might be called anthropological fieldwork among native Americans, the results of which would be deposited with the college.

7. Jefferson complained in his *Autobiography* that under its original charter William and Mary was "an establishment purely of the Church of England; the Visitors were required to be all of that Church; the Professors to subscribe it's 39 articles; it's students to learn it's catechism; and one of its fundamental objects was declared to be to raise up Ministers for that church."

8. According to Brydon, *Virginia's Mother Church*, 2:432–33, the changes greatly weakened the Anglican Church, which for the next forty years "had no institution for training its young men for its own ministry," and served to foster within the college an "attitude of antagonism toward organized religion."

9. The original members of the board included relatives of Jefferson (nephews Peter Carr and Dabney Carr, and son-in-law Thomas Mann Randolph) and two of his close friends, George Divers and Wilson Cary Nicholas. All would have deferred to Jefferson on questions of education.

10. Thomas Jefferson to Thomas Cooper, October 7, 1814.

11. On Rice, see Stoops, "Engrossing the Education of the Country"; and Swift, "Thomas Jefferson, John Holt Rice and Education in Virginia."

12. Rice, "An Excursion into the Country," 547.

13. Rice, review of *The Mountaineer*, 373.

14. Speece, *The Mountaineer*, 189–90. The essays collected and published in this book had been previously published in the weekly *Republican Farmer*.

15. When the commission was appointed, Jefferson wrote to Joseph Cabell (February 26, 1818) that it might be better if Cabell rather than Jefferson were to represent their district, because "there are fanatics both in religion and politics who, without knowing me personally, have long been taught to consider me a raw head and bloody bones, and as we can afford to lose no votes . . . I do think it would be better that you should be named for our district."

16. For all of the questions other than location, the commission, when it convened, elected a subcommittee of six members (consisting of Jefferson, James Madison, Spencer Roane, Archibald Stuart, William Dade, and James Breckenridge) to bring a report to the commission. The report of that subcommittee not only incorporated all of Jefferson's ideas but was also written in his own hand.

17. The mention of languages in this context is gratuitous because Greek and Latin would be taught in any case in the School of Ancient Languages and without any religious purpose, whereas Hebrew, which was customarily taught in denominational schools, is mentioned here specifically for its religious relevance. However, Hebrew was not regularly a part of the University's nineteenth-century curriculum. For details, see below, Appendix B, "The Teaching of Hebrew at the University."

18. The work, entitled *An Essay on the Best System of Liberal Education Adapted to the Genius of the Government of the United States,* went through many editions and had an enormous influence on American education.

19. Knox, *A Vindication of the Religion of Mr. Jefferson.*

20. It is clear from a later letter of Knox's to Jefferson (November 30, 1818) that Knox would have liked an appointment, but equally clear from a letter of Jefferson to Knox (December 11, 1818) that Jefferson was not interested.

21. Cabell, ed., *Early History of the University of Virginia in Letters of Jefferson and Cabell,* 165.

22. Rice, review of Cooper's *Memoirs.*

23. Ibid., 70–73.

24. William H. Cabell to Joseph C. Cabell, March 21, 1820.

25. John Holt Rice to John Hartwell Cocke, January 6, 1820.

26. Thomas Cooper to Thomas Jefferson, March 1, 1820.

27. Thomas Jefferson to Thomas Cooper, March 13, 1820.

28. Thomas Jefferson to John Hartwell Cocke, April 9, 1820, and Thomas Jefferson to Robert B. Taylor, May 16, 1820. To Taylor, Jefferson wrote: "Another subject on this, as on former occasions, gave us embarrassment. You may have heard of the hue and cry raised from the different pulpits on our appointment of Dr. Cooper, whom they charge with Unitarianism as boldly as if they knew the fact, and as presumptuously as if it were a crime, and one for which, like Servetus, he should be burned; and perhaps you may have seen the particular attack made on him in the Evangelical magazine. For myself I was not disposed to regard the denunciations of these satellites of religious inquisition, but our colleagues, better judges of popular feeling, thought that they were not to be altogether neglected, and that it might be better to relieve Dr. Cooper, ourselves and the institution from this crusade."

29. On Cooper's life and career, see Malone, *The Public Life of Thomas Cooper.*

30. Joseph C. Cabell to Thomas Jefferson, January 7, 1822, in Cabell, *Early History of the University,* 230.

31. Rice, *Virginia Evangelical and Literary Magazine* 5 (1822): 185.

32. Report to the President and Directors of the Literary Fund, October 7, 1822, in Cabell, *Early History of the University,* Appendix M, 474–75.

33. If the idea emerged within the board, it would probably have come from John H. Cocke or Chapman Johnson, both devout religious conservatives. A similar scheme had been proposed years earlier by St. George Tucker in his "Sketch of a Plan." See Richard B. Davis, *Intellectual Life in Jefferson's Virginia;* and Roy Honeywell, *The Educational Work of Thomas Jefferson,* 168–69. Differently, John Holt Rice had suggested in his magazine that each of the major sects be invited to endow its own professorship within (not merely adjacent to) the University: "The plan, humbly suggested, is to allow Jews, Catholics, Protestants, Episcopalians, Methodists, Baptists, any and all sects, to endow Professorships, and to nominate their respective professors" ("An Excursion into the Country," 548).

34. Jefferson to Thomas Cooper, November 2, 1822. Joseph Cabell was delighted with this scheme and characterized it as "the Franklin that has drawn the lightning from the cloud of opposition" (Joseph Cabell to Thomas Jefferson, February 3, 1823).

35. This opposition was in part a simple protest by taxpayers against the high cost of building the University, but it was rooted also in the idea that the University was an elitist institution from which only the wealthy and their sons might benefit, while provisions were not being made for educating the less well-to-do.

36. Among the many commentators who have discussed the suggestion of adjacent theological schools, I have been surprised to find so few who regard it as a political ploy rather than a serious proposal. Entirely of that view is Levy, *Jefferson and Civil Liberties,* 11–14.

37. *Minutes of the Board of Visitors,* October 24, 1824. These and other enactments were included in the published *Enactments Relating to the Constitution and Government of the University of Virginia,* 29. There are some curious incoherencies in the regulations: students are said to be "free, and expected to attend regular religious worship" at the theological establishment of their choice on the condition that they do so in the mornings before classes, but they began at 7:30, so that any student wishing to attend a religious service would have to rise very early; and whereas the first regulation suggests that students attend services at an adjacent seminary, the second, together with the following allocation of the Rotunda's rooms, implies that worship services would take place there.

38. "The University of Virginia," *Old Dominion Magazine* 4, part 8 (1870): 655.

39. See below, chap. 4. It is interesting to see that three decades later, Rev. Henry P. Tappan, the first president of the newly established University of Michigan, commented, "Our institution, being a State institution, and, therefore, connected with no particular denomination, cannot establish a Theological School on the University fund. But it is to be hoped that the different denominations will establish professorships in the different branches of theological science in this town. In some of these branches they might unite; in others they would choose to establish separate professorships" (*A Discourse,* 47–48). Tappan's idea seems to be an echo of the Virginia scheme.

40. Trent, *English Culture in Virginia,* 119–21. John Adams was one who disapproved, and he wrote to Jefferson (January 22, 1825): "There are sufficient scholars

in America to fill your Professorships and Tutorships with more active ingenuity and independent minds than you can bring from Europe." Jefferson defended his recourse to Europe in a letter to Edward Everett, July 21, 1825.

41. The letter, written November 23, 1823, also offered Gilmer the professorship in law at the University. Gilmer's response, however, has been preserved: Francis Walker Gilmer to Thomas Jefferson, December 3, 1823.

42. "Agenda for the University of Virginia," April 26, 1824.

43. Gilmer's letters indicate that clergy were disqualified *de jure:* he refers to "the incapacity of being of clerical character" (Francis Walker Gilmer to Thomas Jefferson, September 15, 1824, in Richard B. Davis, ed., *Correspondence of Thomas Jefferson and Francis Walker Gilmer*). Gilmer's letter to George Long (August 27, 1824) reassures him on the subject of religion: "Allay your fears, I pray, about religion. Far from requiring uniformity, we scrupulously avoid having clergymen of any sort connected with the University, not because we have no religion, but because we have too many kinds. All that we shall require of each professor is that he shall say nothing about the doctrines which divide the sects" (Trent, *English Culture in Virginia*). John Adams, in his letter to Jefferson of January 22, 1825, complained: "Europeans are all deeply tainted with prejudices, both ecclesiastical and temporal, which they can never get rid of. They are all infected with Episcopal and Presbyterian creeds and confessions of faith. They all believe that great principle which has produced this boundless universe, Newton's universe, and Hershell's universe, came down to this little ball to be spit upon by the Jews. And until this awful blasphemy is gotten rid of there will never be any liberal science in the world." Adams was arguing against hiring European professors, but his strongly expressed opinion comported with Jefferson's determination not to hire any clergymen.

44. Tucker, Bonnycastle, Long, Key, and Dunglison were Anglicans, Blaetterman was a Lutheran, Emmet was Catholic. Henry Tutwiler, a member of the first class at the University, later commented, "It is now well known that in selecting the first faculty, which was done by Mr. Jefferson, no inquiry was made as to their religious beliefs; and if any of them were not believers in the Christian religion, it was certainly not known to students" (*The Early Years of the University of Virginia*, reprinted in the *Alumni Bulletin* as "The Early Years of the University of Virginia," an address delivered by Tutweiler to the alumni association of the University, June 29, 1882).

45. On the scope and aims of "moral philosophy," see Wilson Smith, *Professors and Public Ethics*, 3–43; Holifield, *The Gentleman Theologians*, 127–54; and Reuben, *The Making of the Modern University*, 19–23.

46. Jefferson had written to his nephew, Peter Carr (August 10, 1787), concerning moral philosophy: "I think it lost time to attend lectures in this branch. He who made us would have been a pitiful bungler if he had made the rules of our moral conduct a matter of science."

47. Chapman Johnson to John H. Cocke, October 5, 1827, Cocke Family Papers, University of Virginia Library, Special Collections. It appears, however, from Cabell's letter to Jefferson of January 7, 1822 (quoted above), that Cabell did *not*

think that clergy should be excluded from the faculty, and that he and Chapman Johnson were agreed in this. But Cabell may have felt obliged, nevertheless, to follow Jefferson's rule.

48. Madison had written to Edward Everett (March 9, 1823), expressing his agreement with Jefferson's exclusion of clergymen from the faculty: "I am not surprised at the dilemma produced at your University, by making Theological Professorships an integral part of the System. The anticipation of such an one, led to the omission in ours; the Visitors being merely authorized to open a public Hall for religious occasions, under *impartial* regulations; with the opportunity to different sects to establish their Theological Schools, so near that Students of the University may respectively attend the religious exercises in them. . . . A University with Sectarian professorships, becomes of course, a Sectarian monopoly: with professorships of rival sects, it would be an arena of Theological Gladiators: without any such professorship, it must incur, for a time at least, the imputation of irreligious tendencies if not designs. The last difficulty was thought more manageable, than either of the others."

49. *North American Review* 10 (1820): 115–36, quotation on 130.

50. George Pierson to Albert Pierson, November 2, 1825, University of Virginia Library, Special Collections, MS 11897.

51. Hawks, "The Character of Jefferson," 19. The next year the *Southern Literary Messenger,* which was located in Richmond, published a review of this review, seeking to salvage Jefferson (and the University) from Reverend Hawks's attack.

52. Tyng, "To the Episcopal Recorder."

53. George Tucker, "Defence of the Character of Thomas Jefferson," 25–26.

54. See Neufeldt, "Religion, Morality, and Schooling."

55. Rice, *Virginia Evangelical and Literary Magazine* 3 (1820): 587.

56. Thomas Jefferson to Thomas Cooper, November 2, 1822. Jefferson expressed similar misgivings about student discipline in a letter to George Ticknor, July 16, 1823.

57. George Tucker, *The Life of Thomas Jefferson,* 2:478–79.

58. Hasler, "On College Government"; Radbill, ed., "The Autobiographical Ana of Robley Dunglison," 29–30.

59. A full account of student disorder at the University is given by Bruce, *History of the University of Virginia,* 2:246–317. See also Wall, "Students and Student Life"; Wagoner, "Honor and Dishonor at Mr. Jefferson's University"; and the recent account of Bowman and Santos, *Rot, Riot and Rebellion.*

60. Philodemos, "Letter VII," *Virginia Evangelical and Literary Magazine* 9 (1826): 350–54.

61. On student disorder at other institutions in the early nineteenth century, see Allmendinger, *Paupers and Scholars;* Kett, *Rites of Passage,* 51–61; and Novak, *The Rights of Youth.*

62. Tutwiler, *Early Years of the University,* 6.

63. *Virginia Evangelical and Literary Magazine* 11 (1828): 303–8.

64. Robert Lewis Dabney, *A Memorial of the Christian Life and Character of Francis S. Sampson,* 8.

65. Godbold, *The Church College of the Old South*, 147–51. The University's disappointing enrollments in its first two decades were attributed to "injurious impressions as to the irreligious tendencies of the institution" by the "Report from the Committee of Schools and Colleges," Document No. 41 in the *Journal of the House of Delegates of the Commonwealth of Virginia, 1844–1845*. See also "A Short Historical Notice of the University of Virginia," *Corks and Curls* 1 (1888): 23.

3. The Early Years

1. Originally, the room was the western oval room on the main (middle) floor of the Rotunda; see *Enactments Relating to the Constitution*, 57. Subsequently, beginning in 1841 or 1842, religious services were held in the eastern basement room of the Rotunda, which was more commodious. See further below.

2. Madison's religious views are, if anything, more furtive than Jefferson's. For what can be said about Madison's religious ideas, see Munoz, "Religion in the Life, Thought, and Presidency of James Madison"; Holmes, *The Faiths of the Founding Fathers*, 91–98; and Olree, "'Pride, Ignorance and Knavery.'"

3. He was the rector of what is now Grace Episcopal Church, in Keswick.

4. He was the pastor of the South Plains Presbyterian Church, in Keswick.

5. Meade, *Sermon Delivered in the Rotunda*, 21.

6. Ibid., 22–23.

7. *Minutes of the Faculty*, vol. 2, for May 25, 1829.

8. Meade, *Old Churches*, 2:56.

9. John B. Minor, "Historical Sketches of Virginia," 260.

10. Oddly, Meade attributed his alienation from the University not to Virginians, or even to Americans, but to "foreigners, who were allowed to forbid a minister of Virginia to be heard in the University of Virginia" (*Old Churches*, 2:56). He must have been referring to the professors recruited from England.

11. *Journal of the Chairman of the Faculty*, University of Virginia, vol. 1, entry for November 2, 1829.

12. The University's *Catalogue of Officers and Students* for the session of 1831–32 lists the title "Chaplain" at the end of the list of faculty, but supplies no name of a chaplain. This at least signals that the idea of a University chaplain had some currency, and that some official status, if not faculty status, was attached to it. It is noteworthy, however, that in subsequent issues of the *Catalogue of Officers and Students* reference to a chaplain does not occur again until the session of 1835–36, when at the end of the list of faculty we find "Rev. Robert Ryland, Chaplain."

13. Robert Lewis Dabney, *Memorial of the Christian Life of Francis S. Sampson*, 16–17.

14. Papers of the Proctors of the University of Virginia, 1819–1905, University of Virginia Library, Special Collections, RG 5/3/2737 3730.

15. *Minutes of the Board of Visitors*, July 10, 1833.

16. He is mentioned in the chairman's *Journal* already in the entry for January 13, 1833. The chairman noted that "Mr. Ryland, the principal of a manual labour

school, and who has during the vacation been attending the lectures of several of the Schools of the University, has permission to preach in the Rotunda today and as long as he stays here." The "manual labour school" was the Virginia Baptist Seminary, which Ryland established in 1832 at Spring Farm in Henrico County, and which was the precursor of Richmond College and the University of Richmond. Ryland, a native of King and Queen County, after gaining preparatory education at an academy called Humanity Hall in Hanover County, attended Columbian College in Washington (later to be known as George Washington University), obtaining an A.B. degree in 1826 and an A.M. in 1831. Licensed to preach in 1825, and ordained to the Baptist ministry in 1827, he was pastor of a church in Lynchburg from 1827 to 1831 before becoming superintendent of the Virginia Baptist Seminary. Ryland later went on to a distinguished career as a preacher, educator, and scholar, but in 1833, while he was attending lectures at the University, he was a willing and available preacher.

17. The terms "nonsectarian" or "unsectarian" seem to have been coined only between 1825 and 1835. The concept of nonsectarianism took root in the early nineteenth century in connection with whether and how religion might be taught in public schools. See Steven K. Green, *The Second Disestablishment*, chap. 3. Jefferson often spoke of "sects," but he seems to have applied that term to whole religious systems as well as to particular "denominations" within those systems.

18. See Buckley, "After Establishment," esp. 474–80.

19. On "nonsectarianism" as itself a Protestant Christian conception, see Feldman, "Non-Sectarianism Reconsidered," esp. 65–81. Nonsectarianism was "a response to the increased religious heterogeneity within states in the aftermath of the Second Great Awakening," which had fueled the proliferation, growth, competition, and conflict of Protestant groups.

20. *Journal of the Chairman*, vol. 5, entries for October 28 to November 1, 1833. Reverend Hammett seems to have been agreeable to reelection, and stated to the chairman that he wanted to remain at the University if funding could be obtained that would be equal to what he would be paid if elected chaplain to the U.S. Congress.

21. Ibid., entry for June 24, 1834.

22. Ibid., vol. 6, entry for January 13, 1835.

23. Letter of J. W. Goss, Charlottesville, Virginia, December 30, 1835, as appearing in the Campbellite publication *Millennial Harbinger* 7 (1836): 86. The contentious split of the Charlottesville Baptist church between Baptists and Campbellites is discussed by Darst, *Ante-Bellum Virginia Disciples*, 50–51.

24. *Journal of the Chairman*, vol. 8, entry for November 3, 1838.

25. Ibid., entry for November 6, 1838.

26. For a clear account of the complicated early history of the Disciples, see Conkin, "Restoration Christianity." On the Disciples, see further below, chaps. 4 and 5.

27. *Journal of the Chairman*, vol. 5, entry for October, 1833. What was in question was presumably religious choral music.

28. Ibid., entry for February 6, 1833. According to Robert Lewis Dabney, another student, Francis S. Sampson, was "the most active agent in originating the first Sabbath

school in the University, and was its superintendent" (*Memorial of the Christian Life of Francis S. Sampson*, 17). Permission for the Sunday school was granted, but the request to hold it in the Rotunda was denied. Subsequently, however, the Board of Visitors empowered the chairman of the faculty to permit the use of rooms "in any of the public buildings" for Sunday school meetings (*Minutes of the Board of Visitors*, July 10, 1833).

29. *American Annals of Education*, 3rd series, 5 (1835): 302–3.

30. John B. Minor, "Historical Sketches," 262.

31. Tyng, "To the Episcopal Recorder."

32. Minor, "University of Virginia," 53.

33. Meade, *Old Churches*, 2:56.

34. Thomas Jefferson to Arthur S. Brockenbrough, April 21, 1825.

35. The most thorough treatment of the history of the University Chapel is by Dashiell, "Between Earthly Wisdom and Heavenly Truth." His study naturally emphasizes the architectural questions but touches on religious attitudes in the University. The history of the chapel is also sketched in the "University Chapel Historic Structures Report," Final Report, January 2008, prepared by Quinn Evans, Architects (chap. 2, "A Brief History").

36. At least some members of the Board of Visitors happily received and supported this initiative by the faculty. W. C. Rives wrote to Tucker (March 23, 1835) with "great satisfaction in expressing my entire approbation" of the project to procure for the University "the advantages of regular and impressive religious services." Letters of George Tucker, University of Virginia Library, Special Collections, MS 8332.

37. *Minutes of the Board of Visitors*, July 8, 1835.

38. This seems to have been part of Visitor James M. Mason's refusal to give his assent to Tucker's proposal: James Mason to George Tucker, March 29, 1835, Letters of George Tucker, University of Virginia Library, Special Collections, MS 8332.

39. This too was a concern of James Mason, who commented to Tucker that there was no authority "to erect any building within the confines of the University" (ibid.).

40. Renewed attention to the question may have been prompted by a student petition for the construction of a chapel at the University. This lengthy petition, composed in 1837 by Professor Bonnycastle on behalf of the students, was contained in a communication from B. B. Minor in the *Alumni Bulletin of the University of Virginia* 3 (1897): 102–3. It is noted there that the petition was not prepared in time to get enough student signatures and so was not formally presented to the board, but that the board was informed of it. The petition is reproduced in Appendix A below.

41. Benjamin B. Minor, "University of Virginia," 54.

42. This is shown by various posters (broadsides) announcing meetings in "the chapel" by the Philomathean Society, the Jefferson Society, the Aesculapian Society, and the Parthenon Society; University of Virginia Library, Special Collections, V7, V72 (1850), U75 (1851–52), A47 (1852), P27 (1852). The *Minutes of the Board of Visitors* for June 26, 1867, contain the notice that "the use of the Chapel (from the commencement of the next session) is hereby granted to the Washington Society for the purpose of holding their meetings. Upon the express conditions that the Society at its own

expense shall furnish the room suitably—keep it at all times in proper condition for publick worship or morning prayer meetings, and surrender it upon due notice from the Board of Visitors."

43. See Schweiger, *The Gospel Working Up*, 24 and 55–64.

44. The certificate is preserved as "Drawings of a Proposed Plan for a University of Virginia Chapel, 1858–1862," University of Virginia Library, Special Collections, RG 31/1/2:1.771.

45. In a letter to Madison (November 30, 1824) Jefferson describes the content of moral philosophy as "mental science generally, including ideology, general grammar and ethics."

46. For biographical details, see Moore, "Gen. John Hartwell Cocke of Bremo 1780–1866."

47. Cocke's evolving and devolving views on slavery are explored in detail by Coyner, "John Hartwell Cocke of Bremo," 1:305–71, 2:372–590. Ultimately, late in his life and under the duress of the Civil War, Cocke returned to a pro-slavery position.

48. On Cocke's temperance work, see Lucien Minor, "General John H. Cocke of Virginia."

49. Jefferson responded with a note expressing admiration for the Harrisons' filial piety and extending the invitation for a following weekday.

50. Barringer, Garnett, and Page, eds., *The University of Virginia*, 1:130.

51. Broadus, "A Memorial of Gessner Harrison," 370.

52. Grayson, "Old Christ Church, Charlottesville," 53.

53. Stephen Smith, in *Addresses Commemorative of James L. Cabell*, 40.

54. William S. Forbes, in ibid., 6.

55. Godbold, *The Church College of the Old South*, 157.

56. See Sullivan, *William Holmes McGuffey*.

57. Westerhoff, *McGuffey and His Readers*, 103–4.

58. Bruce, History of the University, 3:135.

59. Patteson, "William H. McGuffey," 14.

60. "The University of Virginia," *Virginia Historical Register, and Literary Advertiser* 2 (1849): 56–57. The substance of this piece is on the religious and moral condition of the University, and it includes the comment that "I doubt whether there is found in any College in our country a more decided, strong, and salutary religious influence."

61. McGuffey did serve as the regular supply pastor at the Charlottesville Presbyterian Church from the fall of 1863 to the spring of 1866.

62. Thornton, "The Life and Services of William Holmes McGuffey."

63. The dispute played out over several months in the pages of the *Religious Herald*, beginning in the issue of January 13, 1859, with a piece titled "The University of Virginia a Pedobaptist Institution?" Defenses of McGuffey and the University appeared in the issues of March 17 and March 31. John Broadus, a firm Baptist, inquired about the matter to McGuffey, a staunch Presbyterian, and McGuffey defended himself in a letter to Broadus of March 5, 1859, University of Virginia Library, Special Collections, MSS File 3458.

64. Culbreth, *The University of Virginia,* 435. Cf. Lamb, "John B. Minor" (a pamphlet of tribute originally published by the Virginia Law Register, 1895), 8–9. Lamb remarks that Minor's "firm hold of the Christian faith and his constant effort to live by its teaching was the animating spirit of his life and work."

65. Culbreth, *The University of Virginia,* 431–32.

66. Lamb, "John B. Minor," 128; and cf. "Christian Work in the University," *Alumni Bulletin of the University of Virginia* 6, no. 3 (1899): 75.

67. On the tradition of "evidences of Christianity," see Bozeman, *Protestants in an Age of Science,* 139–43; and Holifield, *The Gentlemen Theologians,* 85–96.

68. The book consists of the Cole Lectures, delivered at Vanderbilt University. See also Smith's shorter works, *Thoughts on the Discord and Harmony; Nature, A Witness for the Unity;* and *The Bible: God's Last and Best Revelation.* In contrast to these studies seeking to reconcile science and the Bible, Smith published only one of straightforward science, *Outlines of Physics,* a summary of his lectures.

69. Thornton, "The Devout Natural Philosopher," 11.

70. Professor Smith became an emeritus professor on his retirement, but because of an oversight by President Alderman was permitted to continue residence in his Pavilion until his death in 1928. Consequently, he held, and will forever hold, the record for the occupancy of a Pavilion, having resided in Pavilion V for 69 years, from 1859 to 1928.

71. A. T. Robertson, *The Life and Letters of John Albert Broadus,* 106.

72. See Thornton, "John Albert Broadus." In Robertson's biography, *The Life and Letters of John Albert Broadus,* Broadus's time in Charlottesville and at the University is treated on pp. 55–74 and 96–167. Broadus was a very productive scholar. Among his books were *The Preparation and Delivery of Sermons* (1870), *Lectures on the History of Preaching* (1876, rev. 1896), *Commentary on the Gospel of Matthew* (1886), *Sermons and Addresses* (1886), *Jesus of Nazareth* (1890), *Memoir of James Petigru Boyce* (1893), and *Harmony of the Gospels* (1893).

73. *Watchman of the South* 4, no. 50 (August 5, 1841): 198, cols. 4–6. The paper, published in Richmond, described itself as "Devoted to the promotion of practical piety, the diffusion of religion and general intelligence, and the propagation of the distinctive tenets and institutions of the Presbyterian Church."

74. *Life and Letters of William Barton Rogers,* 1:192.

75. See Feuer, "America's First Jewish Professor," esp. 185–87 and 190–94. Feuer, without saying so, at least insinuates that anti-Semitism was a factor in Sylvester's departure from Virginia. Parshall, *James Joseph Sylvester: Jewish Mathematician,* 76, is not inclined to think anti-Semitism played a role, save as a dimension of his foreignness. It is clear from his letters, however, that Sylvester's Jewishness was a contributing factor in his failure to secure a position at Columbia University in 1843. See Parshall, *James Joseph Sylvester: Life and Work in Letters,* 13, with n. 37. Unable to secure appointment at other American universities, Sylvester returned to England and worked as an actuary until he became professor of mathematics at the Royal Military Academy in 1855, subsequently professor of mathematics at Johns Hopkins University (1876), and then at Oxford University (1883). He died in 1897.

76. William R. Johnson to William Barton Rogers, February 14, 1845, in *Life and Letters of William Barton Rogers*, 1:241.

77. This exemption had already been set forth in the *University of Virginia Catalogue* for 1833–34, but without elaboration.

78. *Southern Literary Messenger* 22 (1856): 241–69, on 260.

79. See above, chap. 2.

80. For the history of the seminary, see Sweetser, *A Copious Fountain*. The study makes no reference, however, to the discussions between the synod and the University.

81. The lectures were published as W. H. Ruffner, ed., *Lectures on the Evidences of Christianity*—a hefty volume of more than 600 pages.

82. *Minutes of the Board of Visitors*, March 17, 1859.

83. Ibid., June 25, 1859.

84. Ibid.

85. Ibid., June 30, 1860.

86. "The University of Virginia," *Old Dominion Magazine* 4 (1870): 655.

87. The last issue of the *University of Virginia Record* to carry this notice was for 1936–37.

88. *Southern Literary Messenger* 20, no. 2 (February 1854): 74.

89. John Holt Rice, "Review of *The Mountaineer*," 371–73, emphases in the original.

90. The "Report from the Committee of Schools and Colleges" to the House of Delegates in 1845 stated that for the suspicion of irreligion at the University "no shadow of a pretext now exists, or has for many years existed," and went on to say that "in no similar institution in this country is there a greater degree of respect voluntarily accorded to the ministers and ordinances of christianity, and in few are more numerous instances to be found of devout piety as well among the students as the professors and their families." *Journal of the House of Delegates of the Commonwealth of Virginia 1844–1845*, "Document No. 41," 5.

91. Barringer, Garnett, and Page, *The University of Virginia*, 1:170.

92. Ruffner, in his introduction to *Lectures on the Evidences of Christianity*, ix–x.

93. Andrew Dickson White, *Autobiography*, 1:271–72.

4. From the Civil War to World War I

1. On the religious background and aftermath of the conflict, see, among many studies, Charles R. Wilson, *Baptized in Blood*, summarized in his "The Religion of the Lost Cause"; Faust, *The Creation of Confederate Nationalism;* R. M. Miller, Stout, and Wilson, eds., *Religion and the American Civil War;* and Noll, *The Civil War as a Theological Crisis*.

2. Bishop Atticus Haygood opined in 1880 that since the Civil War, "the controlling sentiment of the southern people in city and hamlet, in camp and field, among the white and the black, has been religious" (quoted in Woodward, *Origins of the New South*, 169).

3. A full discussion of the war years is provided by Bruce, *History of the University*, 3:256–340; see also Jordan, "The University of Virginia during the Civil War," accessed online February 11, 2019. A brief account by an observer is Francis H. Smith's in Barringer, Garnett, and Page, *The University of Virginia*, 1:171–73.

4. For the effects of the war on Southern colleges and universities, see esp. Stetar, "In Search of a Direction"; and Wagoner, "Higher Education and Transitions in Southern Culture."

5. In 1865, 258 students enrolled, less than half the prewar number. Enrollments at the University did not reach antebellum levels until 1904.

6. On the development in America of the research university, see Veysey, *The Emergence of the American University;* Hofstadter, "The Revolution in Higher Education"; Rudolph, *The American College and University;* Pierson, "American Universities in the Nineteenth Century"; Goodchild and Wechsler, eds., *The History of Higher Education*, part 4: "The Rise of American Universities"; and Geiger, *The History of American Higher Education*, 315–64.

7. Still useful on the origins and nature of the research university is Walter P. Metzger, *Academic Freedom in the Age of the University*, originally published in Richard Hofstadter and Walter P. Metzger, *The Development of Academic Freedom in the United States* (New York: Columbia University Press, 1955), and later separately published under its own title.

8. Andrew Dickson White, the president of Cornell and a staunch advocate of free scientific inquiry, put a sharp point on the issue with his two-volume work *A History of the Warfare of Science with Theology in Christendom* (1896). White differentiated between religion and theology, considering theology as dogmatic and antiscientific. The conflict thesis he espoused has few advocates today among historians of science. See, e.g., Lindberg and Numbers, *God and Nature.*

9. Turner, in *Without God, Without Creed,* points up how the effort by religionists to base religious knowledge on a scientific epistemology ultimately backfired and tended instead to promote agnosticism and advance secularization.

10. For a careful account of the demise of concern with religion and morality, see Reuben, *The Making of the Modern University.*

11. Hawkins, "Charles W. Eliot, University Reform and Religious Faith," 194.

12. Ross, "Religious Influences in the Development of State Colleges"; and see the apologia provided by James Angell, president of the University of Michigan, in "Religious Life in Our State Universities."

13. It was perhaps symptomatic that when the Association of American Universities was formed in 1900, the University of Virginia was not included. It was not thought to be an academically distinguished institution at the beginning of the twentieth century and had not yet attained the status of a research university. Subsequently, the University of Virginia became the first Southern institution to gain membership. At the time, the University of Virginia was comparatively quite poor: of the thirty institutions with endowments of as much as a million dollars in 1900, only two were in the South, and they were Tulane and Vanderbilt.

14. Virginia continued to be headed by its Board of Visitors and a rotating chairmanship of the faculty, while research universities developed under the bold leadership of reform-minded, forward-looking presidents such as Charles Eliot of Harvard, Daniel Gilman of Johns Hopkins, James Angell of Michigan, and Andrew Dickson White of Cornell. Virginia finally opted for a president. He was Edwin A. Alderman, installed in 1904. Although in the late nineteenth century the University benefited from some philanthropic support and some internal reforms, they made no large or lasting differences. See James T. Moore, "The University and the Readjusters."

15. The standard history of the YMCA is Hopkins, *History of the Y.M.C.A.*

16. For the history of the dispute, consult the well-informed comments of McIlhany, "Founding of the First Young Men's Christian Association." The founding date is usually taken to be October 12, 1858, when the constitution and bylaws were adopted. Of further interest in the same issue are "Reminiscences of the Young Men's Christian Association," by three of the founding members of the group: J. William Jones, John L. Johnson, and L. M. Blackford. A general history of the YMCA at the University was written by Milton R. Allen, "A History of the Young Men's Christian Association."

17. See Long, *The Revival of 1857–58.*

18. Letter of J. N. Cullingworth to Prof. Charles W. Kent, September 28, 1908, University of Virginia Library, Special Collections, MS 1360.

19. McIlhany, "Founding of the First Young Men's Christian Association," 50.

20. Shedd, *Two Centuries of Student Christian Movements,* 98–100, discusses the YMCA at the University of Virginia. For contemporary evidence, see "Religion in the University of VA," *The Review* 1, no. 6 (May 18, 1860); "Religious Intelligence," *Richmond Daily Dispatch,* February 13, 1860, 2; July 10, 1860, 1; and *Virginia University Magazine* 5 (April 1861): 380–81.

21. *University of Virginia Catalogue,* 1878–79, 55–56.

22. *Minutes of the Board of Visitors,* November 15, 1883.

23. *Virginia University Magazine,* n.s. 23, no. 3 (December 1883): 191.

24. *Virginia University Magazine,* n.s. 23, no. 8 (May 1884): 492, reported that "through the active exertions of Mr. Glazebrook and of our busy ladies, more than $12,000 has been secured, and Mrs. Chas S. Venable has generously made up the amount to the $15,000 required."

25. *Virginia University Magazine,* n.s. 23, no. 8 (May 1884): 492–93.

26. *Minutes of the Board of Visitors,* June 26, 1884. It is a fair inference that "injury to University property" meant, among other things, intrusion on the Jeffersonian lawn area.

27. The original construction drawings for the chapel have been lost, but a rather full description based on them is provided in the article "Our New Chapel," *Virginia University Magazine,* n.s. 25, no. 2 (November 1885): 104–7.

28. Schele de Vere, *An Address delivered by M. Schele de Vere, L.L.D.*

29. The figure $15,000 comes from "Summary of the Week," *American Architect and Building News,* November 15, 1884, 240 (cited by "University Chapel Historic Structures Report, Final Report," January 24, 2008, 2.4), but the article "The New Chapel,"

Virginia University Magazine 24, no. 1 (October 1884): 53, suggests that this amount was to cover only the stone walls and the roof, and that up to $5,000 more would be needed to complete the building.

30. *Virginia University Magazine*, n.s. 25, no. 6 (March 1886): 367; no. 7 (April 1886): 424; and no. 8 (May 1886): 492–93.

31. *Virginia University Magazine*, n.s. 30, no. 8 (December 1886): 193–95.

32. *Virginia University Magazine*, n.s. 32, no. 3 (December 1888): 228–32, gives an extensive description.

33. Schele de Vere, in his address at the laying of the cornerstone, eulogized Glaze-brook as "the Man to do the great work. . . . And no sooner did he appear among us than all men felt how richly he had been gifted from on high. What burning zeal for the glory of his Master, what powerful, persuasive eloquence, what irresistible earnestness he displayed in the cause which he had so zealously and so successfully made his own." *Virginia University Magazine*, n.s. 24, no. 7 (April 1885): 416, speaks of Glazebrook as "our popular and efficient Chaplain, to whose untiring efforts we owe the erection of the beautiful building, which will ever keep his memory green at this University." Glazebrook (1845–1931) was indeed an able and accomplished man. A decorated Confederate soldier, he was a graduate of VMI and of the Episcopal Theological Seminary of Virginia. Glazebrook left the University in 1885 to become a rector, and thereafter served major parishes in Maryland, Georgia, and New Jersey. He was a member of the Foreign Service from 1914 until his retirement in 1927, serving for a time in Jerusalem. See Kark, *American Consuls in the Holy Land*, 333–34. He was also, incidentally, one of the founders of the Alpha Tau Omega fraternity.

34. *Minutes of the Board of Visitors*, June 27, 1890.

35. The organ room, which was an addition, was a gift of Reverend Glazebrook, and the organ was a gift of alumni in Kentucky. For details on the windows and the organ, see Dashiell, *Between Earthly Wisdom and Heavenly Truth*, 39–43.

36. The old University bell that Jefferson had designed and that had hung in the porch of the Rotunda had cracked and become useless in 1886. Professor Francis Smith sought with the Ladies' Chapel Aid Society to have it recast and hung in the chapel, but that plan appears to have come to nothing. See the correspondence of Francis H. Smith with Johnson Barbour, March 7, 1889, University of Virginia Library, Special Collections, MS 1486: and the *Minutes of the Board of Visitors*, June 27, 1887, and June 24, 1889.

37. Obituary in the *Alumni Bulletin of the University of Virginia* 3 (November 1896): 75–76.

38. *Catalogue of the University of Virginia 1896–97, Announcements 1897–98*, 155.

39. A similar arrangement had been in use at Harvard, where responsibility for supervising worship services rotated among a multidenominational "Board of Preachers." See Hawkins, "Charles W. Eliot," 208–12.

40. The YMCA handbook developed at Virginia was among the earliest. On these handbooks, see Finnegan and Alleman, "The YMCA and the Origins of American Freshman Orientation Programs," esp. 99–104.

41. With the authorization and aid of the International Committee of the YMCA, Professor Davis bought four acres from Caroline H. Davis on November 15, 1887, and an additional acre on May 5, 1888. Funds for the purchase were raised through the International Committee, Cyrus McCormick, New York alumni, current students, and friendly neighbors. The total cost of the five acres was $1,900. This land remained the property of the YMCA until 1931. The purchase of this land by the YMCA was positively commended by the board in 1890 as an enterprise "which cannot fail to contribute materially to the physical well-being of the young men here & ultimately advance the interests of the University," and the Board resolved to render free of charge the use of "carts, workmen etc. of the University" to improve the property (*Minutes of the Board of Visitors*, June 27, 1890). In 1893 the Board of Visitors resolved "to accept the title to the Young Men's Christian Association Athletic Grounds at the University upon such reasonable trusts as the present holder of the legal title may prescribe; provided that no use shall be made of said grounds that will not be acceptable to the Rector and Visitors; and provided further that no expense be absolutely imposed upon the University, but that the sums the University may expend on the said grounds shall be left to the discretion of the Rector and Visitors" (*Minutes of the Board of Visitors*, July 20, 1893). No such transfer of title took place, however. Again in 1899 the board resolved to enter into negotiations with the International Committee of the YMCA and the local board of trustees, "looking to the practicability of the purchase by the Rector & Visitors of the Campus for the uses of the students of the University" (*Minutes of the Board of Visitors*, March 2, 1899). These negotiations also came to nothing. Finally, in 1921, as the University sought a site for a new gymnasium, an agreement was drawn up for the University to purchase from the YMCA "the northern section of the tennis courts" (that is, the northern three-quarters of the YMCA Athletic Campus behind Madison Hall) for $5,000, but the conditions proposed by the YMCA were unacceptable to the University, and, in addition, the site was judged unsuitable (*Y.M.C.A. Board of Directors Minute Book*, May 19, 1921, 99, Papers of the University of Virginia, YMCA, 1859–1922, University of Virginia Library, Special Collections, RG-28; and *Minutes of the Board of Visitors*, May 18, May 31, and November 29, 1921). It is apparent in all this that the University coveted the property but that the YMCA was unwilling to part with it. Finally, in 1931 the financial condition of the YMCA required it to offer for sale the land lying behind Madison Hall (*Minutes of the Board of Visitors*, April 10, 1931).

42. *University of Virginia Catalogue*, 1896–97, 154–55.

43. McIlhany's predecessors were I. C. Harrison (1894–96), a former student president of the association; William McNair, secretary of the YMCA in Louisville and a student at Princeton Theological Seminary, who served from 1896 to 1898; J. M. Brodnax (1898–1900); Herbert D. Gallaudet (1900–1901); and Robert C. Beale (1901–2).

44. Good studies of muscular Christianity are provided by Hall, ed., *Muscular Christianity;* and Putney, *Muscular Christianity.* An evangelical perspective is found in Ladd and Mathisen, *Muscular Christianity.* Among prominent American advocates of muscular Christianity were Theodore Roosevelt (Sr. and Jr.), Henry Ward Beecher, and Dwight L. Moody.

45. For the incorporation of muscular Christianity into the YMCA, see esp. Putney, *Muscular Christianity*, 64–72.

46. The general secretary had his office at #13 West Lawn, a lecture room was used by the YMCA for meetings, and space was loaned to house its Reading Room. The request for space by the YMCA—both for a reading room and a meeting room—and the assignment of it by the Board of Visitors seems to have first occurred in 1878. See the *Minutes of the Board of Visitors*, June 24, 1878, and September 12, 1878.

47. The *Minutes of the Board of Visitors* for June 28, 1886, refer to assurances of L. D. Wishard, college secretary of the International Committee of the YMCA, "that at least $25,000 can be secured for a YMCA building at the University of Virginia provided certain conditions be complied with in the way of guarantees that the building will always be used for the purpose contemplated in the Constitution of the College Young Men's Christian Association." The board hastened to make the needed guarantees, authorized Davis and two students to transmit them to the International Committee, and paid the way of the students to travel to New York City for that purpose. This overture had no result. When, a few years later, the University Chapel fell short of funds during construction, an appeal for assistance was made to the international office of the YMCA, on condition that the chapel plan be enlarged to provide permanent space for the YMCA. The appeal was unsuccessful, but it again brought to the attention of the international office the University YMCA's need for its own quarters.

48. By the time Madison Hall was built, more than thirty other collegiate YMCA chapters already had their own buildings, the first of which was Murray Hall at Princeton (1879). But almost all of these YMCA buildings were constructed, like Madison Hall, through the generosity of a single donor or donor family. The University chapter of the YMCA was formally incorporated on December 10, 1904, as The Young Men's Christian Association of the University of Virginia, Inc., and the five acres of land and the new building were deeded to the corporation on October 16, 1905.

49. A report on the activities of the YMCA in the *Alumni Bulletin of the University of Virginia*, series 3, vol. 1 (1908): 295, says, "The home of the Association, Madison Hall, has become more and more the acknowledged meeting place, not alone of the Publication Boards and the Athletic Committees, but also of musical organizations, state clubs, fraternities, debating teams and other student organizations." Madison Hall formally became the Student Union only in 1933, but it had functioned as such, under the auspices of the YMCA, from the time of its construction.

50. The University was the legal owner of the Parsonage, the Cottages (numbers 3 and 4 on Dawson's Row), and Temperance Hall (which was later replaced by the so-called Entrance Building), but they came to be referred to as YMCA properties. None of these structures had any original connection with the YMCA, but because they were intended to promote religion or morality, the University felt a "moral obligation" to turn over the rental incomes of these buildings to the YMCA. See the letter of William Forrest to President John Newcomb, April 28, 1937, President's Papers, General Records, Subseries III 1937–38, University of Virginia Library, Special Collections, RG-2/1/2/491. In 1937 this rental income amounted to almost $2,000 annually.

51. *University of Virginia Catalogue,* 1904–5, 84.

52. *College Topics,* October 3, 1906, 4.

53. On the discontinuance of University-sponsored services in the chapel, see below, chap. 5.

54. In a tribute, "What the Young Men's Christian Association Owes to Mr. Davis," *Alumni Bulletin of the University of Virginia,* series 3, vol. 3 (1910): 402–3, it is said, "For over twenty-five years his Sunday lectures on the Life of Christ, the Life of St. Paul, and the Book of Psalms, were attended by an aggregate of thousands of men. He used the largest lecture room in the University, and seldom spoke to fewer than one hundred students."

55. This phenomenon was by no means unique to the University of Virginia. See Finnegan and Alleman, "The YMCA and the Origins of American Freshman Orientation Programs," who show that "the primary and generally the only orientation opportunities for college students at hundreds of institutions prior to the 1920s" were provided by collegiate YMCA organizations.

56. In addition to the work cited in the previous note, see, Finnegan and Alleman, "Without Adult Supervision"; Finnegan, "'Believe You Have a Mission in Life'"; and Finnegan, "College Life and the YMCA."

57. Lengthy memorial recollections of Professor Kent are gathered in "Charles William Kent, Professor of English Literature, University of Virginia," *Alumni Bulletin of the University of Virginia,* series 3, vol. 12 (January 1919): 3–45.

58. William Forrest to John Cary White, May 9, 1930 (in an attachment), gives figures for the individual contributions to the creation of the Bible lectureship, totaling $13,887.58, to which was later added the $10,000 contribution on behalf of John B. Cary. Forrest apparently drew his figures from the papers of Charles Kent, who was the point person on the University faculty in promoting the creation of the lectureship.

59. See D. B. Hull, "Christian Woman's Board of Missions."

60. See Flowers, *The Bible Chair Movement in the Disciples of Christ Tradition,* which is summarized in his "The Bible Chair Movement: An Innovation of the Disciples of Christ," and, more briefly, in his "Bible Chair Movement"; and McCormick, "The Bible Chair Movement." The Bible Chair movement among the Disciples of Christ was the root of the later-developing and transdenominational campus ministry enterprise.

61. Quoted from a series of excerpts made from *Missionary Tidings* (the publication of the CWBM), probably made by William M. Forrest (but possibly by S. V. McCasland), with the heading "John B. Cary Memorial Chair of Biblical History and Literature, University of Virginia, Charlottesville, Virginia," preserved among the papers of Selby Vernon McCasland, "Religion Department Administration and Cary Chair Material, 1930–1963," University of Virginia Library, Special Collections, MS 12755-a. The excerpts, which date from 1896 to 1909, appear to have been made by way of documenting the early stages in the development of the School of Biblical History and Literature at the University. This quotation is from *Missionary Tidings* 14 (July 1896): 55.

62. *Missionary Tidings* 14 (December 1896): 205.

63. *Missionary Tidings* 15 (June 1897): 37–38.

64. *University of Virginia Catalogue,* 1897–98, 122–23.

65. *Minutes of the Board of Visitors,* March 2, 1899. During the nineteenth century, Hebrew was only intermittently available, and then only if a sufficient number of students asked for it, in spite of Jefferson's original proposal that it should be offered along with Greek and Latin. For details, see below, Appendix B, "The Teaching of Hebrew at the University."

66. Subsequently, Young moved to Chicago and joined the staff of the *Christian Oracle,* a journal of the Disciples of Christ, which was soon renamed *The Christian Century* and became a highly respected and enormously influential religious periodical during the twentieth century.

67. *Minutes of the Board of Visitors,* June 13, 1900.

68. In *Missionary Tidings* 15 (April 1898): 304–5, a report of the local "advisory committee," led by Professor Kent, recommended that the CWBM assume financial responsibility, along with the existing endowment for the John B. Cary Bible Lectureship, for supporting instruction in Bible at the University, and informed the missionary agency that "as your committee is assured by Mr. T. Archibald Cary, on behalf of his mother, Mrs. Columbia Cary, Miss Gillie Cary, Mrs. Lizzie Daniel, Mrs. Alfie White and himself, that $10,000 will be given to the Christian Woman's Board of Missions as the minimum amount for the endowment of the University of Virginia Bible Lectureship founded by John B. Cary, we recommend that the Bible teaching at the University of Virginia be considered a permanent part of our Bible Chair work."

69. *Minutes of the Board of Visitors,* March 2, 1899.

70. *University of Virginia Catalogue,* 1900–1901, 160.

71. *University of Virginia Catalogue,* 1901–2, 160.

72. Ibid.

73. An emphasis on nonsectarianism had always been characteristic of the University's posture in religious matters. But in contrast to the chaplaincy, for which nonsectarianism had (supposedly) been achieved by rotating the appointment among four principal denominations, the lectureship has no denominational reference, but the lecturer must be Protestant ("evangelical").

74. That the board was under rather constant religious pressure may be inferred from comments by Rev. J. William Jones in the *Alumni Bulletin of the University of Virginia* 3 (1897): 96–97: "It is a matter of very great satisfaction to all friends of evangelical religion that for many years the public sentiment in Virginia, and among the friends of the University, has been so strong in favor of evangelical influences that no Board of Visitors would have ventured to elect a known infidel as professor in the University, and the result has been that nearly all of the Faculty have been members of some evangelical church, and there have been among them as noble specimens of the Christian scholar as ever graced any institution."

75. A brief sketch of Forrest's early career was given by Professor Charles W. Kent in *Alumni Bulletin of the University of Virginia,* n.s., 3 (1903): 183–84. Forrest left behind, in typescript, an extraordinarily detailed autobiography, written when he was eighty

years old, entitled "The Tide of Years: An Autobiography 1868–1950" (University of Virginia Library, Special Collections, MS 3660). This he deposited in Alderman Library at the University of Virginia, with the instruction that it not be read until after his death. It offers an interesting account of his personal and professional life.

76. Forrest, "Tide of Years," 106, says that he told the CWBM that he would not want to continue at Virginia "unless we could get academic recognition for Bible classes."

77. Ibid., 107–15.

78. Ms. Gillie Cary to Charles W. Kent, December 29, 1904, University of Virginia Library, Special Collections, "Additional Papers of Charles W. Kent," MS 3847.

79. William Forrest to T. A. Cary, July 22, 1905, ibid.

80. *Minutes of the Board of Visitors,* June 12, 1905.

81. Helen Moses to Charles W. Kent, February 23, 1905, University of Virginia Library, Special Collections, "Additional Papers of Charles W. Kent," MS 2589; William Forrest to T. A. Cary, July 22, 1905; and Forrest, "Tide of Years," 106–7.

82. *Minutes of the Board of Visitors,* June 11, 1906.

83. Ibid., June 15, 1908.

84. This remains true, even though the funding mechanism for the professorship and school was distinct. There were Bible chairs at other public universities, and some of those universities would follow Virginia's example of allowing courses taught by the holders of those chairs to count for degree credit. This was done by the University of Missouri in 1906–7, the University of Texas in 1910–11, the University of Kansas in 1921–22, the University of Indiana in 1953–54. Only at Virginia, however, was the Bible chair so soon made into a school (i.e., department) of the University. See Flowers, "Bible Chair Movement."

85. *Alumni Bulletin of the University of Virginia,* n.s., 3 (1903): 121–23.

86. *Alumni Bulletin of the University of Virginia,* 3rd series, 3 (1910): 469–73.

87. Ibid., 472.

88. Professor McCasland, Forrest's successor, worked up a table of enrollments in Bible courses from the beginning of the school in 1906 up to 1945. Four students were enrolled (i.e., took a course) in 1906, five in 1907–8 and in 1908–9, six in 1909–10, and five in 1910–11. After that, enrollments grew with the increasing size of the student body, but were never very large, exceeding 100 only eight times (in 1919–12, 1925–28, 1929–30, 1932–33, and 1935–36). In the whole period the average number of students taking Bible courses in a given year was usually between twenty and forty. The tabulations are found in McCasland's essay "The John B. Cary Memorial School of Religion of the University of Virginia," University of Virginia Library, Special Collections, MS 12755-a, "Religion Department: Administration and Cary Chair Material 1930–1963."

89. Alderman, "Religious Ideals of the University," 452–53. Alderman struck the same theme in his "Welcoming Address to the Presbyterian Synod of Virginia, West Virginia, Maryland and the District of Columbia" in Charlottesville (n.d.). Years later in a speech titled "Relations between the Church and State Institutions of Higher Learning," given to the General Assembly of the Presbyterian Church in the United

States on May 26, 1930, Alderman averred that the separation of church and state should *not* entail the separation of religion from education.

90. A number of bulletins were issued in 1913–14 in a series called Bulletins of the Bureau of Extension of the University of Virginia before the series was renamed The University of Virginia Record Extension Series and volumes were numbered, beginning with vol. 1 in 1915. The bulletin entitled "The Country Church" was published in 1913. The volume on religious activities and advantages at the University appeared in vol. 1, no. 4 (1915), the program for observing country church day appeared in vol. 1, no. 5 (1916), the syllabus for Bible study in vol. 2, no. 1 (1916), and the address to the Chautauqua Society in vol. 2, nos. 6–7 (1917). Religious topics were fairly frequent. The annual Rural Life Conferences always included considerations of the country churches. In vol. 8, no. 4 (1923) a play was published for use in Virginia high schools, "The Christmas Pageant of the Holy Grail."

91. For the early part of Alderman's administration, see Dennis, "Reforming the 'Academical Village.'"

92. Metcalf et al., eds., *The Centennial of the University of Virginia*, 3.

93. Barr, "Religion at the University of Virginia." Barr's address was also published in the *Alumni Bulletin*, 3rd series, 14 (1921): 59–72. It is worth noting that the centennial proceedings included "Departmental Alumni Conferences"—Law, Medical, Engineering, College, etc.—and that one of these was "The Clerical Alumni," even though, in contrast to the others, there was no clerical (or theological) department. For presentations to that group, see Metcalf et al., *The Centennial of the University of Virginia*, 140–49.

94. Metcalf et al., *The Centennial of the University of Virginia*, 6.

95. The perspective is well represented by Angell, "Religious Life in Our State Universities." For other state institutions, see Longfield, "From Evangelicalism to Liberalism."

96. So, for example, Francis Smith, the professor of natural philosophy (that is, science) from 1853 until 1907, maintained throughout his career the unity and compatibility of scientific truth and biblical revelation, Darwin and the progress of science notwithstanding. A broad deference to biblicism caused the faculty in 1878 to prevent students from inviting speakers for fear they might "utter objectional sentiments about politics and religion, and also about science, so far as it bore on the origin of man and the age of the world" (Bruce, *History of the University*, 4:126). Or, for another example, moral philosophy, which was predicated on the unity of all truth, both religious and scientific, had been dropped from most university curricula by the 1880s, but the School of Moral Philosophy persisted at Virginia until the retirement of Professor Noah Davis in 1906. Moreover, the University did not experiment with any courses that treated religion from a scientific point of view, but remained content with straightforwardly teaching the Bible into the late 1930s. The YMCA also flourished at Virginia until the 1930s.

5. The Twentieth Century

1. On the role of religion in the war, and the war's consequences for religion, see now Jenkins, *The Great and Holy War;* and A. Gregory, "Beliefs and Religion."

2. In 1900 the plan was developed to have the visiting minister be in residence at the University for a month rather than a single Sunday, and to hold two Sunday services, lead daily prayer meetings, and otherwise fraternize with students and faculty. But the plan was too ambitious and did not last long.

3. *Minutes of the Board of Visitors,* May 15, 1918.

4. The cornerstone of the permanent brick edifice was laid in 1926. There was much wrangling over the design of the permanent building. Against the original architects there was an insistent demand that the church should be architecturally harmonious with University buildings, that is, be constructed of brick and have a columned portico. This indicates how close the church's relationship to the University was meant to be. So also does the very name of the church. It is called "Memorial" because McIlhany's original fund-raising scheme was the "Memorial Plan," which solicited contributions with the idea that the church would be, as he put it, "a sort of Westminster Abbey at the University, where memorials of distinguished alumni and friends who were also prominent in church life may be placed from time to time as they pass on to their reward." For a concise history of the church, see Kettlewell, "A History of St. Paul's Memorial Church."

5. Reverend Tucker was succeeded in 1920 by Noble Powell. Both men were alumni of the University, interacted closely with the faculty and student body, and were warmly regarded by the University community. On Powell's work in Charlottesville, see Hein, *Noble Powell and the Episcopal Establishment,* 36–62.

6. *Minutes of the Board of Visitors,* April 15, 1925.

7. The dispute is reviewed by Allen, "A History of the Young Men's Christian Association," 235–48. The primary source is the *YMCA Board of Directors Minute Book,* January 18, 30, February 14, 1928, 120–34, University of Virginia Library, Special Collections, "Archives of the YMCA, 1904–1966," RG 28/2/1.

8. The growth and decline of the YMCA at Virginia followed a larger pattern that is described by Setran, *The College "Y."* See also his earlier essay, "Student Religious Life." Setran delineates three periods in the evolution of the intercollegiate YMCA. The first (1858–88) was one of growth and expansion, with a strongly personal evangelical emphasis; the second (1889–1915) embraced the halcyon days of the movement, consolidating broad institutional influence, with a more religiously liberal and socially conscious program; and the third (1916–34) was a period of decline and diminishing influence during which the Y aligned itself with liberal Protestantism, focused on collective social ideals, and took little interest in personal evangelism. He argues persuasively that although the collegiate YMCA was intended as a bulwark against academic secularism, it ultimately became, ironically, a mechanism of secularization.

9. *YMCA Board of Directors Minute Book,* May 26, 1931, 183.

10. *YMCA Board of Directors Minute Book,* October 21, 1931, 186; Papers of the President of the University of Virginia, Office Administrative Files 1930–1934,

University of Virginia Library, Special Collections, RG 2/1/2.491 I, Box 15, Folder YMCA.

11. *YMCA Board of Directors Minute Book*, October 17, 1933, 205; "Madison Hall as Student Union," *Association Record*, University of Virginia, 1932–33, 3–4, offers a clear and thorough explanation. Rent paid by the University was $1,500, which was actually less than the annual allocation made by the University to the YMCA for the maintenance and utilities costs of Madison Hall.

12. In his "Foreword" to the *Association Record* for 1932–33, the president of the YMCA, Jere King, forthrightly acknowledged that religion had lost much of its appeal for the student body. He wrote: "Students of the post-war generation, determined not to be 'taken in,' are wary of all devotions, perhaps as a result of their realization that devotions, unless vested with really intelligent content, are likely to end in a haze of sentimental vaporizing, or worse still, in fanaticism. This problem has caused many students to let religious devotions go by the board as incapable of intelligent content, while others have become satisfied with 'contents' quite cut off from religious implications, [for] movements either humanitarian or social."

13. These developments followed a broad national trend. See Seymour A. Smith, *Religious Cooperation in State Universities*, esp. chaps. 3 and 4.

14. *YMCA Religious Emphasis Week Brochure*, 1949, Clippings File, Alderman Library, University of Virginia.

15. Charlottesville *Daily Progress*, November 4, 1958, Clippings File, Alderman Library, University of Virginia. The speakers were Paul Lehmann of Harvard; Brooks Hays, president of the Southern Baptist Convention; Martin D'Arcy of Campion Hall, Oxford; and Rabbi Ephraim Fishoff of Lynchburg.

16. YMCA Preliminary Report of the Program and Planning Committee, November and December 1964, Papers of Selby Vernon McCasland, University of Virginia Library, Special Collections, MSS 12755, Box 1, Folder "Notes on the History of the YMCA." In these reports there is manifest dissatisfaction with the explicitly Christian identity of the YMCA and with traditional YMCA programs.

17. *Minutes of the Board of Visitors*, December 10, 1913.

18. *Minutes of the Board of Visitors*, October 26, 1935.

19. Anna Atwater to Edwin Alderman, May 27, 1915, Papers of the President, 1881–1918, Office Administrative Files 1915–1919, University of Virginia Library, Special Collections, RG 2/1/2.471 III, Box 2.

20. William Forrest to Anna Atwater, July 6, 1915, ibid.

21. Forrest, "Tide of Years," 136.

22. William M. Forrest to Stephen J. Corey, April 25, 1930, University of Virginia, Comptroller's Office, "John B. Cary Lectureship" folder. "If you count up the hundreds of thousands of dollars given by the Carys to the organized interests of our church, I think you will agree that they deserve better at your hands than to have you go as far as you are able to destroy a memorial to their father."

23. Gillie Cary McCabe to Mary Campbell, May 12, 1930, University of Virginia, Comptroller's Office, "John B. Cary Lectureship" folder.

24. Forrest, "Tide of Years," 132–34, 136, mentions "several occasions" when the missionary society considered withdrawing its funds from the Virginia enterprise. The 1929–30 episode seems to have been the most serious.

25. Forrest's publications included *Fires of Desire: A Tragedy of Modern India* (Boston: Clark, 1907); *India's Hurt and Other Addresses* (St. Louis: Christian Publishing Company, 1909); *Do Fundamentalists Play Fair?; Biblical Allusions in Poe* (New York: MacMillan, 1928); and *King or Shepherd? The Song of Solomon Newly Rendered and for the First Time as a Complete Drama* (Boston: Stratford, [ca. 1928]).

26. For an overview of the controversy, see Marsden, *Fundamentalism and American Culture.* One of the University's alumni, Charles Augustus Briggs, became a focal figure in that controversy. On Briggs, see below, Appendix B.

27. Forrest, "Tide of Years," 132–33, and see his critique of fundamentalism in his little volume, *Do Fundamentalists Play Fair?* In a letter to President Alderman, Forrest refers to denominational "complaints that I am a dangerous higher critic." William Forrest to Edwin Alderman, June 2, 1915, Papers of the President, 1881–1918, Office Administrative Files 1915–1919, University of Virginia Library, Special Collections, RG 2/1/2.471 III, Box 2.

28. *Minutes of the Board of Visitors,* January 27, 1940.

29. McCasland's books were *The Resurrection of Jesus* (New York: Thomas Nelson, 1932); *By the Finger of God: Demon Possession and Exorcism in Early Christianity* (New York: Macmillan, 1951); *The Religion of the Bible* (New York: Crowell, 1960); *The Pioneer of Our Faith: A New Life of Jesus* (New York: McGraw-Hill, 1964); and, as coauthor, *Religions of the World* (New York: Random House, 1969).

30. The high school text was *The Bible in Our American Life* (Bridgewater: Virginia Council for Religious Education, 1942).

31. McCasland had the help of a part-time instructor from 1947 to 1960: first John Fischbach (1947–54), then T. Y. Mullins (1954–60), then David Cammack (1960–62). Forrest only rarely had such assistance.

32. A convenient and readable history of the movement is provided by Conkin, "Restoration Christianity." For related topics, see also Foster et al., eds., *The Encyclopedia of the Stone-Campbell Movement.*

33. For the activity of the Disciples in Virginia, see Darst, *Ante-Bellum Virginia Disciples;* and Hodge, *The Plea and the Pioneers in Virginia.* The Charlottesville congregation was formed in 1835, in large part split off from the Charlottesville Baptist church; the Scottsville congregation (which originally met in Concord near Scottsville) was formed in 1836.

34. Selby V. McCasland to Edgar F. Shannon, April 4, 1966, Papers of the President 1965–1966, University of Virginia Library, Special Collections, RG 2/1/2.691, Box 39, "Religion."

35. Frank L. Hereford, undated typescript notes, University of Virginia Office of the Vice President and Provost, Office Administrative Files 1964–1981, University of Virginia Library, Special Collections, "Religion."

36. Frank L. Hereford to Lester Beaurlein, June 13, 1966, Papers of the President 1965–1966, University of Virginia Library, Special Collections, RG 2/1/2.691, Box 53.

37. Lester Beaurlein to Robert Harris, November 1, 1966, Papers of the President, Office Administrative Files, 1965–1966, University of Virginia Library, Special Collections, RG 2/1/2.691, "Religion," and December 6, 1966, Office Administrative Files, 1966–67, RG 2/1/2.701, "Religion."

38. *Minutes of the Board of Visitors*, February 18, 1967. The relevant papers are retained at the University of Virginia, Comptroller's Office, "John B. Cary Lectureship" folder. See also the correspondence between President Shannon and Virgil Sly, president of the missionary agency, Papers of the President of the University of Virginia, Office Administrative Files, 1966–67, University of Virginia Library, Special Collections, RG 2/1/2/701, Box 42, "Religion."

39. Among many studies of the history and nature of the academic study of religion, see Smart, *Secular Education and the Logic of Religion;* Harrison, *"Religion" and the Religions in the English Enlightenment;* Shephard, *God's People in the Ivory Tower;* Sharpe, *Comparative Religion;* Capps, *Religious Studies;* and Wiebe, *The Politics of Religious Studies.* D. G. Hart, a strong critic of the study of religion in secular institutions, offers a useful history in *The University Gets Religion.* See also his earlier essay, "American Learning and the Problem of Religious Studies." Hart highlights not only the history of the field but also the wide range of opinions and deep disagreements about the definition of the subject, about appropriate theory and method, and about its relation to other disciplines.

40. Abington School District v. Schempp 374 U.S. 203 (1963).

41. Justice Tom Clark, in his majority opinion wrote, "In addition, it might well be said that one's education is not complete without a study of comparative religion or the history of religion and its relationship to the advancement of civilization. It certainly may be said that the Bible is worthy of study for its literary and historic qualities. Nothing we have said here indicates that such study of the Bible or of religion, when presented objectively as part of a secular program of education, may not be effected consistently with the First Amendment. But the exercises here do not fall into those categories. They are religious exercises, required by the States in violation of the command of the First Amendment that the Government maintain strict neutrality, neither aiding nor opposing religion" (*Abington School District,* at 225). Justice Goldberg's concurring opinion furnished the handiest distinction, noting the "propriety . . . of the teaching *about* religion, as distinguished from the teaching *of* religion, in the public schools" (ibid., at 306). For this and other rulings affecting the teaching of religion in public schools, see William L. Miller, *Supreme Court Decisions on Church and State.* With specific reference to higher education and the effects of the Schempp decision, see Fellman, "Religion, the State and the Public University"; Alexander, "Religious Studies in Higher Education since Schempp"; Clark, "The Legal Status of Religious Studies Programs"; and Griffin, "'We Do Not Preach, We Teach.'"

42. Claude Welch, *Graduate Education in Religion,* vii, 17, considered that the Schempp case settled the legality of the academic study of religion in public institutions,

an opinion eagerly embraced by most faculty in the field. Jonathan Z. Smith characterized the Schempp case as the "'Magna Carta' for religious studies within state universities" ("'Religion' and 'Religious Studies,'" 231–32). See also Cherry, *Hurrying toward Zion*, 90. The significance of the Schempp decision has probably been overestimated, since other societal factors were also at work. See Imhoff, "The Creation Story."

43. For the growth and distribution of programs, see Welch, *Religion in the Undergraduate Curriculum*, 49–85. He observes that between 1966 and 1970 no fewer than forty-four programs in religion were created in public colleges and universities (50). See also McLean and Kimber, *The Teaching of Religion in State Universities;* and the follow-up by McLean, ed., *Religious Studies in Public Universities*. Different departmental models had developed in different universities before 1965. For these, see Michaelson, *The Study of Religion in American Universities*.

44. The search committee had previously favored other candidates. Originally its second choice, should Buck decline, was E. Earle Ellis, also a biblical scholar, then teaching at New Brunswick Theological Seminary. Untethered from a focus on the Bible, the committee was impressed by Harned's broad and interdisciplinary conception of the field of religion.

45. David. B. Harned to Robert J. Harris, August 25, 1967, University of Virginia, Files of the Department of Religious Studies. An unambiguous designation for the enterprise has been hard to come by. "Religious Studies," which is the most widely used name, could be taken to mean that the activity is itself religious. More cumbersome, but less liable to be misconstrued, is "the Study of Religions."

46. Scott and his wife, Charlotte, were appointed in 1976, he as Kenan Professor of Religious Studies, she as a professor of business administration and commerce in the Darden School. They were the first tenured African Americans on the University faculty.

47. Graduate work in religion at Virginia was attractive to students of other states not least because of the existence at that time of the "Academic Common Market." This was an agreement among states of the southeastern region that permitted a student of one state to attend the state university of another state at in-state tuition rates if a particular degree program were not available in the student's home state. The University of Virginia discontinued its participation in this program in 1998. When Virginia initiated its Ph.D. program, the only other public universities offering a Ph.D. in religion were Iowa, Penn State, and the University of California at Santa Barbara.

48. On these points, see R. S. Hart, "Religious and Theological Studies in American Higher Education." This is a self-study by the academy. For a concise general overview of the field of religious studies in American higher education, see Nord, *Religion and American Education*, 304–19.

49. On the denominational campus ministry movement, see Shedd, *The Church Follows Its Students*, with a focus on public universities and large private universities; and more recently, Sloan, *Faith and Knowledge*, esp. 72–86. Further perspectives are found in McCormick, *Campus Ministry in the Coming Age;* and Shockley, *Campus Ministry*. A brief but useful assessment is given by Stokes, "Denominational Ministry on University

Campuses." Three principal reasons for the general demise of denominational identity and activity in higher education are ecumenism, pluralism, and secularism.

50. Drafts of a letter from President Shannon were prepared by Francis Berkeley and Paul Saunier, and Shannon's letter, relying on Berkeley's draft, was sent on August 30; Papers of the President of the University of Virginia, Office Administrative Files, 1966–67, University of Virginia Library, Special Collections, RG 2/1/2/701, Box 42, file "Religious Organizations: Use of University Facilities." The reassertion of the prohibition of student religious groups from University facilities was reported in the *Cavalier Daily*, September 15, 1966, and a scathing editorial, "A Secular University?" published on September 28, accordingly called attention to the University's long alliance with the YMCA as "an affront to the Jeffersonian tradition."

51. On this provision, see above, chap. 2, pp. 41–44.

52. The relevant correspondence is collected in Papers of the President, University of Virginia Library, Special Collections, RG 2/1/2.751, Box 55, folder "Calendar and Scheduling 1972–73." The students who pressed the case with strong arguments were Beat Steiner and James Keim. The Committee on Calendar and Scheduling, after reviewing aspects off the University's past interactions with student religious groups and the policies of other public institutions, and after soliciting the opinion of the University legal adviser, supported the students' request, and the Student Council put its weight behind the recommendation of the committee.

53. The Lemon test is named for an earlier case, Lemon v. Kurtzman, 403 U.S. 602, 91 S. Ct. 2105, 29 L. Ed. 2d 745 (1971), which defined the scope of the Establishment Clause. In that case the court ruled that a state policy or practice does not violate the Establishment Clause if (1) it serves a secular purpose; (2) its principal effect is not to promote or inhibit religion; and (3) it does not create an excessive entanglement of the state with religion. On the *Widmar* case, see L. Leparulo, "The Rights of Student Religious Groups"; L. M. Newell, "Use of Campus Facilities"; and D. Howarth and W. D. Connell, "Student Rights to Organize and Meet."

54. Rosenberger v. Rector of the University of Virginia, 515 U.S.819 (1995), at 825.

55. In addition to the Court's opinion, see also Office of the Legal Advisor, Case File of the Legal Advisor Pertaining to Wide Awake, 1991–1995, University of Virginia Library, Special Collections, RG 2/2/1.111.

56. In a dissenting opinion Justice Souter considered that the ruling "approves direct funding of core religious activities by an arm of the state"; Rosenberger v. Rector of the University of Virginia, at 863. He reasoned that the student fee was in effect a tax that, in accordance with the ruling, would subsidize a publication engaged in religious proselytizing.

57. Special Committee to Consider Wide Awake Decision (March 20, 1996), in University of Virginia Board of Visitors, Standing and Special Committee Records, 1967–2010, University of Virginia Library, Special Collections, RG 1/1/3/131.

58. www.uvastudentcouncil.com/safguidelines.

59. Urofsky, *Commonwealth and Community*, argues that historically there has been no *effective* anti-Semitism in Virginia. But it is difficult to deny that anti-Semitic prejudice existed.

60. "Annual Reports to the President, 1926–27," Papers of the President, University of Virginia Library, Special Collections, RG 2/1/1.381. The University's hospitable attitude toward teaching about Judaism is confirmed by Simon, "Religion at a State University." Representing the Chautauqua Society, Simon gave lectures on Jewish education and Jewish history during two summer sessions, and he spoke very positively about the welcome and interest he received.

61. The issue is fully treated by Karabel, *The Chosen.* See also Steinberg, "How Jewish Quotas Began." Urofsky, *Commonwealth and Community,* acknowledges instances of anti-Semitism, including such nativist reactions to Eastern European Jewish immigration as the imposition of quotas at the University, exclusion from social clubs, etc., but regards these as isolated and minor.

62. On Christian study centers, see now Cotherman, "Awakening the Lay Evangelical Mind"; his chaps. 6 and 7 detail developments in Charlottesville. A Consortium of Christian study centers, comprising more than twenty such organizations, was formed in 2008.

63. Everson v. Board of Education, 330 U.S. 1 (1947). Jefferson's "wall" metaphor for the separation of church and state was first used in this case by the Supreme Court.

64. For this view, see Marsden, *The Soul of the American University;* Marsden and Longfeld, eds., *The Secularization of the Academy;* Schwehn, *Exiles from Eden;* and Burtchaell, *The Dying of the Light.*

65. This is in keeping with the conclusions drawn from some sample studies at various institutions by Cherry, DeBerg, and Porterfield, *Religion on Campus;* and, more generally, Jacobsen and Jacobsen, *No Longer Invisible;* and Schmalzbauer and Mahoney, *The Resilience of Religion.*

66. A helpful introduction and overview of the discussion is Gorski et al., eds., *The Post-Secular in Question.*

67. Gordon wrote a passionate poem on the theme and read it when Old Cabell Hall was dedicated. The poem is entitled "The Fostering Mother" and is found in Gordon, *For Truth and Freedom,* 43–50. Its theme is "the gift of God is freedom." It is also reported that Gordon wanted the quotation to be in English, but that White insisted on Greek, to comport with the classical style of the building.

Appendix B. The Teaching of Hebrew at the University

1. Report of the Rockfish Gap Commission.

2. Report to the President and Directors of the Literary Fund, October 7, 1822.

3. For the letters, see Trent, *English Culture in Virginia.* The letters are also reproduced by Thomas FitzHugh, "The Letters of George Long," *Alumni Bulletin of the University of Virginia* 9 (1916): 525–56, on 529–30 and 533–35.

4. On Toy, see "Professor Crawford Howell Toy," in the Eminent Alumni series, *Alumni Bulletin of the University of Virginia* 4 (November 1897): 90–92; and Lyon, "Crawford Howell Toy."

5. Toy, "A Student's View."

6. For Toy's father and early background, see Thomas, *History of Freemason Street Baptist Church*, 8.

7. *University of Virginia Catalogue*, 1865–66, 13.

8. *Minutes of the Board of Visitors*, May 26 and 27, 1856.

9. Gildersleeve, *Letters*, 31–35.

10. For an upsurge in religious fervor at the University in this period, see above, chap. 3.

11. See Briggs, "A Sketch of Dr. Charles Augustus Briggs"; Ludlow, "American Old Testament Scholars"; Forrest, "Charles Augustus Briggs"; and Henry Preserved Smith, "Charles Augustus Briggs." Briggs was long well known to any student of biblical Hebrew by being one of the editors of Gesenius's Hebrew lexicon, *Hebrew and English Lexicon of the Old Testament*, ed. Francis Brown, S. R. Driver, and Charles A. Briggs (Oxford: Clarendon Press, 1907), or, to cognoscenti, "BDB" for short. Briggs was also editor of the distinguished biblical commentary series, The International Critical Commentary.

12. *Address by Rev. Charles A. Briggs on the Occasion of his Inauguration as Davenport Professor of Hebrew and the Cognate Languages, Union Theological Seminary, New York City* (New York: Rogers and Sherwood, 1876), 12.

13. *Minutes of the Board of Visitors*, July (June?) 27, 1876.

14. *University of Virginia Catalogue*, 1887–88, 21; 1898–99, and 1899–1900, 63. On Charles Young, see above, chap. 4, pp. 123–24.

15. Muller, "The Sunday Schools of the Young Men's Christian Association," 18–19.

Bibliography

Primary Sources

Alumni Bulletin of the University of Virginia
Cavalier Daily
College Topics
Corks and Curls
Founders Online. https://founders.archives.gov
Journal of the Chairman of the Faculty, University of Virginia
Madison Hall Notes
Minutes of the Board of Visitors, University of Virginia
University of Virginia Alumni News
University of Virginia Catalogue
University of Virginia Magazine

Secondary Sources

Adams, Dickson W., and Ruth W. Lester, eds. *Jefferson's Extracts from the Gospels: "The Philosophy of Jesus" and "The Life and Morals of Jesus."* The Papers of Thomas Jefferson, Second Series. Princeton: Princeton University Press, 1983.

Addresses Commemorative of James L. Cabell, Delivered at the University of Virginia, July 1, 1890. Charlottesville: Published by the Faculty, 1890.

Alderman, Edwin. "Religious Ideals of the University." *Alumni Bulletin of the University of Virginia*, 3rd series, 3 (October 1910): 452–54.

Alexander, Kathryn O. "Religious Studies in Higher Education since Schempp: A Bibliographic Essay." *Soundings* 71 (1988): 389–412.

Allen, Milton R. "A History of the Young Men's Christian Association at the University of Virginia." Dissertation, Department of History, University of Virginia, 1946.

Allmendinger, David. *Paupers and Scholars: The Transformation of Student Life in Nineteenth-Century New England.* New York: St. Martin's Press, 1975.

Angell, James B. "Religious Life in Our State Universities." *Andover Review* 13 (1890): 365–72.

Austin, C. Grey. *A Century of Religion at the University of Michigan: A Case Study in Religion and the State University.* Ann Arbor: University of Michigan, 1957.

Barnett, S. J. *Idol Temples and Crafty Priests: The Origins of Enlightenment Anticlericalism*. New York: St. Martin's Press, 1999.

Barr, William Alexander. "Religion at the University of Virginia." In *The Centennial of the University of Virginia, 1819–1921*, edited by John Calvin Metcalf et al., 4–14. New York: G. P. Putnam's, 1922.

Barringer, Paul, James M. Garnett, and Rosewell Page, eds. *The University of Virginia: Its History, Influence, Equipment and Characteristics*. 2 vols. New York: Lewis Publishing Company, 1904.

Barton, David. *The Jefferson Lies: Exposing the Myths You've Always Believed about Thomas Jefferson*. Nashville: Thomas Nelson, 2012.

Beiser, Frederick C. *The Sovereignty of Reason: The Defense of Rationality in the Early English Enlightenment*. Princeton: Princeton University Press, 1996.

Beliles, Mark. "The Christian Communities, Religious Revivals, and Political Culture of the Central Virginia Piedmont, 1737–1813." In *Religion and Political Culture in Jefferson's Virginia*, edited by Garrett W. Sheldon and Daniel Dreisbach, 3–40. Lanham, Md.: Rowman & Littlefield, 2000.

Beliles, Mark A., with Jerry Newcombe. *Doubting Thomas? The Religious Life and Legacy of Thomas Jefferson*. New York: Morgan James, 2015.

Bell, Sadie. *The Church, the State, and Education in Virginia*. Philadelphia: Science Press Printing, 1930.

Bellah, Robert. "Civil Religion in America." In *American Civil Religion*, edited by Russell E. Richey and Donald Jones, 21–44. New York: Harper & Row, 1974.

Boles, John B. *The Great Revival: Beginnings of the Bible Belt*. Lexington: University Press of Kentucky, 1996.

Bond, Edward L., ed. *Spreading the Gospel in Colonial Virginia: Sermons and Devotional Writings*. Lanham, Md.: Lexington Books, 2004.

Bowers, J. D. *Joseph Priestley and English Unitarianism in America*. University Park: Pennsylvania State University Press, 2007.

Bowman, R., and C. Santos. *Rot, Riot and Rebellion: Mr. Jefferson's Struggle to Save the University that Changed America*. Charlottesville: University of Virginia Press, 2013.

Boyd, Julian P., et al., eds. *Papers of Thomas Jefferson*. Princeton: Princeton University Press, 1950–.

Bozeman, Theodore Dwight. *Protestants in an Age of Science: The Baconian Ideal and Antebellum American Religious Thought*. Chapel Hill: University of North Carolina Press, 1977.

Bratt, David. "Southern Souls and State Schools: Religion and Public Higher Education in the Southeast, 1776–1900." Dissertation, Yale University, 1999.

Briggs, Emily Grace. "A Sketch of Dr. Charles Augustus Briggs." *Alumni Bulletin of the University of Virginia* 5 no. 4 (1899): 91–101.

Broadus, John A. "A Memorial of Gessner Harrison." *Alumni Bulletin of the University of Virginia*, 3rd series, 10 (1917): 339–71.

Brown, J. W. *The Rise of Biblical Criticism in America, 1800–1870*. Middletown, Conn.: Wesleyan University Press, 1969.

Brown, Samuel W. *The Secularization of American Education: As Shown by State Legislation, State Constitutional Provisions, and State Supreme Court Decisions.* New York: Teachers College, Columbia University, 1912.

Bruce, Philip A. *History of the University of Virginia 1819–1919: The Lengthened Shadow of One Man.* 5 vols. New York: Macmillan, 1920–22.

Brydon, George M. *Virginia's Mother Church and the Political Conditions under Which It Grew.* 2 vols. Philadelphia: Church Historical Society, 1952.

Buckley, Thomas E. "After Establishment: Thomas Jefferson's Wall of Separation in Antebellum Virginia." *Journal of Southern History* 61 (1995): 445–80.

———. "The Political Theology of Thomas Jefferson." In *The Virginia Statute for Religious Freedom: Its Evolution and Consequences in American History,* edited by Merrill D. Peterson and Robert C. Vaughan, 75–107. Cambridge Studies in Religion and American Public Life. Cambridge: Cambridge University Press, 1988.

Bulman, William J., and Robert G. Ingram, eds. *God in the Enlightenment.* New York: Oxford University Press, 2016.

Burtchaell, James. *The Dying of the Light: The Disengagement of Colleges and Universities from Their Christian Churches.* Grand Rapids: Eerdmans, 1998.

Butler, John, ed. *Religion on Campus.* New Directions for Student Services, no. 46. San Francisco: Jossey-Bass, 1989.

Butler, Jon. *Awash in a Sea of Faith: Christianizing the American People.* Cambridge, Mass.: Harvard University Press, 1990.

Cabell, N. F., ed. *Early History of the University of Virginia as Contained in the Letters of Thomas Jefferson and Joseph C. Cabell.* Richmond: J. W. Randolph, 1856.

Capps, Walter. *Religious Studies: The Making of a Discipline.* Minneapolis: Fortress Press, 1995.

Caron, Nathalie, and Naomi Wulf. "American Enlightenments: Continuity and Renewal." *Journal of American History* 99 (2013): 1072–91.

Champion, Justin. *The Pillars of Priestcraft Shaken: The Church of England and Its Enemies 1660–1730.* Cambridge: Cambridge University Press, 1992.

Cherry, Conrad. *Hurrying toward Zion: Universities, Divinity Schools, and American Protestantism.* Bloomington: Indiana University Press, 1995.

Cherry, Conrad, Betty DeBerg, and Amanda Porterfield. *Religion on Campus.* Chapel Hill: University of North Carolina Press, 2001.

Clagett, Martin R. "William Small, Teacher, Mentor, Scientist." Dissertation, Virginia Commonwealth University, 2003.

Clark, W. Royce. "The Legal Status of Religious Studies Programs in Higher Education." In *Beyond the Classics? Essays in Religious Studies and Liberal Education,* edited by Frank E. Reynolds and Sheryl L. Burkhalter, 109–39. Atlanta: Scholars Press, 1990.

Conkin, Paul. *American Originals: Homemade Varieties of Christianity.* Chapel Hill: University of North Carolina Press, 1997.

———. "Priestley and Jefferson: Unitarianism as a Religion for a New Revolutionary Age." In *Religion in a Revolutionary Age,* edited by R. Hoffman and P. J. Albert, 290–307. Charlottesville: University Press of Virginia, 1994.

———. "The Religious Pilgrimage of Thomas Jefferson." In *Jeffersonian Legacies*, edited by Peter S. Onuf, 19–49. Charlottesville: University Press of Virginia, 1993.

———. "Restoration Christianity: Christians and Disciples." In Conkin, *American Originals: Homemade Varieties of Christianity*, 1–56. Chapel Hill: University of North Carolina Press, 1997.

Cotherman, Charles E. "Awakening the Lay Evangelical Mind: Francis Schaeffer, James Houston, and the Christian Study Movement in North America." Dissertation, University of Virginia, 2017.

Coyner, M. Boyd, Jr. "John Hartwell Cocke of Bremo: Agriculture and Slavery in the Antebellum South." Dissertation, Department of History, University of Virginia, 1961.

Cragg, Gerald R. *The Church in the Age of Reason, 1648–1789*. Baltimore: Penguin Books, 1960.

Culbreth, David M. R. *The University of Virginia: Memories of Her Student-Life and Professors*. New York: Neale Publishing Company, 1908.

Dabney, Robert Lewis. *A Memorial of the Christian Life and Character of Francis S. Sampson, D.D.* Richmond: Enquirer Book and Job Press, 1855.

Dabney, Virginius. *Mr. Jefferson's University: A History*. Charlottesville: University Press of Virginia, 1981.

Darst, H. Jackson. *Ante-Bellum Virginia Disciples: An Account of the Emergence and Early Development of the Disciples of Christ in Virginia*. Richmond: Virginia Christian Missionary Society, 1959.

Dashiell, David, III. "Between Earthly Wisdom and Heavenly Truth: The Effort to Build a Chapel at the University of Virginia, 1835–1890." Thesis, School of Architecture, University of Virginia, 1992.

Davis, Derek H., ed. *The Oxford Handbook of Church and State in the United States*. Oxford: Oxford University Press, 2010.

Davis, Richard B., ed. *Correspondence of Thomas Jefferson and Francis Walker Gilmer, 1814–1826*. Columbia: University of South Carolina Press, 1946.

———. *Intellectual Life in Jefferson's Virginia, 1790–1830*. Chapel Hill: University of North Carolina Press, 1964.

D'Elia, Donald J. "Jefferson, Rush, and the Limits of Philosophical Friendship." *Proceedings of the American Philosophical Society* 117 (1973): 333–43.

Dennis, Michael. "Reforming the 'Academical Village': Edwin A. Alderman and the University of Virginia, 1904–1915." *Virginia Magazine of History and Biography* 105 (1997): 53–86.

Dyer, Thomas G. *The University of Georgia: A Bicentennial History, 1785–1985*. Athens: University of Georgia Press, 1985.

Emerson, Roger L. "Latitudinarianism and the English Deists." In *Deism, Masonry and the Enlightenment: Essays Honoring Alfred Owen Aldridge*, edited by J. A. Leo Lemay, 19–48. Newark: University of Delaware Press, 1987.

Enactments Relating to the Constitution and Government of the University of Virginia. Charlottesville: Cary, Watson & Co, 1831.

Faust, Drew Gilpin. *The Creation of Confederate Nationalism: Ideology and Identity in the Civil War South.* Baton Rouge: Louisiana State University Press, 1988.

Feldman, Noah. "Non-Sectarianism Reconsidered." *Journal of Law and Politics* 65 (2002): 65–117.

Fellman, David. "Religion, the State and the Public University." *Journal of Church and State* 26 (1984): 73–90.

Feuer, Lewis S. "America's First Jewish Professor: James Joseph Sylvester at the University of Virginia." *American Jewish Archives* 36 (1984): 151–201.

Finnegan, Dorothy. "'Believe You Have a Mission in Life and Steadily Pursue It': Campus YMCAs Presage Student Development Theory, 1894–1930." *Higher Education in Review* 6 (2009): 11–41.

———. "College Life and the YMCA: The Young Men's Christian Association and Higher Education," 2005. http://resources.razorplanet.com.

Finnegan, Dorothy, and Nathan F. Alleman. "Without Adult Supervision: Campus YMCAs as an Ancestor of Student Affairs." Paper presented at the Association for the Study of Higher Education, Philadelphia, November 2005.

———. "The YMCA and the Origins of American Freshman Orientation Programs." *Historical Studies in Education* 25 (2013): 95–114.

Flowers, Ronald B. "Bible Chair Movement." In *The Encyclopedia of the Stone-Campbell Movement,* edited by Douglas A. Foster et al., 91–92. Grand Rapids: Eerdmans, 2004.

———. "The Bible Chair Movement: An Innovation of the Disciples of Christ." *Discipliana* 26 (1966): 8–13.

———. "The Bible Chair Movement in the Disciples of Christ Tradition: Attempts to Teach Religion in State Universities." Dissertation, University of Iowa, 1967.

Forrest, William M. "Charles Augustus Briggs." *Alumni Bulletin of the University of Virginia,* 3rd series, 6 (1913): 640–44.

———. *Do Fundamentalists Play Fair?* New York: Macmillan, 1926.

———. "The Tide of Years: An Autobiography 1868–1950." Unpublished typescript, University of Virginia Library, Special Collections, MS 3660.

Foster, Douglas A., et al., eds. *The Encyclopedia of the Stone-Campbell Movement.* Grand Rapids: Eerdmans, 2004.

Frazer, Gregg. *The Religious Beliefs of America's Founders.* Lawrence: University Press of Kansas, 2012.

Gaustad, Edwin S. *Great Awakening in New England.* New York: Harper & Row, 1957.

———. *Historical Atlas of Religion in America.* New York: Harper & Row, 1962.

———. *Sworn on the Altar of God: A Religious Biography of Thomas Jefferson.* Grand Rapids: Eerdmans, 1996.

Gay, Peter. *The Enlightenment: An Interpretation.* Vol. 1, *The Rise of Modern Paganism.* New York: Knopf, 1966.

Geiger, Roger L. *The History of American Higher Education: Learning and Culture from the Founding to World War II.* Princeton: Princeton University Press, 2015.

Gildersleeve, Basil Lanneau. *The Letters of Basil Lanneau Gildersleeve*. Edited by W. Ward Briggs. Baltimore: Johns Hopkins University Press, 1987.

Gilley, Sheridan. "Christianity and Enlightenment: An Historical Survey." *History of European Ideas* 1 (1981): 103–21.

Godbold, A. *The Church College of the Old South*. Durham: Duke University Press, 1944.

Goodchild, Lester, and Harold Wechsler, eds. *The History of Higher Education*. Part 4, "The Rise of American Universities and Other Post-Secondary Institutions during the Nineteenth and Early Twentieth Centuries," 203–375. 2nd ed. Needham Heights, Mass.: Simon and Schuster, 1997.

Gordon, Armistead. *For Truth and Freedom: Poems of Commemoration*. Staunton, Va.: A. Shultz, 1898.

Gorski, Philip S., et al., eds. *The Post-Secular in Question: Religion in Contemporary Society*. New York: Social Science Research Council and New York University Press, 2012.

Grasso, Christopher. *Skepticism and American Faith: From the Revolution to the Civil War*. New York: Oxford University Press, 2018.

———. "Skepticism and American Faith: Infidels, Converts, and Religious Doubt in the Early Nineteenth Century." *Journal of the Early Republic* 22 (2002): 465–508.

———. "The Religious and the Secular in the Early American Republic." *Journal of the Early Republic* 36 (2016): 359–88.

Grayson, Jennie Thornley. "Old Christ Church, Charlottesville, Virginia, 1826–1895." In *Papers of the Albemarle County Historical Society*, vol. 8 (1947–48). Charlottesville: Albemarle County Historical Society, 1940–51.

Green, Edwin L. *A History of the University of South Carolina*. Columbia: The State Company, 1916.

Green, Steven K. *The Second Disestablishment: Church and State in Nineteenth-Century America*. New York: Oxford University Press, 2010.

Gregory, A. "Beliefs and Religion." In *The Cambridge History of the First World War*, edited by J. Winter, 418–44. Cambridge: Cambridge University Press, 2014.

Griffin, Leslie. "'We Do Not Preach, We Teach': Religion Professors and the First Amendment." *Quinnipiac Law Review* 19 (2000): 1–65.

Grote, Simon. "Religion and Enlightenment." *Journal of the History of Ideas* 75 (2014): 137–60.

Hall, Donald, ed. *Muscular Christianity: Embodying the Victorian Age*. Cambridge: Cambridge University Press, 1994.

Harrison, Peter. *"Religion" and the Religions in the English Enlightenment*. Cambridge: Cambridge University Press, 1990.

Hart, D. G. "American Learning and the Problem of Religious Studies." In *The Secularization of the Academy*, edited by George Marsden and Bradley Longfield, 195–233. New York: Oxford University Press, 1992.

———. *The University Gets Religion: Religious Studies in American Higher Education*. Baltimore: Johns Hopkins University Press, 1999.

Hart, R. S. "Religious and Theological Studies in American Higher Education." *Journal of the American Academy of Religion* 59 (1991): 715–827.

Hasler, F. "On College Government." In *Journal of the Proceedings of a Convention of Literary and Scientific Gentlemen*, 264–65. Reproduction of original edition of 1831. New York: New York University Press, 1931.

Hatch, Nathan. *The Democratization of American Christianity*. New Haven: Yale University Press, 1989.

Hauser, Alan J., and Duane F. Watson, eds. *A History of Biblical Interpretation*. Vol. 3, *The Enlightenment Through the Nineteenth Century*. Grand Rapids: Eerdmans, 2017.

Hawkins, Hugh. "Charles W. Eliot, University Reform and Religious Faith in America, 1869–1909." *Journal of American History* 51 (1964): 191–213.

Hawks, F. "The Character of Jefferson." A review of *The Life of Thomas Jefferson, Third President of the United States, with parts of his correspondence never before published, and notices of his opinions on questions of civil government, national policy and constitutional law*, by George Tucker. *New York Review and Quarterly Church Journal* 1 (1837): 5–58.

Hayes, Kevin. "How Thomas Jefferson Read the Qur'an." *Early American Literature* 39 (2004): 247–61.

Healey, Robert M. "Jefferson on Judaism and the Jews: 'Divided We Stand, United We Fall.'" *American Jewish History* 73 (1984): 359–74.

———. *Jefferson on Religion in Public Education*. New Haven: Yale University Press, 1962.

Hein, David. *Noble Powell and the Episcopal Establishment in the Twentieth Century*. Urbana: University of Illinois Press, 2001.

Herrick, James. *The Radical Rhetoric of the English Deists: The Discourse of Skepticism, 1680–1750*. Columbia: University of South Carolina Press, 1997.

Hodge, Frederick A. *The Plea and the Pioneers in Virginia: A History of the Rise and Early Progress of the Disciples of Christ in Virginia, with Biographical Sketches of the Pioneer Preachers*. Richmond: Everett Waddey Company, 1905.

Hofstadter, Richard, "The Revolution in Higher Education." In *Paths of American Thought*, edited by Arthur M. Schlesinger and Morton White, 269–90. Boston: Houghton Mifflin, 1963.

Holifield, E. Brooks. *The Gentlemen Theologians: American Theology in Southern Culture, 1795–1860*. Durham: Duke University Press, 1978.

———. *Theology in America: Christian Thought from the Age of the Puritans to the Civil War*. New Haven: Yale University Press, 2003.

Holmes, David. *The Faiths of the Founding Fathers*. New York: Oxford University Press, 2006.

Holt, Ann. *A Life of Joseph Priestley*. London: Oxford University Press, 1931.

Honeywell, Roy J. *The Educational Work of Thomas Jefferson*. New York: Russell & Russell, 1964.

Hopkins, Howard. *History of the Y.M.C.A. in North America*. New York: Association Press, 1951.

Howarth, Don, and William D. Connell. "Students' Rights to Organize and Meet for Religious Purposes in the University Context." *Valparaiso University Law Review* 16 (1981): 103–43.

Hudson, Wayne. *The English Deists: Studies in Early Enlightenment*. London: Pickering and Chatto, 2009.

Hull, D. B. "Christian Woman's Board of Missions." In *The Encyclopedia of the Stone-Campbell Movement*, edited by Douglas A. Foster et al., 200–202. Grand Rapids: Eerdmans, 2004.

Hull, G. "William Small 1734–1775: No Publications, Much Influence." *Journal of the Royal Society of Medicine* 90 (1997): 102–5.

Imhoff, Sarah. "The Creation Story, or How We Learned to Stop Worrying and Love Schempp." *Journal of the American Academy of Religion* 84 (2016): 466–97.

Isaac, Rhys. *The Transformation of Virginia, 1740–1790*. Chapel Hill: University of North Carolina Press, 1982.

Jacobsen, Douglas, and Rhonda Hustedt Jacobsen. *No Longer Invisible: Religion in University Education*. New York: Oxford University Press, 2012.

Jenkins, Philip. *The Great and Holy War: How World War I Became a Religious Crusade*. New York: HarperOne, 2014.

Johnson, L. H., III. "Sharper Than a Serpent's Tooth." *Virginia Magazine of History and Biography* 99 (1991): 145–62.

Jones, G. W. *The Public University and Religious Practice: An Inquiry into University Provision for Campus Religious Life*. Muncie, Ind.: Ball State University, 1973.

Jones, J. William, John L. Johnson, and L. M. Blackford. "Reminiscences of the Young Men's Christian Association." *Alumni Bulletin of the University of Virginia*, 3rd series, 2 (1909): 57–70.

Jordan, E. L., Jr. "The University of Virginia during the Civil War." *Encyclopedia of Virginia*. Virginia Foundation for the Humanities, March 24, 2016.

Karabel, Jerome. *The Chosen: The Hidden History of Admission and Exclusion at Harvard, Yale and Princeton*. New York: Houghton Mifflin Harcourt, 2005.

Kark, Ruth. *American Consuls in the Holy Land, 1832–1914*. Detroit: Wayne State University Press, 1994.

Kemeny, P. C. *Princeton in the Nation's Service: Religious Ideals and Educational Practice, 1868–1928*. New York: Oxford University Press, 1998.

Kett, Joseph. *Rites of Passage: Adolescence in America, 1790 to the Present*. New York: Basic Books, 1977.

Kettlewell, Paula. "A History of St. Paul's Memorial Church on the Occasion of Its Eightieth Year as a Parish." www.stpaulsmemorialchurch.org/aboutstpauls/history.

Kidd, Thomas. *The Great Awakening: The Roots of Evangelical Christianity in Colonial America*. New Haven: Yale University Press, 2007.

Knight, E. W., ed. *Documentary History of Education in the South before 1860*. Vol. 3, *Rise of the State University* (1952). 5 vols. Chapel Hill: University of North Carolina Press, 1949–53.

Knox, Samuel. *An Essay on the Best System of Liberal Education Adapted to the Genius of the Government of the United States*. Baltimore: Warner & Hanna, 1799.

———. *A Vindication of the Religion of Mr. Jefferson, and a Statement of his Services in the Cause of Religious Liberty. By a Friend to Real Religion*. Baltimore: W. Pechin, 1800.

Koch, Adrienne. *The Philosophy of Thomas Jefferson*. Gloucester, Mass.: P. Smith, 1957.

Koch, G. A. *Republican Religion, the American Revolution and the Cult of Reason*. New York: Henry Holt, 1933.

Kohlbrenner, Bernard J. "Religion and Higher Education: An Historical Perspective." *History of Education Quarterly* 1 (1961): 45–56.

Ladd, Tony, and James A. Mathisen. *Muscular Christianity: Evangelical Protestants and the Development of American Sport*. Grand Rapids: Baker Books, 1999.

Lamb, James, C. "John B. Minor." *Alumni Bulletin of the University of Virginia* 2, no. 4 (February 1896): 121–30.

Lambert, F. "'God—And a Religious President . . . [or] Thomas Jefferson and No God': Campaigning for a Voter-Imposed Religious Test in 1800." *Journal of Church and State* 39 (1997): 769–89.

Lehmann, Karl. *Thomas Jefferson: American Humanist*. New York: Macmillan, 1947.

Leparulo, Linda S. "The Rights of Student Religious Groups under the First Amendment to Hold Religious Meetings in the Public University Campus." *Rutgers Law Review* 33 (1981): 1008–53.

Lerche, Charles. "Jefferson and the Election of 1800: A Case Study in Political Smear." *William and Mary Quarterly* 5 (1948): 467–91.

Levy, Leonard W. *Jefferson and Civil Liberties: The Darker Side*. Cambridge, Mass.: Belknap Press, 1963.

Lindberg, David C., and Ronald L. Numbers. *God and Nature: Historical Essays on the Encounter between Christianity and Science*. Berkeley: University of California Press, 1986.

Little, David. "The Origins of Perplexity: Civil Religion and Moral Belief in the Thought of Thomas Jefferson." In *American Civil Religion*, edited by Russell Richey and Donald Jones, 185–210. New York: Harper & Row, 1974.

Long, Kathryn T. *The Revival of 1857–58: Interpreting an American Religious Awakening*. New York: Oxford University Press, 1998.

Longfield, Bradley J. "From Evangelicalism to Liberalism: Public Midwestern Universities in Nineteenth-Century America." In *The Secularization of the Academy*, edited by George M. Marsden and Bradley J. Longfield, 46–73. New York: Oxford University Press, 1992.

Louisell, David, and John H. Jackson. "Religion, Theology and Public Higher Education." *California Law Review* 50 (1962): 551–799.

Loux, Jennifer R. "John Hartwell Cocke (1780–1866)." In *Dictionary of Virginia Biography*. Richmond: Library of Virginia (1998–), 2006. http://www.lva.virginia.gov/public/dvb/bio.asp?b=Cocke_John_Hartwell_1780-1866.

Lucci, D. *Scripture and Deism: The Biblical Criticism of the Eighteenth-Century British Deists*. Bern: Peter Lang, 2008.

Ludlow, James M. "American Old Testament Scholars: Charles Augustus Briggs." *The Old and New Testament Student* 12 (1891): 7–12.

Luebke, Fred C. "The Origins of Thomas Jefferson's Anti-Clericalism." *Church History* 32 (1963): 344–56.

Lyon, David G. "Crawford Howell Toy." *Harvard Theological Review* 13 (1920): 1–22.

Mahoney, Kathleen A. "The Rise of the University and the Secularization of the Academy: The Role of Liberal Protestantism." *Higher Education Annual* 16 (1996): 117–31.

Malone, Dumas. *The Public Life of Thomas Cooper, 1783–1839*. New Haven: Yale University Press, 1926.

Marsden, George M. *Fundamentalism and American Culture: The Shaping of American Evangelicalism, 1875–1925*. New York: Oxford University Press, 1980.

———. *The Soul of the American University: From Protestant Establishment to Established Nonbelief*. New York: Oxford University Press, 1994.

Marsden, George M., and Bradley J. Longfield, eds. *The Secularization of the Academy*. New York: Oxford University Press, 1992.

Marty, Martin E. *The Infidel: Freethought and American Religion*. Cleveland: World Publishing Company, 1961.

Mathews, Donald G. *Religion in the Old South*. Chicago: University of Chicago Press, 1977.

May, Henry F. *The Enlightenment in America*. New York: Oxford University Press, 1976.

McCormick, Thomas R. "The Bible Chair Movement: The Foundation of Disciples Campus Ministry." *Discipliana* 47 (1987): 19–23.

———. *Campus Ministry in the Coming Age*. St. Louis: CBPO Press, 1987.

McDonald, Robert M. S. "Was There a Religious Revolution of 1800?" In *The Revolution of 1800: Democracy, Race and the New Republic*, edited by James Horn, Jan Ellen Lewis, and Peter S. Onuf, 173–98. Charlottesville: University of Virginia Press, 2002.

McIlhany, Hugh. "Founding of the First Young Men's Christian Association among Students." *Alumni Bulletin of the University of Virginia*, 3rd series, 2 (1909): 48–56.

McLean, Milton D., ed. *Religious Studies in Public Universities*. Carbondale: Southern Illinois University Press, 1967.

McLean, Milton D., and Harry H. Kimber. *The Teaching of Religion in State Universities*. Ann Arbor: University of Michigan Press, 1960.

Mead, Sidney. *The Lively Experiment: The Shaping of Christianity in America*. New York: Harper & Row, 1963.

Meade, William. *Old Churches, Ministers, and Families of Virginia*. 2 vols. Philadelphia: Lippincott, 1857.

———. *Sermon Delivered in the Rotunda of the University of Virginia on Sunday, May 24, 1829 on the Occasion of the Deaths of Nine Young Men Who Fell Victims to the Diseases Which Visited that Place during the Summer of 1828, and the following Winter*. Charlottesville: F. Carr & Co, 1829.

Merrill, W. M. *From Statesman to Philosopher: A Study in Bolingbroke's Deism*. New York: Philosophical Library, 1949.

Metcalf, John C., et al., eds. *The Centennial of the University of Virginia, 1819–1921*. New York: G. P. Putnam's Sons, 1922.

Metzger, Walter P. *Academic Freedom in the Age of the University*. New York: Columbia University Press, 1961.

Michaelson, Robert. *The Study of Religion in American Universities: Ten Case Studies with Special Reference to State Universities*. New Haven: The Society for Religion in Higher Education, 1965.

Miller, Cynthia L. "William Small and the Making of Thomas Jefferson's Mind." *Colonial Williamsburg* 22 (Autumn 2000): 30–33.

Miller, R. M., H. S. Stout, and C. R. Wilson, eds. *Religion and the American Civil War*. New York: Oxford University Press, 1998.

Miller, William L. *Supreme Court Decisions on Church and State*. Charlottesville: Ibis, 1986.

Minor, Benjamin B. "University of Virginia." *Southern Literary Messenger* 8, no. 1 (January 1842): 50–54.

Minor, John B. "Historical Sketches of Virginia: Literary Institutions of the State: The University of Virginia, Part III." *Old Dominion Magazine* 4 (1870): 260–68.

Minor, Lucien. "General John H. Cocke of Virginia." *American Temperance Magazine* 2 (1852): 129–41.

Moore, James T. "The University and the Readjusters." *Virginia Magazine of History and Biography* 78 (1970): 87–101.

Moore, William C. "Gen. John Hartwell Cocke of Bremo 1780–1866: A Brief Biography and Genealogical Review with a Short History of Old Bremo." *William and Mary Quarterly* 13 (1933): 150–52, 207–18.

Morais, H. M. *Deism in Eighteenth Century America*. New York: Russell & Russell, 1934.

Muller, F. "The Sunday Schools of the Young Men's Christian Association a Dozen Years Ago." *Alumni Bulletin of the University of Virginia* 5, no. 1 (May 1898): 18–22.

Munoz, Vincent P. "Religion in the Life, Thought, and Presidency of James Madison." In *Religion and the American Presidency*, edited by M. Rozelle and G. Whitney, 51–72. New York: Palgrave Macmillan, 2007.

Neufeldt, Harvey. "Religion, Morality, and Schooling: Forging the Nineteenth-Century Consensus." In *Religion and Morality in American Schooling*, edited by Thomas C. Hunt and Marilyn M. Maxson. Washington, D.C.: American University Press, 1981.

Newell, L. M. "Use of Campus Facilities for First Amendment Activity." *Journal of College and University Law* 9 (1982–83): 27–39.

Noll, Mark. *America's God: From Jonathan Edwards to Abraham Lincoln*. Oxford: Oxford University Press, 2002.

———. *The Civil War as a Theological Crisis*. Chapel Hill: University of North Carolina Press, 2006.

Nord, Warren A. *Religion and American Education: Rethinking a National Dilemma*. Chapel Hill: University of North Carolina Press, 1995.

Novak, Steven. *The Rights of Youth: American Colleges and Student Revolt, 1798–1815.* Cambridge, Mass.: Harvard University Press, 1977.

O'Brien, Charles F. "The Religious Issue in the Election of 1800." *Essex Institute Historical Collection* 107 (1971): 82–93.

Olree, Andy G. "'Pride, Ignorance and Knavery': James Madison's Formative Experiences with Religious Establishments." *Harvard Journal of Law and Public Policy* 36 (2013): 211–76.

Onuf, Peter S. *The Mind of Thomas Jefferson.* Charlottesville: University of Virginia Press, 2007.

Onuf, Peter S. and Nicholas P. Cole, eds. *Thomas Jefferson, the Classical World, and Early America.* Charlottesville: University of Virginia Press, 2011.

Outrum, Dorinda. *The Enlightenment.* Cambridge: Cambridge University Press, 1998.

Overholt, William A. *Religion in American Colleges and Universities.* Washington, D.C.: American College Personnel Association, 1970.

Pailin, D. "The Confused and Confusing Story of 'Natural Religion.'" *Religion* 24 (1994): 199–212.

Parshall, Karen. *James Joseph Sylvester: Jewish Mathematician in a Victorian World.* Baltimore: Johns Hopkins University Press, 2006.

———. *James Joseph Sylvester: Life and Work in Letters.* Oxford: Clarendon Press, 1998.

Patteson, C. "William H. McGuffey, D.D., LL.D." *Alumni Bulletin of the University of Virginia* 2, no. 1 (May 1895): 13–15.

Patton, John S. *Jefferson, Cabell and the University of Virginia.* New York: Neale Publishing Company, 1906.

———. *The University of Virginia: Glimpses of Its Past and Present.* Lynchburg: J. P. Bell Company, 1900.

Peterson, Merrill D., ed. *Thomas Jefferson: Writings.* The Library of America, 17. New York: Literary Classics of the U.S., distributed by Viking Press, 1984.

Pierson, George. "American Universities in the Nineteenth Century." In *The Modern University,* edited by Margaret Clapp, 59–94. Ithaca: Cornell University Press, 1950.

Porterfield, Amanda. *Conceived in Doubt: Religion and Politics in the New American Nation.* Chicago: University of Chicago Press, 2012.

Putney, Clifford. *Muscular Christianity: Manhood and Sports in Protestant America, 1880–1920.* Cambridge, Mass.: Harvard University Press, 2001.

Radbill, S. X., ed. "The Autobiographical Ana of Robley Dunglison, M.D." *Transactions of the American Philosophical Society,* n.s., 53 (1963): 3–212.

Ragosta, John. *Religious Freedom: Jefferson's Legacy, America's Creed.* Charlottesville: University of Virginia Press, 2013.

Randall, Henry S. *Life of Jefferson.* 3 vols. New York: Derby & Jackson, 1858.

Reuben, Julie A. *The Making of the Modern University: Intellectual Transformation and the Marginalization of Morality.* Chicago: University of Chicago Press, 1996.

Reventlow, H. G. *The History of Biblical Interpretation.* Vol. 4, *From the Enlightenment to the Twentieth Century.* Leiden: Brill, 2010.

Rice, John H. "An Excursion into the Country." *Virginia Evangelical and Literary Magazine* 1 (1818): 537–51.

———. Review of Cooper's *Memoirs. Virginia Evangelical and Literary Magazine* 3 (1820): 63–74.

———. Review of *The Mountaineer. Virginia Evangelical and Literary Magazine* 2 (1819): 363–75.

Robertson, A. T. *The Life and Letters of John Albert Broadus.* Philadelphia: American Baptist Publication Society, 1910.

Robertson, R. "Religion and Enlightenment: A Review Essay." *German History* 25 (2007): 422–31.

Rogers, William Barton. *Life and Letters of William Barton Rogers.* Edited by his wife, with assistance of W. T. Sedgwick. 2 vols. Boston: Houghton, Mifflin, 1896.

Ross, Earl D. "Religious Influences in the Development of State Colleges and Universities." *Indiana Magazine of History* 46 (1950): 343–62.

Rudolph, Frederick. *The American College and University: A History.* New York: Knopf, 1962.

Rudy, S. Willis. "The 'Revolution' in American Higher Education—1865–1900." *Harvard Educational Review* 21 (1951): 155–74.

Ruffner, W. H., ed. *Lectures on the Evidences of Christianity, Delivered at the University of Virginia, during the Session of 1850–51.* New York: Robert Carter and Brothers, 1852.

Sanford, Charles. *The Religious Life of Thomas Jefferson.* Charlotte: University of North Carolina Press, 1987.

Schele de Vere, M. *An Address delivered by M. Schele de Vere, L.L.D., on the Occasion of the Laying of the Corner-Stone of the University Chapel, March 30, 1885.* Charlottesville: Jefferson Book and Job Printing House, 1885.

Scherr, Arthur. "Thomas Jefferson versus the Historians: Christianity, Atheistic Morality, and the Afterlife." *Church History* 83 (2014): 60–109.

Schlereth, Eric R. *An Age of Infidels: The Politics of Religious Controversy in the Early United States.* Philadelphia: University of Pennsylvania Press, 2013.

Schmalzbauer, John, and Kathleen Mahoney. *The Resilience of Religion in American Higher Education.* Waco: Baylor University Press, 2018.

Schofield, Robert E. *The Enlightened Joseph Priestley: A Study of His Life and Work from 1773 to 1804.* University Park: Pennsylvania State University Press, 2004.

———. *The Enlightenment of Joseph Priestley: A Study of His Life and Work from 1733 to 1773.* University Park: Pennsylvania State University Press, 1998.

Schultz, C. B. "'Of Bigotry in Politics and Religion': Thomas Jefferson's Religion, the Federalist Press, and the Syllabus." *Virginia Magazine of History and Biography* 91 (1983): 73–91.

Schwehn, Mark. *Exiles from Eden: Religion and the Academic Vocation in America.* New York: Oxford University Press, 1993.

Schweiger, Beth B. *The Gospel Working Up: Progress and the Pulpit in Nineteenth-Century Virginia.* New York: Oxford University Press, 2000.

Setran, David. *The College "Y": Student Religion in the Era of Secularization.* New York: Palgrave Macmillan, 2007.

———. "Student Religious Life in the 'Era of Secularization': The Intercollegiate YMCA, 1877–1940." *History of Higher Education Annual* 21 (2001): 7–45.

Sharpe, Eric. *Comparative Religion: A History.* London: Duckworth, 1986.

Shedd, Clarence P. *The Church Follows Its Students.* New Haven: Yale University Press, 1938.

———. *Religion in the State University.* Hazen Pamphlets, no. 16. New Haven: Hazen Foundation, 1948.

———. *Two Centuries of Student Christian Movements: Their Origin and Intercollegiate Life.* New York: Association Press, 1934.

Sheehan, Jonathan. *The Enlightenment Bible.* Princeton: Princeton University Press, 2005.

———. "Enlightenment, Religion and the Enigma of Secularization: A Review Essay." *American Historical Review* 108 (2003):1061–80.

Sheldon, Garret W., and Daniel Dreisbach, eds. *Religion and Political Culture in Jefferson's Virginia.* Lanham, Md.: Rowan & Littlefield, 2000.

Shephard, R. S. *God's People in the Ivory Tower: Religion in the Early American University.* Brooklyn: Carlson, 1991.

Sheridan, Eugene. *Jefferson and Religion.* Monticello Monograph Series. Charlottesville: Thomas Jefferson Memorial Foundation, 1998.

Shockley, Donald G. *Campus Ministry: The Church beyond Itself.* Louisville: Westminster/John Knox Press, 1989.

Simon, Abram. "Religion at a State University." *Religious Education* 12 (1917): 37–39.

Sloan, Douglas. *Faith and Knowledge: Mainline Protestantism and American Higher Education.* Louisville: Westminster/John Knox Press, 1994.

Smart, Ninian, *Secular Education and the Logic of Religion.* New York: Humanities Press, 1968.

Smith, Francis H. *The Bible: God's Last and Best Revelation of Himself.* Richmond: W. E. Jones, 1909.

———. *Christ Regarded as the Center of Science.* New York: Fleming H. Revell, 1906.

———. *Nature, A Witness for the Unity, the Power and the Goodness of God.* Chapel Hill: University Press, 1908.

———. *Thoughts on the Discord and Harmony between Science and the Bible.* New York: Wilbur Ketcham, 1888.

Smith, Henry Preserved. "Charles Augustus Briggs." *American Journal of Theology* 17 (1913): 497–508.

Smith, Jonathan Z. "'Religion' and 'Religious Studies': No Difference at All." *Soundings* 71 (1988): 231–44.

Smith, Seymour A. *Religious Cooperation in State Universities: An Historical Sketch.* Ann Arbor: University of Michigan, 1957.

Smith, Steven D. "Nonestablishment 'Under God'? The Nonsectarian Principle." *Villanova Law Review* 50 (2005): 1–24.

Smith, Wilson. *Professors and Public Ethics: Studies of Northern Moral Philosophers before the Civil War.* Ithaca: Cornell University Press, 1956.

Snider, William D. *Light on the Hill: A History of the University of North Carolina at Chapel Hill.* Chapel Hill: University of North Carolina Press, 1992.

Sorkin, David. *The Religious Enlightenment: Protestants, Jews, and Catholics from London to Vienna.* Princeton: Princeton University Press, 2008.

Speece, Conrad. *The Mountaineer.* 3rd ed. Staunton: Isaac Collett, 1823.

Spellberg, Denise A. *Thomas Jefferson's Qur'an: Islam and the Founders.* New York: Knopf, 2013.

Steele, C. M. "Chapman Johnson." *Virginia Magazine of History and Biography* 35 (1927): 161–74, 246–57.

Steinberg, Stephen. "How Jewish Quotas Began." *Commentary,* September 1, 1971. www.commentarymagazine.com/articles/how-jewish-quotas.

Stetar, Joseph M. "In Search of a Direction: Southern Higher Education after the Civil War." *History of Education Quarterly* 25 (1985): 341–67.

Stewart, Matthew. *Nature's God: The Heretical Origins of the American Republic.* New York: Norton, 2014.

Stokes, Allison. "Denominational Ministry on University Campuses." In *Beyond Establishment: Protestant Identity in a Post-Protestant Age,* edited by Jackson W. Carroll and Wade C. Roof, 173–87. Louisville: Westminster/John Knox Press, 1993.

Stoops, Terry L. "'Engrossing the Education of the Country': John Holt Rice, Presbyterianism, and Educational Competition in the South, 1777–1831." Dissertation, Curry School of Education, University of Virginia, 2010.

Sullivan, Delores. *William Holmes McGuffey: Schoolmaster to the Nation.* Rutherford: Fairleigh Dickinson University, 1994.

Sweetser, William B. *A Copious Fountain: The History of Union Presbyterian Seminary, 1812–2012.* Louisville: Westminster/John Knox, 2016.

Swift, David E. "Thomas Jefferson, John Holt Rice and Education in Virginia, 1815–25." *Journal of Presbyterian History* 49 (1971): 32–58.

Tappan, Henry. *A Discourse Delivered by Henry P. Tappan, at Ann Arbor, Mich., on the occasion of his Inauguration as Chancellor of the University of Michigan, December 21st, 1852.* Detroit: Advertiser Power Press, 1852.

Taylor, Charles. *A Secular Age.* Cambridge, Mass.: Belknap, 2007.

Tewksbury, T. G. *The Founding of American Colleges and Universities before the Civil War.* New York: Teachers College, Columbia University, 1932.

Thomas, Ella M. *History of Freemason Street Baptist Church, Norfolk, Virginia,* Norfolk: Hampton Roads Paper Co., 1917.

Thomson, Robert P. "The Reform of the College of William and Mary, 1763–1780." *Proceedings of the American Philosophical Society* 115 (1971): 187–213.

Thornton, William M. "The Devout Natural Philosopher: A Brief Notice of the Life and Work of Francis H. Smith." *University of Virginia Alumni News* 17, no. 1 (September 1928): 9–13.

————. "John Albert Broadus." *Alumni Bulletin of the University of Virginia* 2 (1895): 1–10.

————. "The Life and Services of William Holmes McGuffey: Philosopher, Teacher, Preacher." *Alumni Bulletin of the University of Virginia*, 3rd series, 10 (1907): 237–57.

Toy, Crawford Howell. "A Student's View of the University of Virginia, 1852–1856." *Alumni Bulletin of the University of Virginia*, 3rd series, 8 (1915): 12.

Trent, William P. *English Culture in Virginia: A Study of the Gilmer Letters and an Account of the English Professors obtained by Jefferson for the University of Virginia.* Baltimore: Johns Hopkins University, 1889.

Tucker, George. "Defence of the Character of Thomas Jefferson, against a writer in the New York Review and Quarterly Church Journal. By a Virginian." *New York Review and Quarterly Church Journal* 2 (1838): 5–46.

————. *The Life of Thomas Jefferson, Third President of the United States, with parts of his correspondence never before published, and notices of his opinions on questions of civil government, national policy and constitutional law.* 2 vols. Philadelphia: Carey, Lea & Blanchard, 1837.

Tucker, St. George. "Sketch of a Plan for the Endowment and Establishment of a State-University in Virginia." January 4, 1805. Tucker Coleman Papers, Swem Library, College of William and Mary.

Turner, James. *Without God, Without Creed: The Origins of Unbelief in America.* Baltimore: Johns Hopkins University Press, 1985.

Tutwiler, Henry. *The Early Years of the University of Virginia: An Address before the Alumni Society of the University of Virginia.* Charlottesville: Chronicle Book and Job Office, 1882. Reprinted as "The Early Years of the University of Virginia," *Alumni Bulletin of the University of Virginia* 7 (1900): 8.

Tyng, S. H. "To the Episcopal Recorder, Charlottesville, June 1, 1850." *The Episcopal Recorder* 18 (1840): 50.

Urofsky, Melvin I. *Commonwealth and Community: The Jewish Experience in Virginia.* Richmond: The Richmond Virginia Historical Society and the Jewish Community Federation of Richmond, 1977.

Veysey, Laurence R. *The Emergence of the American University.* Chicago: University of Chicago Press, 1965,

Vicchio, Stephen J. *Jefferson's Religion.* Eugene, Ore.: Wipf & Stock, 2007.

Wagoner, Jennings L. "Higher Education and Transitions in Southern Culture: An Exploratory Apologia." *Journal of Thought* 18 (1983): 104–18.

————. "Honor and Dishonor at Mr. Jefferson's University: The Antebellum Years." *History of Education Quarterly* 26 (1986): 155–79.

Wall, Charles C. "Students and Student Life at the University of Virginia 1825–1861." Dissertation, University of Virginia, 1978.

Walter, Erich A., ed. *Religion and the State University.* Ann Arbor: University of Michigan Press, 1958.

Walters, K. S. *The American Deists: Voices of Reason and Dissent in the Early Republic.* Lawrence: University Press of Kansas, 1992.

―――. *Rational Infidels: The American Deists.* Wolfeboro, N.H.: Longwood, 1992.

Welch, Claude. *Graduate Education in Religion: A Critical Appraisal.* Missoula: University of Montana Press, 1971.

―――. *Religion in the Undergraduate Curriculum: An Analysis and Interpretation.* Washington, D.C.: Association of American Colleges, 1972.

Wenger, Mark R. "Thomas Jefferson, the College of William and Mary, and the University of Virginia." *Virginia Magazine of History and Biography* 103 (1995): 339–74.

West, John G. *The Politics of Revelation and Reason: Religion and Civic Life in the New Nation.* Lawrence: University Press of Kansas, 1996.

Westerhoff, John. *McGuffey and His Readers.* Nashville: Abingdon Press, 1978.

White, Andrew Dickson. *Autobiography of Andrew Dickson White.* 2 vols. London: Macmillan, 1905.

―――. *A History of the Warfare of Science with Theology in Christendom.* 2 vols. New York: D. Appleton and Company, 1896.

Wiebe, Donald. *The Politics of Religious Studies: The Continuing Conflict with Theology in the Academy.* New York: St. Martin's Press, 1999.

Wigelsworth, Jeffrey R. *Deism in Enlightenment England.* Manchester: Manchester University Press, 2009.

Wilson, Charles R. *Baptized in Blood: The Religion of the Lost Cause, 1865–1920.* Athens: University of Georgia Press, 1980.

―――. "The Religion of the Lost Cause: Ritual and Organization of the Southern Civil Religion, 1865–1920." *Journal of Southern History* 46 (1980): 219–38.

Wilson, Douglas L., ed. *Jefferson's Literary Commonplace Book.* The Papers of Thomas Jefferson, Second Series. Princeton: Princeton University Press, 1989.

Wilson, William. "The Myth of Jefferson's Deism." In *The Elusive Thomas Jefferson: Essays on the Man behind the Myths,* edited by M. A. Holowchak and B. W. Dotts, 118–29. Jefferson, N.C.: McFarland, 2017.

Woodward, C. Vann. *Origins of the New South, 1877–1913.* Baton Rouge: Louisiana State University Press, 1951.

Wright, Conrad. *The Beginnings of Unitarianism in America.* Boston: Beacon Press, 1955.

Wykes, D. L., and I. Rivers, eds. *Joseph Priestley, Scientist, Philosopher, and Theologian.* Oxford: Oxford University Press, 2008.

Index

Baptists (*continued*)

    and, 62–63, 65, 76, 195–96n16; Toy as Hebrew scholar and, 177, 180; in Virginia, 2, 5; Virginia Baptist Seminary, 195–96n16; Virginia Statute for Religious Freedom supported by, 2–3

Barr, William Alexander, 135, 209n93

Beale, Robert C., 204n43

Beaurlein, Lester, 150

Beecher, Henry Ward, 204n44

Bible: authority of, 11, 14, 130, 184n22; critical study of, 130–31, 185n29; establishment of Bible lectureship, 120–27, 132; Jefferson's letter to Peter Carr on how to read, 9; in *Notes on the State of Virginia*, 10; School of Biblical History and Literature, 127–32, 144–47; YMCA, Bible study sponsored by, 121–22, 124

biblicism, 18, 209n96

Bill for Amending the Constitution of the College of William and Mary (Virginia), 26, 34

Bill for Establishing Religious Freedom (1779), 2, 188n52

Bill for the More General Diffusion of Knowledge (Virginia), 26, 27, 29

Bishko, Julian, 150

Blaetterman, George, 45, 89–90, 193n44

Bolingbroke, Henry St. John, Viscount, 7, 16, 184–85n24

Bonnycastle, Charles, 45, 46, 58, 64, 72, 89, 173–74, 193n44, 197n40

Bowditch, Nathaniel, 39–40

Bowman, Francis W., 56–57, 60

Breckenridge, James, 191n16

Briggs, Charles Augustus, 176, 178, 180, 212n26, 216n11

Broadus, John Albert, 76, 80, 81, *88*, 88–89, 103, 122, 176, 177, 198n63, 199n72

Broadus, Maria Harrison, 88

Brockenbrough, Arthur, 69

Brodnax, J. M., 204n43

Brown, J. W., 185n29

Brydon, George M., 190n8

Buck, Harry M., 150

Cabell, James L., 74, 75, 80, 81–82, *82*, 86

Cabell, Joseph C., 30, 36, 37, 39–40, 46, 76, 78, 81, 190n15, 192n34, 193–94n47

Cabell, William H., 37–38

Calvin, John, and Calvinism, 53, 185n30, 187n44

Cammack, David, 212n31

Campbell, Alexander P., 66, 67, 122–23, 147–49

Campbell, Thomas, 66, 148–49

Campbellites and Campbellism, 65–67, 147–49, 196n23. *See also* Disciples of Christ

Carr, Dabney, 190n9

Carr, Peter, 8–9, 11, 28, 189n54, 190n9, 193n46

Cary, Columbia, 207n68

Cary, Gillie (later McCabe), 145, 207n68

Cary, John Baytop, and Cary endowment, 122–26, 128–31, 144–45, 149–51, 153, 206n58, 207n68, 211n22

Cary, Lizzie (later Daniel), 145, 207n68

Cary, T. Archibald, 128, 207n68

Cassell, Charles F., 108

Catholicism: of faculty members, 90–91, 193n44; local Charlottesville churches, 138, 139; Newman Club, 139, 159; priestcraft and, 16; student body, Catholic members of, 141, 165–66, 167

Centennial Celebration (1921) of University of Virginia, 135, 209n93

centennial celebration (1958) of YMCA at UVA, 142

Center for Christian Study, 167

chapel: bell, 111, 138, 202n36; Bonnycastle petition for (1837), on behalf of students, 72, 173–74, 197n40; James L. Cabell's support for, 82; Civil War halting plans for, 77; construction of (1883–90), 106–12, *111*, 133; discontinuation of

regular services at, 138–39; first antebellum proposal for (1835–41), 69–73;
Ladies' Chapel Aid Society, 106, 109–10;
location of, 107–8; organ/organ room,
111, 203n35; second antebellum proposal
for (1855–60), 76–77, 77; YMCA and,
205n47

chaplaincy: discontinuation of, 138;
"Preachers to the University," 112, 138,
210n2; rotating chaplaincy system, 62–69,
73, 195n12, 196n17, 196n19

Charlottesville Woolen Mills, 143

Chesnut, Glen, 153

Childress, James, 153

Christ Regarded as the Centre of Science
(Francis H. Smith), 88, 199n68

Christian Century, 124n66

Christianity: knowledge/interest of Jefferson in, 1; nonsectarianism, Christian,
62–69, 136; religious freedom not limited
to, 2; restorationist approach to, 12–13,
17. *See also specific denominations; specific
doctrines; specific entries at* religion

Christianity as Old as the Creation (Tindall,
1730), 184n22

Christianity Not Mysterious (Toland, 1696),
184n22

Christian Women's Board of Missions
(CWBM), 123–29, 144–45, 149, 207n68,
208n76

Church of England. *See* Episcopalianism

Civil War to World War I, period of,
99–136; academic weakness of UVA
during, 100–102, 134–35, 201n13;
ascendancy of YMCA at UVA, 112–20,
116, 132–33, 209n96; Bible lectureship,
establishment of, 120–27, 132; chapel,
Civil War interrupting plans for, 77;
chapel, construction of (1883–90),
106–12, 111, 133; distance traveled from
Jefferson's vision of secular university
during, 130, 132–36; effects of Civil War
on UVA and religious belief in America,

99–102, 200nn1–2; effects of World War
I on UVA and religious belief in America,
137, 140; Extension Division, activities
of, 134–35, 209n90; public opinion from,
124, 131–32, 133–34, 207n74; School of
Biblical History and Literature, 127–32;
UVA chapter of YMCA, establishment
of, 89, 102–6

Clark, Sheldon, 19

Clark, Tom (Supreme Court Justice), 213n41

classics, Jefferson's interest in, 5, 11, 19,
183n149

clergy: antebellum provisions for students
aiming to become ministers, 92–96;
early American colleges and universities founded to educate, 151; Federalist
clergy and opposition to Jefferson, 15,
16, 187n44; first clergyman appointed to
faculty, 48, 82–85, 130; Jefferson's refusal
to appoint clergy as faculty, 45–48, 78,
80, 82–83, 193–94nn47–48, 193n43;
parsonage for, 73–76, 89, 117, 132, 133,
205n50; twentieth-century provisions
for students aiming to become ministers,
143–44, 157–58. *See also* anticlericalism;
chaplaincy; independent religious schools
close to UVA

Cobbs, Nicholas, 61, 63, 64

Cocke, John Hartwell, 38, 46–47, 75, 78–80,
79, 88, 192n33, 198n47

Coffinberry, Este, 144

Cohen, Gratz, 164

College of William and Mary: Jefferson
attending, 5–6, 8, 11; Jefferson's efforts
to reform, 26–27, 34, 190nn6–8; secular
vision of Jefferson for UVA and, 25–27;
theological orientation of, 5, 25, 183n15

Collins, Anthony, 184n22

Commonplace Book (Jefferson's), 7, 184n24

Congregationalism, 25, 187n44

Cooper, Thomas, 17, 28–29, 36–39, 44, 50,
51, 53, 159, 188n48, 191n28

Correa da Serra, Jose Francesco, 37

literature, 129–30; YMCA, support for, 85, 89, 103, 113, 118–19, 120–21. *See also specific faculty members by name*
Fauquier, Francis, 6
Federalist clergy, 15, 16, 187n44
Feuer, Lewis S., 199n75
First Amendment, 152, 162–64, 168, 213n41. *See also* Establishment Clause
Fischbach, John, 212n31
Fishoff, Ephraim, 211n15
Fletcher, Josh, 159–60
Forrest, William M., 126–28, 130–31, 144–47, 149, 206n58, 207–8nn75–76, 211n22, 212nn24–25, 212n27
Franklin, Benjamin, 8
freedom of religion. *See* religious freedom
French Revolution, 46
Fry, Henry, 186n34
fundamentalist Protestantism, 145–46, 167

Gallaudet, Herbert D., 204n43
Garnett, James M., 122
Garrett, A., 64
gender issues, 168–69
Gibbes, Daniel, 160
Gildersleeve, Basil, 177–78, 179
Gilman, Daniel, 202n14
Gilmer, Francis Walker, 45, 175–76, 179, 193n41, 193n43
Glazebrook, Otis, 106, 107, 110, 202n24, 203n33, 203n35
Goodspeed, E. J., 146
Gordon, Armistead, 171, 216n67
Goss, J. W., 65–66
Grammer, Carl, 124
Granberry, J. C., 122
Great Awakening, 8, 185n25
Great Depression, 140
Great Revival (Second Great Awakening), 8, 18, 53–54, 78, 97–98, 148, 185n25, 188n48

Hamilton, Alexander, 8
Hammett, William, 61, 63, 64, 67, 81, 196n20

Hammond, Lewis, 150
Hampden-Sydney College, 33, 93, 95, 176
Harned, David B., 153–55, 214n44
Harris, Robert, 150
Harrison, Dabney Carr, 94, 103
Harrison, Gessner, 66, 75, 80–81, *81*, 88, 176, 177, 198n49
Harrison, I. C., 204n43
Harrison, Maria (later Broadus), 88
Hart, D. G., 213n39
Hartt, Julian, 154
Harvard University, 25, 100, 165, 176, 202n14, 203n39
Hatch, Frederick, 56, 60
Hawks, Francis L., 48–49, 194n51
Haygood, Atticus, 200n2
Hays, Brooks, 211n15
Healey, Robert M., 189n58
Hebrew language, as university subject, 34, 35, 124, 130, 175–80, 191n17, 207n65
Hereford, Frank, 150
History of the Corruptions of Christianity (Priestley, 1782), 12, 186n34
Hoge, Moses D., 122
Huebner, Emil, 177
Humphreys, Milton W., 178

independent religious schools close to UVA: antebellum UVA and, 92–95; Center for Christian Study, 167; Jefferson's vision of secular university and, 40–44, 192nn33–36, 192n39, 194n48
Industrial Revolution, 102
Islam: Jefferson's knowledge and opinion of, 1; Muslims in early America, 181n2

James W. Richard Lectures/Lectureship of Comparative History, 144
Jefferson, Martha (later Randolph), 182n11, 186n34, 189n54
Jefferson, Thomas, and religion, 1–23; anticlericalism of Jefferson, 16, 45–48, 187n44; classics, interest in, 5, 11, 19,

Jefferson, Thomas (*continued*)
183n149; current religious studies
program, likely opinion of, 157; early
influences and development, 4–12;
in elections of 1796 and 1800, 15, 16,
36; Great Revival, distaste for, 18, 53,
188n48; Gessner Harrison and, 80–81,
198n49; level and extent of interest in
religion, 1, 22–23; mature views, 17–23;
Priestley, influence of, 12–17, 186n31,
186n34; on religious freedom, 2–4, 24, 50,
171, 181–82n8, 188n52; reticence about
revealing personal beliefs, 4, 182n11,
189n57; revealed religions, fundamental
critique of, 3–4; Benjamin Rush, influence
of, 186–87n38; sectarianism, dislike of, 19,
22, 148, 149; troublesome nature of legacy
of, in nineteenth century, x, 54; "wall"
metaphor for separation of church and
state, 216n63. *See also* secular university,
Jefferson's vision of
Jesus, divinity of, 10–11, 13–14, 18
Jesus movement, 166
Jews and Judaism. *See* Judaism
John B. Cary Memorial School/Depart-
ment. *See* religious studies department
Johnson, Chapman, 46–47, 55, 80, 192n33
Johnson, Robert, 66
Jones, J. William, 207n74
Journal of Bible and Religion, 150
Journal of the American Academy of Religion,
150
Journal of the Chairman of the Faculty, 56, 60,
61, 62, 64, 65
Judaism: anti-Semitism, 91, 164,
215–16nn59–61; Extension Division
of UVA and, 134–35; faculty, Jewish
members of, 89–91, 164, 165, 199n75;
Hebrew language, as university subject,
34, 35, 124, 130, 175–80, 191n17, 207n65;
Jefferson's knowledge and opinion of, 1;
Jews in early America, 1, 181n3; quotas
on Jewish students, 164–65; religious

studies at UVA in, 153; student body,
Jewish members of, 141, 164–66; student
religious groups and, 165
Juda's Jewels (Davis), 118

Keim, James, 215n52
Kent, Charles W., 118, *120*, 120–21, 123,
127–28, 145, 206n58, 207n68, 207n75
Key, Thomas, 45, 193n44
King, Jere, 211n12
Knox, Samuel, 35–36, 191n20
Koch, Adrienne, 188n51
Kohlbrenner, Bernard J., 189–90n2
Kraitsir [Kraitzer], Charles, 90, 91

Ladies' Chapel Aid Society, 106, 109–10,
202n24, 203n36
Lamb, James C., 199n64
land-grant schools, 100
latitudinarianism, 183n15, 184n22
Law, Thomas, 189n54
Lehman, Linwood, 164
Lehmann, Paul, 211n15
Lemon test, 162, 215n53
Lettofsky, Allen, 153
Lewis, Albert, 165
"Life and Morals of Jesus of Nazareth, The"
(Jefferson Bible), 14–15
Linfield, Ben-Zion, 164
Little, David, 154, 181n7
Locke, John, 19, 20, 46, 183–84n22
Lomax, John, 45, 58
Long, George, 45, 80, 175–76, 193n44
Lutheran churches in Charlottesville, 138, 139
Luther P. Jackson House (4 Dawson's Row),
76
Lyell, Charles, 87

Madison, James (president of U.S.), 2,
46–48, 55–57, 80, 116, 184n24, 191n16,
194n48, 195n2, 198n45
Madison, Rev. James (president of William
and Mary), 26

as School of Religion, 146–47; student
enrollments in, 131, 154–55, 156, 208n88;
twentieth-century faculty opposition to,
150, 153, 156–57
religious test for professor of biblical history
and literature, 129–30
research universities, development of,
100–102, 134, 202n14
resecularization of UVA in twentieth
century, 168–71
restorationist approach to Christianity,
12–13, 17
revealed religion. *See* natural versus
revealed religion
revivalism in America, 8, 18, 53–54, 78,
97–98, 103, 148, 185n25, 188n48
Rice, John Holt, 30–31, 36–41, 50–51, 96–97,
192n33
Richie, Mr., 46–47
Richman, Daryl, 167
Richmond College, 196n16
Rives, W. C., 197n36
Roane, Spencer, 191n16
Rockfish Gap report, 32–35, 41, 48, 73, 78,
160
Rogers, William and Robert, 90–91
Roman Catholics. *See* Catholicism
Roosevelt, Theodore, Jr., 204n44
Roosevelt, Theodore, Sr., 204n44
*Rosenberger v. Rector and Visitors of the
University of Virginia* (Supreme Court,
1995), 162–64, 215n56
Rosenblum, Marvin, 165
Rotunda, and religious worship at UVA: at
antebellum UVA, 55, 61, 67–68, 69–70,
72–73, 85, 195n1, 197–98n42; Jefferson's
vision of secular university and, 33, 42, 43
Ruffner, William H., 93–94, 97
Rush, Benjamin, 10, 14, 182n11, 184n23,
186–87n36
Rush, Richard, 4
Ryland, Robert, 63, 65–66, 195–96n16,
195n12

Sampey, John, 124
Sampson, Francis S., 176, 177, 196–97n28
Schaeffer, Francis, 167
Schele de Vere, Maximilian, 108–9, 122,
203n33
Schempp decision (*School District of Abington
Township, Pennsylvania, et al. v. Schempp
et al.*, Supreme Court, 1963), 152, 153,
213–14nn41–42
School of Biblical History and Literature,
127–32, 144–47
"scientific" approach to religion, 101, 152,
201nn8–9, 209n96
Scientific Revolution, 6
Scott, Charlotte, 214n46
Scott, Nathan, 154, 214n46
Scottish Enlightenment, 6
Scripture. *See* Bible
Second Great Awakening (Great Revival),
8, 18, 53–54, 78, 97–98, 148, 185n25,
188n48
sectarianism, Jefferson's dislike of, 19, 22,
148
secularism of new research universities, 101
secular university, Jefferson's vision of, ix,
23, 24–54; anticlericalism of Jefferson and
refusal to appoint clergy as faculty, 45–48,
78, 80, 82–83, 193n43, 193–94nn47–48;
architectural layout of UVA, 69, 109;
close connection between higher education and religion in eighteenth century,
24–25, 189–90n2; concept of "secular,"
24, 189n1; Cooper Affair, 35–40; development of, 25–32; distance traveled from,
between Civil War and World War I, 130,
132–36; European professors, Adams's
arguments against hiring, 192–93n40,
193n43; exclusion of religious studies
from curriculum, ix, 29, 34–36, 45–46, 48;
faculty, search for, 35–40, 45–48, 193n44;
Great Revival (Second Great Awakening)
and, 53–54; independent religious schools
close to UVA, compromise of, 40–44,

secular university (*continued*)
192nn33–36, 192n39, 194n48; moral philosophy, professorship of, 35, 45–46, 78,
193n46, 198n45, 209n96; public opinion
and, 48–54, 195n65; religious worship at
UVA and, 33–34, 43, 192n37; resecularization of UVA in twentieth century,
168–71; Rockfish Gap report, 32–35, 41,
48, 73, 78, 160; Schele's refutation of,
109; student discipline and, 50–52; student
religious groups and, 159–60
sensationism, 20
separation of church and state: at antebellum
UVA, 63, 75; during Civil War to World
War I period, 123, 125–26, 136, 209n89;
early American ideas about religion and,
181n7; Jefferson's concept of religion and,
4, 181n7, 182n10; Jefferson's vision of a
secular university and, 25, 41; Jefferson's
"wall" metaphor for, 216n63; Morill Act
and, 151; in twentieth century, 151, 168,
216n63
Setran, David, 210n8
Shannon, Edgar, 149, 151, 152–53, 159–60
Short, William, 2, 10, 11, 19, 187n39, 187n44,
188nn49–50
Simon, Abram, 216n60
Skinner, James H., 143
slavery, African Americans, and racial
issues, 10, 79, 85, 168–69, 198n47, 214n46
Small, William, 5
Smith, Edward Dunlap, 60
Smith, Francis H., 80, *87*, 87–88, 118, 121,
199n68, 199n70, 201n3, 203n36, 209n96
Smith, James, 185n30
Smith, Jonathan Z., 214n42
Society of Biblical Literature, 147
Socinianism, 186n31
Socrates and Jesus Compared (Priestley,
1803), 14
Sons of Temperance, 80
Souter, David (Supreme Court Justice),
215n56

Southern Baptist Theological Seminary,
89, 177
Southern Literary Messenger, 72, 93, 96
Southern Literary Review, 194n51
Sparks, Jared, 17, 185n30
Speece, Conrad, 31–32
Spellberg, Denise A., 181n2
Steiner, Beat, 215n52
Stone, Barton W., and Stone-Campbell
movement, 148–49
Story of the Nazarene, The (Noah K. Davis),
118
St. Paul's Memorial Episcopal Church,
Charlottesville, 138–39, 210n4
Stuart, Archibald, 191n16
Student Council, 159, 162, 164, 215n52
student religious groups, 157–68; access
to UVA facilities, 159–62; "Christian
Houses," 167; denominational campus
ministries, affiliations, and associations,
139, 158–59; evangelical Protestantism
and, 166–67; First Amendment issues,
162–64, 168, 213n41; growing religious
pluralism of student body, 164–66,
167–68; Jefferson's vision of secular
university and, 159–60; local Charlottesville churches and, 139; prayer meetings,
Sunday School, and Bible Society at antebellum UVA, 67–68, 85, 96, 196–97n28;
university funding for (*Rosenberger*
decision, 1995), 162–64
Supreme Court decisions: *Everson v. Board
of Education* (1947), 168, 216n63; *Lemon
v. Kurtzman* (1971), 215n53; *Rosenberger
v. Rector and Visitors of the University of
Virginia* (1995), 162–64, 215n56; *School
District of Abington Township, Pennsylvania, et al. v. Schempp et al.* (1963), 152,
153; *Widmar v. Vincent* (1981), 161–62
Sylvester, James Joseph, 89–91, 164, 199n75

Tappan, Henry P., 192n39
Taylor, Robert P., 191n28

White, Andrew Dickson, 97, 201n8, 202n14

White, Stanford, 171, 216n67

Wickham, McClung, 62, 67

Wide Awake, 162–63

Widmar v. Vincent (Supreme Court, 1981), 161–62

Willett, H. L., 114, 122, 123

William and Mary. *See* College of William and Mary

Wilson, Douglas L., 184n24

Wilson, Woodrow, 116

Wishard, L. D., 205n47

Witech, John, 159

women, admission of, 168–69

World War I and religious belief in America, 137, 140. *See also* Civil War to World War I, period of

Wu, Anthony, 147

Wythe, George, 6, 27

Yale University, 25, 155, 165

Young, Charles, 123–24, 126, 130, 179, 207n66

Young Men's Christian Association (YMCA): ascendancy of, 112–20, *116*, 132–33, 209n96, 210n8; Bible study sponsored by, 121–22, 124, 132, 179; centennial celebration (1958) at UVA, 141–42; chapel at UVA and, 205n47; decline of, 139–43, 210n8, 211n12; evangelical Protestantism, association with, 114, 115, 161; faculty support for, 85, 89, 103, 113, 118–19, 120–21; financial support of YMCA by UVA, 117–18, 132, 205n50, 210n11; foundation and early years, 102–4; land behind Madison Hall owned by, 204n41, 205n48; legacy of, at UVA, 143; Madison Hall, at UVA, 115–17, *116*, 119–20, 132, 140–43, 205nn47–49, 211n11; parachurch groups replacing, 166; physical education and "muscular Christianity," 115; School of Biblical History and Literature and, 129; social and religious agendas, conflict between, 140; *Student Hand Book* and freshman orientation programs, 112, 113, 119, 132, 140, 203n40, 206n55; student religious groups and, 159, 160–61; University Christian Association/University Religious Council, 141–42; UVA chapter, establishment of, 89, 102–6